*f*P

A CRIME SO MONSTROUS

FACE-TO-FACE
WITH MODERN-DAY
SLAVERY

E. BENJAMIN SKINNER

Free Press
New York London Toronto Sydney

Free Press
A Division of Simon & Schuster, Inc.
1230 Avenue of the Americas
New York, NY 10020

First Free Press hardcover edition March 2008

FREE PRESS and colophon are trademarks of Simon & Schuster, Inc.

For information about special discounts for bulk purchases, please contact Simon & Schuster Special Sales at 1-800-456-6798 or business@simonandschuster.com

Maps by Ib Ohlsson

Book design by Ellen R. Sasahara

Manufactured in the United States of America

1   3   5   7   9   10   8   6   4   2

Library of Congress Cataloging-in-Publication Data

Skinner, E. Benjamin.
A crime so monstrous : face-to-face with modern-day slavery / E. Benjamin Skinner.—1st Free Press hardcover ed.
    p. cm.
1. Slavery. 2. Human trafficking. 3. Forced labor. I. Title.
HT871.S45 2008
306.3'62—dc22   2007023483

ISBN-13: 978-0-7432-9007-4
ISBN-10:   0-7432-9007-0

To my mother, who is my conscience, and

To my father, who is my sense of humor

Contents

[T]here is but one coward on earth,
and that is the coward that dare not know.

—W. E. B. Du Bois

Foreword

Of course, we all know what slavery is. We've read about it in countless history books, seen it in documentaries and movies. Slavery is awful. Slavery is inhuman. Slavery is dead.

But that last point isn't true. In fact, slavery is very much alive on every continent. In fact, as Ben Skinner points out, there are more slaves in the world today than ever before, although they represent a smaller percentage of the world's population than in the past.

Widespread calls for abolition, of course, began in the nineteenth century. In those years, slavery was legal and open, and defended or participated in by men like Thomas Jefferson and the powerful English parliamentarian Banastre Tarleton. Today, no one can openly condone any form of slavery. But it still exists, usually ignored by most people and the media. How widespread is it? How can we stop it? These remain huge, shamefully ignored questions. Ben Skinner seeks nothing less than to change that.

But there are complications. Among activists and policymakers, even the definition of slavery is disputed. Some people maintain that every prostitute is a slave; some go so far as to assert that the only present-day slaves are prostitutes. This absurd view in effect consigns to limbo millions of men and women who are, by any standard, living in slavery but not working in the sex trade. In Uganda, for example, when the Lord's Resistance Army seizes a fourteen-year-old girl and forces her to be an unpaid porter and a concubine, that is, by any definition, slavery. In New York City, in the 1990s, one crime family forced hundreds of deaf and mute Mexicans to peddle trinkets on the subway. At the end of each day, if the men and women did not meet their daily quotas, their traffickers beat them or shocked them with stun guns. That too is slavery.

Ben Skinner takes the reader into some of the world's worst hellholes. By going inside the minds of modern-day slaves and traffickers, by taking long, difficult roads to find the roots of the problem, Skinner exhumes ghosts that walk today's world.

Those who understand slavery best have seen slaves or survivors—or escaped bondage themselves. Take Tom Lantos. During World War II, the Nazis forced the sixteen-year-old Lantos into a slave labor unit in his native Hungary. Millions of other Jews never escaped bondage. But Lantos not only survived, he fought the Nazis, and eventually made his way to America. Today he is the only former slave (and only Holocaust survivor) in the U.S. Congress, where he chairs the powerful House Foreign Affairs Committee. Through sponsorship of antitrafficking legislation, Lantos continues to fight for other victims of what he experienced. But Lantos is a rare exception—a man of passion and power and personal experience, who can talk freely about his past.

One must never forget that slaves are first and foremost people. Their lives are filled with sorrow and injustice—but also, as Skinner shows, they are touched with humor and joy. Just like regular people. Just like free people.

Those who profit from the misery of slaves are here too. As the first writer who has observed the sale of human beings on four continents, Skinner lays bare the trade. In Port-au-Prince, a human trafficker offers him a ten-year-old girl for $50. In Bucharest, a pimp proposes to trade a young woman for a used car.

Despite the horrors they endure, some slaves overcome. After a daring rescue, a Haitian child slave recovers, and becomes an internationally acclaimed drummer. An Eastern European sex slave finds freedom, then finds the courage to testify against her traffickers. A young girl freed from bondage in a suburban Miami home performs the ultimate act of defiance by healing herself, getting an education, and daring to dream.

The cause of abolition may sometimes seem hopeless. Slavery is a slippery and confounding evil, and persists despite twelve international conventions banning the slave trade, and over three hundred international treaties banning slavery.

Still, this is a fight we must win. Global abolition must remain a priority until the last slave is freed. Because slavery is a hidden crime, the greatest challenge is to raise consciousness, to expose it in all its forms. When Americans feel it in their gut, they will understand that ending this crime so monstrous is not a political issue; it is an American imperative, and a human responsibility.

This is why there are still modern-day abolitionists. And this is why the rest of us should join them.

—*Richard Holbrooke*

Author's Note

Imagine that Robert E. Lee's staff officer had not lost his three cigars in 1862. Imagine that the general's Antietam battle plans, which were wrapped around those cigars, hadn't wound up in Union hands. Alternatively, imagine that George McClellan hadn't finally used the providential intelligence to stop the rebels in the bloodiest battle in American history. Imagine that a thus disempowered Lincoln was unable to issue the Emancipation Proclamation. Imagine that the South had won and spread slavery to the Western Territories.

Imagine that, eighty years later, Japan limited its racist empire to Asia, rather than attacking Pearl Harbor. Imagine that Hitler, unchecked by the Confederate States of America, rolled back the steady advance of freedom since England abolished the slave trade in 1807.

Imagine, in other words, a world where the ideologies that endorsed slavery still stood.

None of these scenarios happened. And yet: There are more slaves today than at any point in human history.

In his book *Disposable People* (1999), an unassuming scholar named Kevin Bales claimed that there were then 27 million slaves—whom he defined as human beings forced to work, under threat of violence, for no pay—worldwide. His figure was staggering, even when measured against other terrible epochs. At its height under Joseph Stalin, the Soviet Gulag held 5 million slaves. The Nazis enslaved 12 million in total, but culled them so rapidly that far fewer were alive at any given time.

The year 1861 was the only one when the total slave population rivaled today. That year, there were 3.8 million slaves in the United

States—a greater number than in the rest of the world combined. In Russia at the time, though most of Europe had abolished slavery, there may have been 23 million serfs. That estimate, from a Bolshevik writer justifying the excesses of the Communist revolution, is deceptive. A serf was a subject, albeit diminished, under law, and often owned property; a slave was himself mere property under law.

Human bondage is today illegal everywhere. But if we accept that one slave exists in a world that has abolished legal slavery, then, if we look closely, we soon must accept that millions of slaves exist.

Bales acknowledges that his figure is far from exact. John Miller, America's antislavery czar, told me, "These victims don't stand in line, Ben, and wait for a census to count them." Bales pleaded for criticism, hoping to be proved wrong. Subsequent regional studies have only buttressed his claim. A detailed, 2005 International Labour Organization report found 10 million forced laborers in Asia alone. Whatever the total number, it was big. And, to me, meaningless.

"The death of one man is a tragedy," Stalin, who knew something about the subject, supposedly maintained. "The death of a million men is a statistic." Hence the first reason for this book. I could not prove the definite number of slaves, and I would not try. But I might show what their slavery meant.

The second reason for paying attention was because my government did. A week before the 2000 election, President Bill Clinton signed the Trafficking Victims Protection Act. For the first time, an American president assumed global abolition as a national burden. The new law called for programs to eradicate slavery, and mandated that the State Department annually rank countries based on their efforts. Tier One was for those showing progress toward abolition. A Tier Three ranking, reserved for reprobate nations that countenanced bondage, could trigger sanctions. John Miller, whose office wrote the report, intended to "name and shame" foreign governments.

"Name and shame." It's a far cry from the nineteenth-century interdictions of the Royal Navy. Over a period of seventy years, 2,000 British sailors died freeing 160,000 slaves.

But the modern American war on slavery was nonetheless historic. Whereas President Lincoln used emancipation to win foreign government support for the Union, President George W. Bush used the nation's strength to win foreign government support for emancipation. John Miller, his knight in the effort, began working on the issue at the same moment I did. Thus, in this book I have woven his years of discovery in with my own.

Three caveats. First, regarding language. For Bales's statistic to mean anything, "slavery" has to mean something. I adopt his definition. I met dozens of people who described themselves as slaves. Their stories were often tragic. Many were child laborers. Many faced terrible abuse. But, in this book, those who failed to meet all of Bales's three criteria—compelled to work, through force or fraud, for no pay beyond subsistence—are not slaves.

Second, regarding scope. The book is grossly insufficient in its reach. Over five years, I visited twelve countries and recorded interviews with over a hundred slaves, slave dealers, and survivors. They were not a monolithic bunch. They had lives. Herein I tell the stories of only a few. There are millions that I never reached, and dozens of afflicted countries that I never investigated.

Finally, regarding facts. I changed eight names. In Europe, "Tatiana" asked that I use pseudonyms for her and her fellow slaves as well as her traffickers; and I changed the names of my fixers in the Romanian and Turkish underworlds. In India, "Gonoo" asked that I change his name and that of his eldest son. Slaves in preindustrial societies like those in front-line southern Sudan rarely shared a Western sense of time, thus their personal chronologies may be imprecise. I was able to cross-check most of their stories, but not all, and I have noted inconsistencies when they occurred. I converted currencies into dollars, adjusted for inflation. I altered no other details.

The first thing that John Miller ever said to me was that slavery is the greatest human rights challenge of my generation. He was right. But in the first couple of weeks in any new country that I visited, my greatest challenge was finding a single slave. After talking to the right people, often shady characters, I went through the looking glass. Then the slaves were everywhere. I often wondered whether I might have saved those that I found in bondage. With one exception, I did not. I withheld action to save one person, in the hope that this book would later save many more. Writing that now, it still feels like an excuse for cowardice.

A CRIME SO MONSTROUS

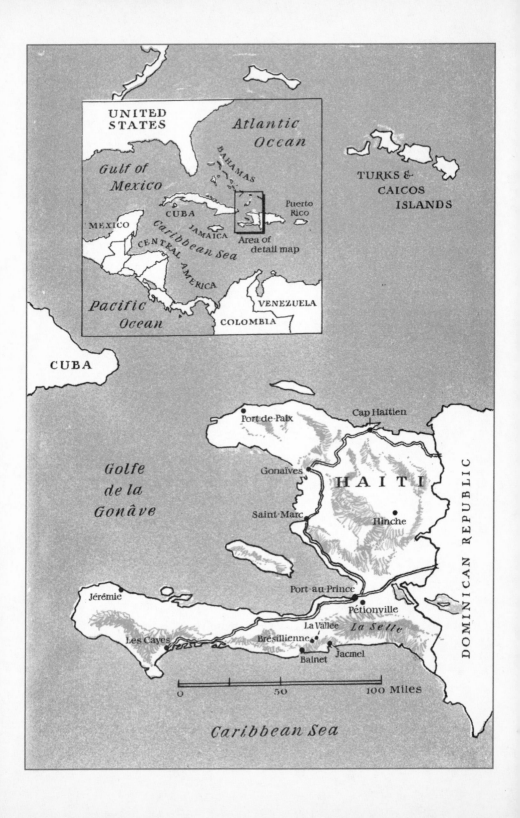

1

The Riches of the Poor

For our purposes, let's say that the center of the moral universe is in Room S-3800 of the UN Secretariat, Manhattan. From here, you are some five hours from being able to negotiate the sale, in broad daylight, of a healthy boy or girl. Your slave will come in any color you like, as Henry Ford said, as long as it's black. Maximum age: fifteen. He or she can be used for anything. Sex or domestic labor are the most frequent uses, but it's up to you.

Before you go, let's be clear on what you are buying. A slave is a human being who is forced to work through fraud or threat of violence for no pay beyond subsistence. Agreed? Good. You may have thought you missed your chance to own a slave. Maybe you imagined that slavery died along with the 360,000 Union soldiers whose blood fertilized the Emancipation Proclamation and the Thirteenth Amendment. Perhaps you assumed that there was meaning behind the dozen international conventions banning the slave trade, or that the deaths of 30 million people in world wars had spread freedom across the globe.

But you're in luck. By our mere definition, you are living at a time when there are more slaves than at any point in history. If you're going to buy one in five hours, however, you've really got to stop navel-gazing over things like law and the moral advance of humanity. Get a move on.

First, hail a taxi to JFK International Airport. If you choose the Queensboro Bridge to the Brooklyn-Queens Expressway, the drive should take under an hour. With no baggage, you'll speed through security in time to make a direct flight to Port-au-Prince, Haiti. Flying time: three hours.

The final hour is the strangest. After disembarking, you will cross the tarmac to the terminal where drummers in vodou getup and a dancing midget greet you with song. Based on Transportation Security Administration warnings posted in the departure terminal at JFK, you might expect abject chaos at Toussaint L'Ouverture Airport. Instead, you find orderly lines leading to the visa stamp, no bribes asked, a short wait for your bag, then a breeze through customs. Outside the airport, the cabbies and porters will be aggressive, but not threatening. Assuming you speak no Creole, find an English-speaking porter and offer him $20 to translate for the day.

Ask your translator to hail the most common form of transport, a tap-tap, a flatbed pickup retrofitted with benches and a brightly colored canopy. You will have to take a couple of these, but they only cost 10 gourdes (25 cents) each. Usually handpainted with signs in broken English or Creole, tap-taps often include the words MY GOD or JESUS. MY GOD IT'S MY LIFE reads one; another announces WELCOME TO JESUS. Many are ornate, featuring windshields covered in frill, doodads, and homages to such figures as Che Guevara, Ronaldinho, or reggae legend Gregory Isaacs. The driver's navigation is based on memory, instinct. There will be no air conditioning. Earplugs are useful, as the sound system, which cost more than the rig itself, will make your chest vibrate with the beats of Haitian pop and American hip-hop. Up to twenty people may accompany you: five square inches on a wooden bench will miraculously accommodate a woman with a posterior the size of a tractor tire. Prepare your spine.

You'll want to head up Route de Delmas toward the suburb of Pétionville, where many of the country's wealthiest thirty families—who control the nation's economy—maintain a pied-à-terre. As you drive southeast away from the sea, the smells change from rotting fish to rotting vegetables. Exhaust fumes fill the air. You'll pass a billboard featuring a smiling girl in pigtails and the words: *Give me your hand. Give me tomorrow. Down with Child Servitude.* Chances are, like the majority of Haitians, you can't read French or Creole. Like them, you ignore the sign.

Heading out of the airport, you'll pass two UN peacekeepers, one with a Brazilian patch, the other with an Argentine flag. As you pass the blue helmets, smile, wave, and receive dumbfounded stares in return. The United Nations also has Jordanians and Peruvians here, parked in APVs fifteen minutes northwest, along the edge of the hyperviolent Cité Soleil slum, the poorest and most densely populated six square miles in the poorest and most densely populated country in the hemisphere. The peacekeepers don't go in much, neither do the national police. If they do, the gangsters that run the place start shooting. Best to steer clear, although you'd get a cheap price on children there. You might even get offered a child gratis.

You'll notice the streets of the Haitian capital are, like the tap-taps, overstuffed, banged up, yet colorful. The road surfaces range from bad to terrible, and grind even the toughest SUVs down to the chassis. Parts of Delmas are so steep that the truck may sputter and die under the exertion.

Port-au-Prince was built to accommodate about 150,000 people, and hasn't seen too many centrally planned upgrades since 1804. Over the last fifty years, some 2 million people, a quarter of the nation's population, have arrived from the countryside. They've brought their animals. Chickens scratch on side streets, and boys lead prizefighting cocks on string leashes. Monstrously fat black pigs root in sooty, putrid garbage piled eight feet high on street corners or even higher in enormous pits that drop off sidewalks and wind behind houses.

A crowd swells out of a Catholic church broadcasting a fervent mass.

Most Haitians are Catholic. Despite the efforts of Catholic priests, most also practice vodou. In the countryside, vodou is often all they practice.

You may see a white jeep or van with a siren, a red cross, and the word AMBULENCE handpainted on it. You might assume this is an ambulance. It is not. These private vehicles only carry dead people. Public health is spotty at best. The annual budget for the health care of the UN peacekeepers in Haiti is greater than the annual budget for the country's Health Ministry. It's a bad idea to get sick here, as I was to find out.

At night, those with homes pack into tin-roofed, plywood, or cinderblock dwellings, on dirt roads bisected by gullies of raw sewage. Most people loot electricity from street wires to enjoy a light or two until rolling blackouts enshroud the city and end the sounds of dancehall reggae and hip-hop. Then total darkness reigns, and total silence, save for the spasmodic barking of dogs, and the nightly gunfire that can be heard from Cité Soleil to Pétionville. Only the generator-driven lights of the fortified UN compounds illuminate the haze over the city.

But now, in the daytime, many Haitians, particularly the 70 percent with no formal employment, will be on the sweaty, steamy, dusty streets. When either gender needs to urinate, they simply find a quiet pole or a ditch. No point going home for relief since few have indoor plumbing. Haitians take great pride in their appearance, but as more than three quarters live on less than two dollars per day, they don't have many pieces in their wardrobe. Some beg, like the thirtysomething woman sitting in the middle of Delmas, one horribly infected breast, glistening with pus, hanging out of her shirt.

Some hustle. There are more than 10,000 street kids, mostly boys as young as six, some selling unprotected sex for $1.75. Haiti has the highest prevalence of HIV infection outside of sub-Saharan Africa, and Haitians who believe sex with virgins protects against, or even cures, AIDS have driven up the price of such intercourse to $5.00. Haiti has also become a magnet for sex tourists and pedophiles. One left a review of the children in an online chatroom: "The younger ones are even more kinker [sic] than the older women. . . . Park on the street and tell them to go at it!!!!!!!!! If anyone sees you they just ignore you. No police but the multi-national military force is still here." Locals say that the main contribution of the peacekeepers to Haiti's economy comes via the brothels. Opposite a UN camp on an otherwise desolate road outside of Port-au-Prince, Le Perfection nightclub does booming business.

Most city dwellers who work do so on an ad hoc basis. A doubled-over, shirtless man strains under a donkey cart laden with the burnt-out carcass of a car. An elderly woman balances a hundred eggs in five tiers on her head and nimbly navigates a pulverized side road. A young man pushes up the bustling sidewalk with two queen-sized mattresses on his head. The tinkling of shoeshine bells is constant. An old man—probably no more than fifty-seven, the average life span for a Haitian—pushes a wheelbarrow filled with empty bottles. He catches you smiling at his threadbare, oversized T-shirt bearing an image of Snoopy, Woodstock, and the words WORLD'S MOST HUGGABLE GRANDMA. Bubbling with good humor, he shoots back a toothless grin. Many peddle trinkets, bouillon cubes, single-shot plastic bags of water, plantain chips, "Mega-watt" energy soda, or vegetables in various states of decay.

A man hawks cell phone chargers with which he swats stray dogs as they slink by. Another man on Delmas sells cowhide *rigwaz* whips and leather martinets. Those are for beating a different kind of creature. "*Timoun se ti bet,*" a Haitian saying relates: "Children are little animals." "*Ti neg se baton ki fe I mache,*" goes another: "It is the whip which makes the little guy walk."

You are now about halfway up Delmas, and slaves are everywhere. Assuming that this is your first trip to Haiti, you won't be able to iden-tify them. But to a lower-middle-class Haitian, their status is "written in blood." Some are as young as three or four years old. But they'll always be the small ones, even if they're older. The average fifteen-year-old child slave is 1.5 inches shorter and 40 pounds lighter than the aver-age free fifteen-year-old. They may have burns from cooking for their overseer's family over an open fire; or scars from beatings, sometimes in public, with the martinet, electrical cables, or wood switches. They wear faded, outsized castoffs, and walk barefoot, in sandals or, if they are lucky, oversized shoes.

If you arrive in the afternoon, you may see their tiny necks and delicate skulls straining as they tote five-gallon buckets of water on their heads while navigating broken glass and shattered roads. Or you might see them picking up their overseer's smartly dressed children from school.

These are the *restavèks*, the "stay-withs," as they are euphemistically known in Creole. Forced, unpaid, they work from before dawn until deep night. The violence in their lives is unyielding.

These are the children who won't look you in the eyes.

At Delmas 69, yell "*merci*," hop out, pay the driver, and turn left onto the relatively well-kept side street with overhanging but not overgrown trees. Any time of day, you will find here a group of four or five men, standing in front of Le Réseau (The Network) barbershop.

As you approach, one man steps forward. "Are you looking to get a person?" he asks.

Meet Benavil Lebhom. Hail-fellow, he smiles easily, and is an easy man to do business with, if not an easy man to trust. Benavil, thirty-eight, has a trim mustache and wears a multicolored striped polo shirt, a gold rope suspending a coin and a cross, and Doc Martens knockoffs. His colleagues approach. One extends his hand, offers his card, and introduces himself as a "businessman."

Benavil is what is known in Haiti as a *courtier*, a broker. He holds an official real estate license and calls himself an employment agent. But most employees he places are atypical job seekers. Two thirds of his sales are child slaves.

Like most Haitians, Benavil is from the countryside, but he moved to Port-au-Prince twenty-five years ago. He started in construction, but in 1989 he switched to real estate sales and founded a company called SOPNIBEL. Soon he discovered a more lucrative commodity: human beings. The biggest year for child selling was 1995, shortly after

President Jean-Bertrand Aristide returned to power, and UN sanctions were lifted. In the cities, people had a bit more money, and could afford small luxuries again. Benavil sold twenty to thirty kids in a good week then, and made upward of $200 per month. Nationwide the number of restavèks ballooned from 109,000 in 1992 to 300,000, or one in ten Haitian children, in 1998, to 400,000 in 2002.

Originally from a hamlet called La Vallée in the underdeveloped and forbidding southern highlands of La Selle, Benavil sired two children there although he never married. It is from those fertile mountains that he and his fellow *courtiers* harvest their best-selling crops.

Benavil's business works like this: A client approaches him about acquiring a restavèk. Normally, this client is lower middle class—a UNICEF study found the average income for a slaveowning household in Haiti was under $30 per month. After per capita GDPs were torpedoed by the economic chaos that followed two coups, sanctions, and colossal government mismanagement even in peacetime, the monthly incomes sank further. Lower-class urbanites also acquire restavèks, but, unable to afford a middleman like Benavil, a friend or relative performs his service free of charge.

A child's price is negotiable, but Benavil is bound by agreements—which he won't detail for you—with the capital's other *courtiers*, whom he estimates number at least 3,000. "We do have a formula," he says.

Clients then place their order. Some want boys; most want girls. Some want specific skills. "They'll ask for someone who knows how to bake," says Benavil; "sometimes they'll ask for a boy who knows how to work an oven." Most want children from the countryside. No one wants children from urban blights like Cité Soleil. Although their parents would give them away, clients know street-smart kids would escape at the earliest opportunity. Older kids, too, are out of favor as even rural ones will be willful, independent. Most children Benavil sells are around age twelve. The youngest slaves he brokers, he claims, are seven.

After a client has ordered, Benavil's colleague in La Vallée begins working to convince an impoverished rural family to give up its child. Normally, all it takes is the promise that the child will be well nourished and educated. Urban Haitians are poor; rural families are dirt-poor. Out of every 1,000 urban children, 112 will die before age five; in the countryside, the figure is 149. By comparison, in the neighboring Dominican Republic, it's 35; in war-torn Congo, 108.

Rarely are the parents paid. They yield their children because *court-iers* dangle the promise of school like a diamond necklace. More than 80 percent of Haiti's schools are private, and urban high schools cost $385 per year; this sum is beyond the annual income of the typical Haitian, and particularly out of reach for rural parents, most of whose income goes toward food. The average Haitian boy receives 2 years of schooling; the average girl, 1.3. In the countryside, where only a handful of schools exist, most children never attend school at all.

But the dangled diamond necklace is a fake, as 80 percent of restavèks do not go to school. Those who do must fight to go, are only allowed to attend when they finish their labor, and have to find the tuition money on their own. The slave's role in the master's house is to work, not to learn.

Occasionally, when parents agree to give up their child, Benavil treks to the countryside to ensure that he is providing a quality product to his clients. "Sometimes I go out to make sure it's a healthy child I'm giving them," he says. Then he makes his delivery. Sometimes the customer isn't satisfied. "They say, 'Oh, that's not the person I want,'" he sniffs. Benavil tells them: "You can't say, 'I don't want this one,' because you didn't have any to begin with, so how do you know you don't want this one?" Some refuse to pay. Some of his clients take their slaves with them to the north. "Some to the States, some to Canada. They continue to work for the person. And sometimes, once the person brings them over there, they'll let them figure out how to live. They'll give them their freedom. Sometimes."

But not always. Restavèks live as slaves to this day in Haitian communities across the United States. Most don't make headlines. One little girl in Miami was an exception. On September 28, 1999, police rescued a twelve-year-old from the suburban Miami home of Willy and Marie

Pompee. The Pompees acquired the girl in their native Haiti, and took her to the United States, where they forced her to keep their $351,000 home spotless, eat garbage, and sleep on the floor. Like many female restavèks, she was also considered a "*la-pou-sa-a*" or a "there-for-that." In other words, she was a sex toy. When police, acting on a tip, rescued her that day in September, she was suffering from acute abdominal pain and a venereal disease: since age nine, the couple's twenty-year-old son, Willy Junior, had regularly raped her.

Like many human traffickers, Benavil describes his work in euphemistic, even humanitarian terms. He claims that what he does helps the children. "Because the child can't eat" while they're in the countryside; "because there are people of good faith that will help them." He claims to tell clients, "Life is something spiritual, it's not something in a store you can buy." "I don't sell children," he says without prompting, "although it would seem like it." He "places" them.

But, Benavil admits, "you have people that mistreat" the children he doesn't sell. When he drops children off, he notes they often will be forced to sleep on the floor with any other domestic animals the client has.

It's time to buy a slave. Your negotiation might sound a bit like the following exchange.

"How quickly do you think it would be possible to bring a child in? Somebody who could clean and cook?" you ask. You don't want to stay in Haiti too long. "I don't have a very big place; I have a small apartment. But I'm wondering how much that would cost? And how quickly?"

"Three days," Benavil says.

"And you could bring the child here? Or are there children here already?"

"I don't have any here in Port-au-Prince right now," says Benavil, his eyes widening at the thought of a foreign client. "I would go out to the countryside."

"Would I have to pay for transportation?"

"*Bon*," says Benavil. "Would you come out as well?"

"Yeah, perhaps. Yes, I would if it's possible."

"A hundred U.S."

"And that's just for transportation?" you ask, smelling a rip-off.

"Transportation would be about a hundred Haitian," says Benavil, or around $13, "because you'd have to get out there. Plus food on the trip. Five hundred gourdes." You'll be traveling some distance, to La Vallée. A private car, Benavil explains, would be faster but pricier. You'll have to pay for gas, and that will cost as much as $40. Plus hotel and food.

"Okay, five hundred Haitian," you say. Now the big question: "And what would your fee be?"

You just asked the price of the child. This is the moment of truth, and Benavil's eyes narrow as he determines how much he can milk from you.

"A hundred. American."

"A hundred U.S.!" you shout. Emote here—a sense of outrage, but with a smile so as not to kill the deal.

"Eight hundred Haitian."

"That seems like a lot," you say. "How much would you charge a Haitian?"

"A Haitian? A Haitian?" Benavil asks, his voice rising with feigned indignation to match your own. "A hundred dollars. This is a major effort."

"Could you bring down your fee to fifty U.S.?" you ask.

Benavil pauses. But only for effect—he knows he's got you for way more than a Haitian would pay for a child. "*Oui*," he finally says with a smile. The deal isn't done.

"Let me talk it over. It's a lot of money, but I understand that you're the best," you say.

"*Oui!*"

He gives you his number, and, as he's left his business cards at the office, writes down his name for you as well. Benavil leans in close and whispers: "This is a rather delicate question. Is this someone you want as just a worker? Or also someone who will be a 'partner.' You under-stand what I mean? Or is it someone you just really want to work?"

Briefed as you are on the "*la-pou-sa-a*" phenomenon, you don't blink at being asked if you want the child for sex as well as housework.

"I mean, is it possible to have someone that could be both?" you ask.

"*Oui!*" Benavil responds enthusiastically.

"I think probably a girl would be better."

"Just one?" Benavil asks, hopefully.

"Just one."

"When do you need it by?" he asks.

"I can't say that right now, but you say you could have one ready in three days?"

"Um-hmm." He nods.

"I'm not actually sure whether a girl or boy would work better," you, the doubting consumer, say. A slave is a serious purchase. Best to acquire the right one the first time. "I'll decide that later. Do you want to ask me any other questions about what I want?"

"What age?" Benavil asks.

"Younger better," you say. "Probably somewhere between nine and eleven."

"What kind of salary would you offer?"

Unlike the sex question, this surprises you. But you figure it's just Benavil doing his humanitarian shtick again. "I could give food and I could give a place to stay, and I might be able to pay for school. But in terms of salary, even though I'm American, I'm a poor writer. But per-haps school and food."

"Perhaps when you leave the country, would you take the person with you?"

"I think I could probably do that. It depends on visa issues, but I think I could probably work it out. Any more questions?"

Benavil tells you that he can "arrange" the papers to make it look as if you've adopted the child. That will make it easier to take your purchase home. He offers you a thirteen-year-old girl.

"That's a little bit old," you say.

"I know of another girl who's twelve. Then ones that are ten, eleven, and twelve," he responds.

You say you'd like to see what's on offer in the countryside. But then you tell him not to make any moves without further word from you.

Here, 600 miles from the United States, and five hours from the desk of the UN Secretary-General, you have successfully bargained a human being down to the price of the cab fare to JFK.

I **didn't** make up these descriptions and conversations, though they read like a perverted travel tale. They were recorded in October 2005 in Haiti, and like slavery itself, they can only be absorbed if you think of them at a distance. But in Haiti as elsewhere, a slave is no metaphor.

And conjured literary irony cannot compare to the cruel irony of Haiti's history. The French colony of Saint-Domingue was once "the pearl of the Antilles," the richest colony in the hemisphere, with a GDP greater than that of the United States. Today, Haiti is the poorest nation in the Americas. Haitian blacks, who then comprised over 90 percent of the colony's population, forged the region's second free republic by staging, in 1791, the modern world's first, and only, successful slave revolt.

Now Haiti has more slaves than any nation outside of Asia, and more than toiled on the entire island of Hispaniola (including Haiti and the Dominican Republic) when the revolution began.

In 1685, the king of France laid the groundwork for a system of child slavery that mutated but continued for 330 years. One hundred and seventy years after black slaves first were taken to the island, Louis XIV, the absolutist "Sun King," declared black children in Saint-Domingue to be property of their mother's master. Masters were free to sell the offspring or give them to other family members. From age eight, the slaves minded the master's children. At age twelve, they joined their parents in the field.

A century later, in the midst of Haiti's bloody and protracted revolution, revolt leader Toussaint L'Ouverture drafted a new constitution abolishing slavery. His new nation became the first in the western hemisphere, and second in the world, to make abolition the law of the land. But L'Ouverture worried that a rising trend would allow slavery to survive. Rural parents, he noted with concern, were sending "their boys and girls to the city on the pretext of gaining the education which they will never attain in the cities." Already, the restavèk phenomenon was simmering. Article 68 of the 1801 Constitution called for schools throughout the countryside.

L'Ouverture's successors failed his vision, betrayed the new constitution, and realized his fears. The first leaders of Haiti created only a handful of schools, restricted to those whose parents "rendered high services to the country." The president himself had the final say on whose children got in. School became the exclusive domain of the elite.

The January 1, 1804, declaration of independence brought economic chaos. The revolution destroyed the plantations, which the new leaders tried to revive by forcing citizens back into slavery. But, as Haitians say, "when a chicken lays an egg, you cannot put it back." Haitians resisted violently. Haiti's leaders continued to try, through such blunt tools as the Rural Code of 1864, which introduced *corvée* labor on the rural population to force them to work on large plantations. Despite these efforts, Haiti became a nation of subsistence farmers, pauperized by a 150-million-franc debt to France to compensate for "colonial losses."

Haiti's rural children, as they always had done and always would, felt that chaos and debt most dearly.

On October 9, 1779, 750 freed black Haitians fought for the Continental Army against the redcoats at the Siege of Savannah. But for most Americans, Haitians were no brothers in arms, and Haiti represented danger, chaos, a Satanic evil reflected in its dominant religion of Vodou, and its new name, nearly homonymic with Hades.

The prospect of the state formed of its slave revolt menaced America, and what scared Americans most was the idea that a similarly violent uprising might happen in the United States. In *Uncle Tom's Cabin*, the most influential novel of the nineteenth century, Harriet Beecher Stowe captured U.S. sentiment toward Haiti before the Civil War with the commentary of her self-satisfied slaveholder, Alfred St. Clare. Alfred clashes with his brother, Augustine, who abhors slavery but continues to hold slaves. One day, after witnessing the beating of a slave, Augustine uses the insurrection in Haiti as a cautionary tale.

"O, come, Augustine!" snapped Alfred. "As if we hadn't had enough of that abominable, contemptible Hayti!"

Seeking, in President Thomas Jefferson's words, to "confine the pest to the island," the U.S. government embargoed Haiti for sixty years. But when legal American slavery entered its final spasmodic throes, the United States ran out of excuses for isolating Haiti. "If any good reason exists why we should persevere longer in withholding our recognition of the independence and sovereignty of Hayti and Liberia," Abraham Lincoln said in 1861, "I am unable to discern it."

A year later, after the U.S. Congress recognized Haiti, Lincoln enunciated a use for the black republic: a dumping ground for freed American slaves. He encouraged blacks to migrate to Haiti and Liberia to seek the freedom and independence he thought they would never fully realize in the United States. Lincoln sent Frederick Douglass as counselor minister to Haiti to lead the way. But other freedmen did not follow.

The public recognition of Haiti as an independent republic, of course, did not mean that Americans privately recognized Haitians as equals, worthy of the same human rights as whites. In the fall of 1906, President Theodore Roosevelt eyed Haiti from his leisure cruise aboard the USS *Louisiana*. He remarked to his son Kermit that a century after the slave revolt, the nation had successfully transformed itself "into a land of savage negroes, who have reverted to vodouism and cannibalism." "Universal suffrage in Hayti," he later wrote, "has not made the Haytians able to govern themselves in any true sense."

Woodrow Wilson agreed, and in 1915, he did something about it.

After one of Haiti's seasonal coups, Wilson, warning of potential German infiltration through the island, sent 330 Marines to take charge. The Americans stayed for nineteen years. As many Haitians actively resisted the occupation, the Marines had to reach into Haiti's past to get laborers to build roads. They revived the *corvée* system, tying Haitians together in chain gangs, and executing resisters. After shooting the insurgent leader, Charlemagne Péralte, Marines in blackface strung up his corpse in a public square on All Saints' Day.

While reinstating adult slavery, the occupiers highlighted child slavery as a reason for being there in the first place. In 1921, an American aristocrat named John Dryden Kuser—who had married seventeen-year-old Brooke Russell (later known as Brooke Astor), the daughter of Haiti's high commissioner, Brigadier General John H. Russell—wrote a book called *Haiti: Its Dawn of Progress After Years in a Night of Revolution.* The work, in addition to being a hagiography of Kuser's father-in-law, justified the U.S. occupation in part because of the preexisting system of child slavery on the island. Four years later, at a meeting of the League of Nations' Temporary Slavery Commission, the commission's most outspoken and independent member cited Kuser to criticize Haiti for the restavèk system. Haiti's former minister of agriculture, Louis Dante Bellegarde, responded indignantly that peasants were simply arranging for wealthier Haitians to pay for their children's education in exchange for light labor.

The issue was not raised again in an international forum for over half a century.

The martyr Péralte's bust is today engraved on Haiti's fifty-cent piece, and in the Haitian national memory, the end of the American occupation in 1934 was a great moment. For the child slaves, however, the worst was still to come.

Over the next seventy years the restavèks, hitherto degraded, became crushed. Before independence, some had status as au pairs and maids in upper-class households. As wealthy Haitians became able to pay adult domestic workers, restavèks became the slaves of the urban lower middle classes. The national government's gross economic mismanagement and urban-oriented educational policies compounded natural disasters to bury rural populations. A decade after independence, the supply of restavèks exceeded demand. While restavèk abuse occasionally offended bourgeois sensibilities, the government never enforced the half-dozen laws that it passed in order to curtail such exploitation.

Starting in 1957, the dictatorships of François "Papa Doc" Duvalier and his son "Baby Doc" rendered Haiti a thug state. With his *Tontons Macoutes* death squads, the father institutionalized terror. Under the son, tens of thousands of Haitians were sold as slaves—some tricked at recruiting centers, others simply dragooned—to sugar consortiums in the neighboring Dominican Republic. "It is the destiny of the people of Haiti to suffer," Baby Doc once explained.

Five years to the day after rural Haitians overthrew Baby Doc in a bloody coup, they carried a populist named Jean-Bertrand Aristide to power. Haiti's first democratically elected president looked like the champion of the restavèk. A Roman Catholic slum priest who ran an orphanage, Aristide invited hundreds of destitute children to his inauguration: "Children of Haiti," he told them, "this year you have a little friend who is president."

But Aristide was president for less than a year. The remnants of the *Tontous Macoutes* overthrew the "little friend" in an orgiastically violent coup, in which they publicly displayed several Aristide supporters with their severed genitals in their mouths. Aristide fled into exile, where he denounced the plotters and tried to position himself once again as a defender of the poor. In so doing, he addressed the restavèk issue, calling it a by-product of underdevelopment and Western greed. U.S. officials in Port-au-Prince were unimpressed:

"The Haitian left, including President Aristide and his supporters in Washington and here," the embassy cabled Washington, "consistently manipulate or even fabricate human rights abuses as a propaganda tool."

Still, no one in Clinton's administration liked the new junta. Nancy Ely-Raphel, the Deputy Assistant Secretary of State for Human Rights, said, "They're slowly turning Haiti into hell." On September 19, 1994, a U.S.-led multinational force secured the ground for Aristide's return. A week before the intended restoration, Representative Phil Crane, a conservative Republican from Illinois, rose on the House floor to blast the plan: "Haiti is not worth one American life," he said, echoing Bob Dole's earlier statement in the Senate. "Let us go to China, the greatest slave state in history. Instead of bestowing Most Favored Nation [status] on them, let us teach them about democracy." But the Republicans had been out of power in Congress for forty years, and his words fell on deaf ears in the Clinton administration.

"The egg is back! The egg is back!" Aristide's supporters shouted upon his return to the presidential palace. The proverb had been disproved and the chicken had indeed taken back the egg; but the egg turned out to be rotten. The Aristide restored by the multinational force was not the same Aristide elected by the people. Cowed by the demands of international financial institutions, he abandoned his programs for the poor. Terrified by the prospect of another paroxysmal coup, he employed the thug tactics of the Duvaliers.

Aristide proved adept at paying lip service to the restavèks. Two months after the restoration, he ratified the UN Convention on the Rights of the Child, and he later acknowledged that the restavèk system is "one of the cancers on our social body in Haiti that keep democracy from growing." But in practice, Aristide did little to free the slaves, save for proposing more meetings, and unveiling, with great pomp, a hot line to report restavèk abuses. The hot line was normally unmanned, and currently boasts a perpetual busy signal.

At the time, the United States was undergoing a seismic political shift of its own. A week after Crane's comment in the fall of 1994, Newt Gingrich's GOP colleagues won control of Congress and consolidated their power over the next five elections. In the second Bush administration, modern slavery mattered, and Aristide was the thug who perpetuated it in Haiti.

Shortly before George W. Bush took office, a soft-spoken man named Jean-Robert Cadet stirred American consciences about Haitian slavery. Cadet turned what had been a biographical letter to his newborn son into an elegant and painful book chronicling his years as a restavèk. He revealed in detail the torture and sexual abuse that he endured from his earliest memories until his mistress took him to the United States. On September 28, 2000, Cadet offered graphic testimony before Jesse Helms and the Senate Foreign Relations Committee's hearing on modern slavery: "I believe it is the moral obligation of this great nation to help Haiti solve the restavèk problem," he concluded.

Since the first Bush administration, the State Department had included reports of child slavery in its yearly assessment of the human rights situation in Haiti. Now, State took a harder look. In 2003, his first year at the helm of the American antislavery office, John Miller dropped Aristide's government to Tier Three of the *Trafficking in Persons Report*—a ranking that could trigger sanctions. In an eleventh-hour move, the Haitian Senate proposed an amendment to the constitution to outlaw the restavèk system.

Embassy officials in Port-au-Prince enlisted Roger Noriega, the new Assistant Secretary for Western Hemisphere Affairs, to convince Secretary of State Colin Powell to upgrade Haiti. The embassy argued that if the United States imposed sanctions on Haiti, a country dependent on aid for all public works, the nation would veer sharply toward becoming a full-on failed state. Swayed by these arguments and the importance of Haitian cooperation in stemming the flow of immigrants and narcotics, Secretary Powell recommended upgrading Haiti to Tier Two, where it would not face sanctions.

Shortly after Bill Nathan was born in 1984, his father died of malaria. To honor him, Bill's mother, Teanna, gave the baby an American-sounding name. His father was Haitian, but had worked for an American cargo company based in coastal Cap Haitien. Widowed at forty, Teanna became, like 60 percent of Haitian mothers, the sole supporter of her children. With Bill and his three-year-old sister Shayla, she headed south in search of work, settling in Hinche, a town in the central plateau of the country. There she met Sister Caroline, an American nun who helped her find a small home. Teanna earned money by doing laundry and cooking food for wealthier neighbors. She didn't make much, but it was enough to feed her children rice, beans, and, when she could, chicken.

Teanna had never been to college, but she dreamed of giving her children that chance, and with Sister Caroline's help, Bill was able to start kindergarten at age three. His mother worked hard; still, she made sure that her children enjoyed their childhood. When she got home from work, no matter how exhausted she was, she always warmed water to shower them. If the children misbehaved, she would ground them, but never hit them.

"Sundays, after church, my mom would cook different foods like fish, bananas, some salad," Bill recalled. "She would make something special for us to make us feel happy and comfortable, showing us the way she cared about us. And she would take us out and go to the public park to play with other kids. She was a good lady."

Shortly after Teanna moved the family to Hinche, her brother followed. Young Bill never completely understood why, but sharp tension existed between his mother and uncle. Bill and Shayla once went over to their uncle's house, and he grabbed them angrily. "What are you doing here?" he asked. "Where is your mother?"

When Teanna heard the story, she decided that if anything happened to her, her brother would be an unreliable caretaker for her children. She expressed her concerns to the two neighborhood families that employed her.

One sweltering July evening in 1991, Teanna fed the children, and tucked them in bed. Bill, who was seven at the time and just learning to read, fell sound asleep. In the middle of the night, his mother began to wail. "Bill! Shayla! I love you, my babies," she told her children. "I don't know what's wrong with me. I feel like I'm dying." It was the last thing she said.

The day after she died, Sister Caroline came to their house to offer her condolences. The two neighbors Teanna had worked for bickered over who would take the children. They compromised by splitting up the siblings. Immediately after the funeral, Bill, still in shock, moved in with the Gils. Wilton and Sealon Gil owned a restaurant and had two boys and two girls of their own. They were a lower-middle-class family, with no car but enough to eat. Although his sister moved in with a nearby family, Bill rarely saw her.

Everyone assumed that the children would be well cared for, as the two families had seemed compassionate when Teanna was alive. And for the first two months, perhaps out of sympathy, the Gils treated Bill decently, letting him attend school and giving him a comfortable bed, which he shared with the other two boys. All of the kids had chores, but there was a paid servant in the household who cooked and cleaned. After the first month, Sealon began treating Bill less like a family member and more like a slave. "Day by day, there were certain things like carrying water that they made me do," he said. Still, Wilton was a gentler soul, and tempered a simmering rage in his wife.

Politics, as so often in Haiti, intervened to make things more miserable. On September 30, 1991, Aristide fell, and the purges of his supporters began. Wilton, a member of Aristide's Lavalas ("Avalanche") political party, knew Aristide personally. One night, paramilitaries came to the Gils, demanded to see Wilton, fired shots into the house, and broke down the door. Wilton surrendered. He was hog-tied, imprisoned, and tortured. After a month he escaped via Port-au-Prince to the United States, where he soon took up with an American woman.

With his sole protector now gone, Bill's life changed drastically. In the disastrous post-coup economy, the restaurant sank. Sealon could no longer afford the servant, so she made Bill do her work, and more. Starting at five every morning, he mopped the floors, swept the yard, boiled the water. Then, even in torrential rains, he worked outside for several hours, feeding and watering the pig and tending to the vegetables. He was no longer allowed time or water to bathe, and could not sit at the table with the others to eat. Sometimes Sealon gave him leftovers. He became dangerously malnourished. His new bed was a pile of rags on the floor in Sealon's mother's house. When his clothes grew threadbare, Sealon gave him the other children's castoffs.

On some days, Bill was allowed to attend school for a few hours, as Sister Caroline still paid his tuition. Seeing that he was underfed, the school director funded his school lunches as well. Sealon permitted him to go only if he finished his other tasks, and did not allow him any time to study at home. He fell far behind. But school provided something more important for Bill. There, no one teased him about being a restavèk. There, for a few moments each week, he was a boy, not an animal.

"*Petit paw lave yon Bo, Kite yon bo,*" goes a Haitian proverb: "Your child is not my child, and I don't have to do anything for him because he's not mine." While Sealon's children were at school, Bill had to negotiate with vendors at the market and work at the restaurant. When they came home, they called him "slave" and beat him with switches or their fists for the slightest infraction or none at all. As they were bigger than he was, Bill could not fight back.

Sealon routinely yelled at him, even in public. One time at the market, he lost her money to buy groceries. "I know you, Bill. You ate the money!" Sealon shouted when he came home. She reached for the leather martinet. During the beating, one of many, he did not scream. Afterwards, his chin quivering, the eight-year-old was defiant.

"*Mon Dieu bon,*" he told her. "God is good, and one day I won't be a restavèk anymore."

"Do you think you've got somewhere else to go?" Sealon laughed. "You're never going to be anything in your life. Never. You will still be a restavèk, going in the street and cleaning cars. At best you'll be a thief." Bill longed to escape, but couldn't. As a child, his world was too small.

Months later, Sealon decided to teach the boy to work faster. She gave him 20 Haitian dollars and told him to get rice, beans, and other foodstuffs from the market. Then she spit on the floor. "By the time that spit dries," she told him, "you'd better be back here."

He ran so fast that his lungs burned by the time he reached the market. Overstimulated from the long sprint, and seeing no line for the vendors, he got distracted from his task. A young man's hands whirled over three wooden shells, one of which concealed a picture. Other kids stood around gaping at the man and his shell game.

"Hey, little man," the huckster said to Bill, "if you put down four dollars and see the wood with the picture beneath it, just touch it, and you'll get eight dollars back." The other kids egged him on: "Play! Play! You'll have more money to buy things anyway."

The man stopped, and all eyes were on Bill. In a flash he put $4 in front of the left shell. He lost. A pang of pure fear melted his stomach. Nauseous, he immediately realized that he could not afford all of Sealon's shopping list because of the $4 HA (about 50 U.S. cents) that he had lost. Shame piled on shame when he approached the vendors, who saw Bill regularly but didn't know him. Through welling tears, he revealed more than he cared to about his life. He lived with people who weren't his family, he said, and they had sent him. This was a polite way of confessing that he was a restavèk. He begged them to give him the items, explaining that his *granmoun*, his grown-up, would kill him. They refused.

Bill curled up under a mango tree, his mind white with fear, desperately trying to think of lies that would spare him the beating he knew was in his future. Unbeknownst to him, word had already reached Sealon of his peccadillo. When he got home, the spit was dry.

"You bet the money!" Sealon screamed. "And you know we don't have any money in the house!"

Bill tried to speak but choked on tears instead. She kicked him to his knees. Then she handed him two rocks, one in either hand, and told him to hold his arms extended, and not to drop the rocks or she would kill him.

The martinet first fell on his back. He held his tongue, and held on to the rocks. Then she beat him harder. As Bill screamed, she whipped him everywhere—his head, even his eyes. The other children watched in horror. After twenty minutes, Bill's blood lay in pools on the cement floor. The rocks were still in his hands.

On January 1, 2004, Aristide told a small crowd assembled in front of the gleaming white presidential palace that Haiti was "the mother of liberty" in the world. But the world had seen enough of Aristide's brand of liberty. Dozens of national leaders were invited to mark Haiti's bicentennial: only the prime minister of the Bahamas and South Africa's president, Thabo Mbeki, showed up.

Haiti, too, had seen enough of Aristide. It was coup season again. Reminiscent of Baby Doc's last days, mass protests spread from the countryside as rebels seized Cap Haitien, where the original slave revolt had begun against the French. They mauled Aristide supporters, and shot at Mbeki's helicopter. Rebel leader Louis-Jodel Chamblain explained that he intended to "liberate" Haiti, and compared Aristide to Napoleon's brother-in-law, who had failed to quell the slave revolt.

On February 29, a U.S. aircraft once again ushered Aristide into exile. Over the next ten months, foreign donors recalled millions of dollars in pledged aid. Haiti's GDP shrank nearly 4 percent while its population grew by 2.3 percent. Parts of Haiti fell out of government control entirely. The coup, combined with the Iraq War, pulled American attention away from the restavèks. Rural children once again slipped into the shadows, entering bondage in greater numbers than ever before.

The U.S. Agency for International Development (USAID) funded awareness campaigns to discourage child slavery, but the bulk of the money went toward billboards for a population that could not read, and television and radio jingles for a population without electricity. Three State Department officials monitored human trafficking part time, but department regulations curtailed their ability to find enslaved children and families.

For its 2004 report, the Trafficking in Persons (TIP) office begged off placing Haiti into its tier system, citing the lack of an organized government. The following year, TIP's evaluation was a confused and contradictory rehash of previous statements: "The Interim Government of Haiti does not fully comply with the minimum standards for the elimination of trafficking; however, it is making significant efforts to do so. Haiti is placed on Tier 2 Watch List for its failure to show evidence of increasing efforts to combat trafficking in persons over the past year."

UN organizations approached the issue of Haitian slavery as they handled modern slavery in many other countries. Without drama, without creativity, without effectiveness. The UN Human Rights Commission continued, as it had for fifteen years, to "express concern." From its air-conditioned and heavily fortified headquarters in Port-au-Prince, UNICEF issued lengthy studies on the problem of "children in domesticity," dancing around the issue of slavery, but explicitly refusing to employ the term.

Renel Costumé, muscular and clean-cut, wore a trim mustache and several gold rings. He looked several sizes too large for his airless office in a police precinct next to the national airport. Costumé, as head of the twenty-three-man Brigade for the Protection of Minors (BPM), led the national effort to combat the restavèk system. A 1995 graduate of Haiti's national police academy, Costumé soon learned why the UNICEF-funded BPM was a joke among his fellow officers.

As we spoke, he reached past his nonfunctional computer and fiddled mindlessly with my tape recorder, looking down and answering in low tones. At one point in the conversation, the electricity died, and we continued in darkness without even a fan to cut through the sweltering heat.

A dumpy office was the least of Costumé's problems. In theory, BPM was the first-response agency, fielding restavèk abuse reports, and galloping to the rescue. But the agency's landline was out of order, and its cell phone was out of scratch card minutes. Even if, theoretically, a message got through, BPM had one car, and anywhere beyond the capital was beyond its reach.

Were an officer to investigate, unless he found the most egregiously abusive bondage, he couldn't do much. Like the United States, Haiti pursued drug traffickers with much more zeal than slave traders. Human trafficking was still legal, as was forced, unpaid labor for children between the ages of twelve and fifteen. A law requiring the registration of unpaid domestic servants was never enforced. Under Aristide, when the BPM had a bit more money and actually could conduct investigations, its officers still had no authority to arrest masters, and could only scold them for mistreating their slaves. On occasion, a child ran away and a good soul would take her to the BPM. Brigade offices then would put her into an adult detention facility.

When I told him about Benavil Lebhom and his child-selling business, Costumé was phlegmatic. "If it's a pact between two families, we don't have to intervene," he said. "Look, we know the domesticity phenomenon is illegal," using the euphemism preferred by the Haitian government and the UN, "but it's not in our capacity to end it by ourselves." Stunningly, he even acknowledged that he had restavèk children living with him.

"But I don't rape them."

The morning after meeting Benavil, I set out for the mountains of La Selle, from where he would acquire the girl to sell to me. I went on my own, with the goal not of buying a girl but of exploring why parents would give theirs away to a stranger.

Now, in the life cycle of every bad idea, there comes a point where it reveals itself as such. Unfortunately, this is rarely at the birth of the idea. If I believed in omens, the enormous tarantula that leisurely crept across my path as I set out at five in the morning might have provided that epiphany. But for me, the revelation never occurred until nine and a half hours later, at the peak of the arc as I flew between my motorcycle and the jagged mountain rocks below.

That morning, my translator, Serge, and I boarded a tap-tap before sunrise. Downtown Port-au-Prince was already humming. A woman in a dress and an updo strode past, preaching apocalyptic gospel to no one in particular. Pressed against the tap-tap windows, vendors hawked all manner of goods balanced in huge baskets on their heads—tiers of plantain chips, crates of eggs, baskets of apples. One enterprising boy peddled medicines with a bullhorn. Hands reached through an open window behind me to tug at my arm, with pleas of *"Blanc! Blanc!"*

Children scurried past. Some wore uniforms and backpacks, heading for school. Others, the restavèks, escorted them or carried water. The tap-tap was larger than normal, but that didn't make us any more comfortable. The plastic school bus seats were crammed together, allowing no leg room, and less than a foot to pass down the center aisle. People squeezed six to a seat, along with screaming babies, terrified chickens in plastic bags, and unwieldy sacks of grain. The collector packed in more passengers so he could make more money. Then everyone began to yell.

Gargantuan speakers broadcast a chill gospel song by Losharimi, a Haitian pastor, which calmed passengers, until the collector demanded in voice stentorian to see one old woman's ticket. Her chin quivered. "The monkey handed me a ticket," she said, "and now the monkey wants to see it." As soon as the collector filled the last square inch, two corpulent women at the back of the tap-tap squeezed their way between the seats, descended, and urinated by the tire well.

On top of an adjacent tap-tap, a goat stood like a hood ornament. Our roof was piled several feet high with luggage, barrels, and people. Inside, everything was covered with ugly, 1970s green plaid wallpaper. The side windows bore American flags, and the rear window—the place of honor on tap-taps—an elaborate handpainted portrayal of Moses parting the Red Sea with his staff, leading his people to freedom.

A few enterprising vendors managed to invade the bus. In a rare moment of thematic unity in an otherwise random scene, a buxom young woman in a low-cut V-neck T-shirt hawked long French baguettes, which she called "Moses sticks." The collector tucked a few gourdes between the hawker's breasts but, unimpressed, she quickly threw them back at him. A man outside the bus bellowed at her for monopolizing the lucrative indoor spot.

As dawn crept over the mountains, the area around the bus seemed to explode, as the sea of humanity around us became illuminated. The music switched from melodious gospel to ear-splitting hip-hop, and the bass tube beneath our seat crackled. The driver started the engine, and we pushed through the crowd toward the swirling slums of Carrefour. Another onboard hawker held aloft such drugstore items as ginseng and aspirin, and extolled their virtues at the top of his lungs, introducing each with a deadpan *"Mes amis . . ."*

After an hour, the air cooled as we drove up into the winding, lush mountains, past small terraced farms, the tap-tap careering dangerously close to 90-foot drop-offs. Modernity seemed to evaporate in the mountain air as naked children buzzed around shacks unconnected to any road, removed from any farmland.

Descending, the driver pumped the wheezing brakes as we hurtled toward the sea. The air became sticky as we arrived in Jacmel, a sleepy, fading tourist town on the ocean. Parts of Jacmel were charming—like Old Havana or antediluvian New Orleans. Over the last decade, narco-traffickers from Colombia had begun to launder their money through property here, providing sorely needed, if morally questionable, investment. But most of the town, like Port-au-Prince, was crumbling.

After a quick lunch of gamey pigeon, we filled our water bottles, and took scooters three miles to tiny Dumez, where we rented much more powerful motorized dirt bikes for the next leg of the journey. There were no helmets available and the forthcoming "road"—better described as an extended gash of mud and jagged rocks—was designed for nothing like wheels.

A few hundred meters along, a raging brown river consumed the road entirely. Serge and I—along with three locals who had joined us-raised our feet and plowed through, blindly hoping that it was no more than one or two feet deep. At one point, our bikes became stuck next to an already stalled tap-tap, precariously close to a ten-foot waterfall. Using the larger vehicle as a fulcrum, we pulled ourselves past.

As we passed the first small town, the road disintegrated into slush. Climbing higher, the views became spectacular, though difficult to enjoy

ngerously close to the cliff's edges. The shocks on the
g dead, and my stomach, already savaged by giardia, felt
e being repeatedly uppercut into my throat. We ascended into
og, which lent everything a soft, mystical quality. Mostly though, it
made it impossible to see more than fifteen feet ahead. We slowed to 25
miles per hour, squeezing the brakes on the downhills and revving the
throttle on the uphills.

Fortunately, the accident happened during the latter process, so
I wasn't going fast. Serge had sped ahead, and in an attempt to catch
up, I hit an inconveniently placed rock, toppled diagonally, and landed
ungracefully on my side. My left foot broke the bike's fall, but my left
hand was a bloody mess. Locals who saw the crash took immediate
interest, but were more fascinated with a *blanc* all the way out here than
with my health. No broken bones, so I kicked the front fender back into
place, tucked the smashed rearview mirror in my pack, and rejoined
Serge, who had stopped to relieve himself.

We rode on past increasingly rural and far-spread outposts, which
looked like spaghetti western sets in decline. Everywhere we rumbled
past men, agape at my presence, with machetes; and gawking women
with loads on their heads, a whip in their hands, and a donkey leading
the way.

After three hours, we reached a two-building outpost called Bainet.
There we left the bikes and met Trajean LaGuerre, who had been waiting for us all morning. Tall, graceful, wearing well-worn dress shoes
and a white shirt, Trajean would be our guide on the three-hour walk
to Brésillienne, the tiny town which he led. We descended into La Selle,
over white broken rocks that soon turned to treacherous, slushy red
mud. We passed a few more men of all ages walking effortlessly over
the terrain that was causing me to wobble like a nonagenarian. At
spots the pleasant scent of moist earth was punctured by the familiar
smell of donkey manure, or dried by woodsmoke from nearby cooking fires.

The red mud turned dark brown. The inclines along the edge of the
path quickly became more severe, and at a few places, the track dis-

appeared entirely, sliding off into precipices below. The surrounding green was fiercely vibrant. As we came around a long turn, we breached the fog and could see over the jagged hills to the sea.

Half an hour into the trek, a light rain turned into a downpour. My foot, swelling from the crash, gave way and I went down in the ankle-deep mud, covering myself from head to toe. We turned off the road, down a nine-foot steep slickrock, stumbling into a different world. We came into a tin-roofed shack and asked the farmer for shelter. The farmer had a scruffy beard, gentle eyes; he was missing all of his front teeth. He sat on the floor with his neighbor, separating corn kernels from their cobs. They both wore straw hats, filthy shirts, and overalls. The place smelled heavily of kerosene from the only light source—a lamp in the next room. Save for a couple of plastic water jugs and a girl's jelly sandals, nothing would have been out of place in mid-nineteenth-century rural America.

We sat in silence as the rain poured down and the farmer's wife, mostly cloistered in the other room, filled up buckets of water from several leaks in the rusted tin roof. The farmer gave us the only chairs in the house, handmade out of straw and unfinished wood. At one point, he wordlessly ordered me to turn around, unsheathed a sickle, and cut mud from the back of my pant leg. The farmer's young son sat in the corner, wearing a threadbare tunic. A dog stood near the opposite hut, its eyes shut, willing itself to be dry. Finally, the rain eased up, I thanked the farmer with 25 gourdes, and we headed on.

I was retted on the outside from rain, and inside from sweat. Exhausted, we climbed the last several hundred meters to Brésillienne's town hall—a simple reed and log church, with a dirt floor and floating, hand-carved pews. We were at the highest point of the surrounding hills. From this elliptical plateau, we looked out to the ocean and 360 degrees of the fog-shrouded, rugged green hills. Christopher Columbus described this land but saw it only from the sea.

The view temporarily made me forget the poverty all around. Tra-jean reminded me with a coconut, which he opened with a machete and handed to me. He did so because, like 77 percent of rural Haiti,

Brésillienne has no access to safe water. As a comparison, in Burundi, the poorest country in the world, 31 percent have no clean water.

People here live much as they would have in L'Ouverture's day. Everyone farms, but only occasionally sell their yucca and potatoes in Bainet. The worst harvest in local memory was in 2003, but 2004 and 2005 were also terrible. One crop, however, never faltered.

"Timoun se richès malere," say Haitians: "Children are the riches of the poor." Nationwide, the average woman has 4.8 children. Every family in Brésillienne has at least two children under the age of fifteen; one household produced eighteen children in a single generation. Men won't use condoms here, and women avoid the pill, claiming it makes them sick and takes away their appetites. But the real reason families have so many children lies in the two-in-five childhood mortality rate, and an understanding that, as long as the crops come up, extra hands mean extra food.

Trajean blew a conch from the edge of the plateau to draw everyone close, and soon locals of all ages filed into the church. They said I was the third *blanc* in modern history to visit. (Two French doctors made the trek four years earlier.) Only one Haitian aid group, Limyè Lavi ("Light of Life"), which did remarkable work with scant funds, had visited them recently. Without that visit, the families would be mostly ignorant of the dangers posed by *courtiers*, for whom their young *"richès"* have a far more pecuniary definition.

The heads of each of Brésillienne's thirty-two families were present. The elders sat on the pews which they pulled around us on all sides; the younger men and women stood at the back. Trajean led a brief prayer, all heads bowed.

Then we talked, town hall style. Fear, shame, and regret poured out of the parents, all of whom save one had allowed a total stranger to walk away with one of their children. Most of the interlopers claimed some connection with the families. But why had these men and women given their children to people whose faces they had never seen before and would never see again? Many just looked down when I asked the question.

"We are not capable of helping our children," exclaimed one man, "and this man came and we thought he was going to treat the child well!"

The children who were sent away were often the brightest ones who held the greatest promise. Their parents felt they would take best advantage of the blessing of education. Now, most mothers had no contact with their kids. Four children had run back home after horrendous ordeals. Those children were taciturn, ashamed to tell their parents the extent of their abuse.

"How can you say to your mother or father that you were raped?" a Limyè Lavi organizer had explained earlier.

The villagers dispersed, but one mother named Litanne Saint-Louis stayed. Her face was wan, her legs scarred from years of hard labor. Born in Brésillienne, she was unsure of her exact age, guessed she was in her fifties, but looked older. In her youth, she saw other children get sent away as restavèks, but none from her family.

Litanne had eight children. She recalled the birth of the first two, Eva and Camsease Exille, as being difficult: "Oh, they hurt!" But the girls themselves were anything but a pain. Camsease cried, but no more than the other children. "Children in the countryside are stronger than children in the cities," said Litanne. At seven months, Camsease was walking. In her early years, she was strikingly affectionate. Whenever she was given food, regardless of who gave it to her, Camsease would run up to her and say: "Thank you, Mommy, thank you!"

As Camsease entered adolescence, the market for her family's crops evaporated. Litanne and her husband worried that soon they would be unable to feed their children at all. Still, they managed to scrape together school tuition for Eva and Camsease. Camsease squeezed in playtime with classmates in the small hours of the morning before class began; but one by one, those classmates disappeared. Camsease was scared.

In early 2003, when Camsease was eleven and Eva twelve, a man and his sister came from the city. Obese, in jeans, they looked to Litanne like the quintessence of well-fed modernity. And their words rang like a blessing. The woman, Alette, held Litanne's hand: "I'll help your child, *mami*. I'll put her in school."

Alette explained that her husband had just left for the Dominican Republic and she was looking for someone to live with her. Camsease, then in third grade, was terrified. But Litanne overrode her daughters' objections, hearing in Alette's words a once-in-a-lifetime opportunity. "I'd like one for my sister, and one for me," the woman said. Litanne sent off Eva and Camsease. Tearfully, Litanne and her husband embraced the two children, not knowing when or if they would see them again.

A few months later, Eva came back. Looking several years older, she explained that her mistress had never allowed her to go to school, instead making her work in the house sixteen hours every day. She and the husband beat her with a martinet, and the beatings got worse when they discovered that she wanted to leave. During the beatings, Eva's mistress would remind the girl how lucky she was to have been brought to the city, telling her that she didn't deserve it and could always be replaced. "You're worthless," the woman would say.

Horrified, Litanne envisioned Camsease enslaved in some other urban lair. She had no idea where Camsease was, but early in 2005 an old acquaintance showed up. He explained that Camsease had seen him on the streets of Port-au-Prince; his was the first face she recognized since her bondage began, and she asked him to take a message to her mother: Camsease wanted to come home. Lacking details, Litanne knew her daughter was enduring abuse, and was out of school.

As Litanne and I spoke, clouds threatened more torrents. Night fell, and Serge and I felt our way over the rocks to Trajean's house, some 600 feet away. His wife's sister sat on the dirt floor of a side shack, preparing food over an open flame. Pigs rooted outside, and chickens pecked at the edges: Trajean, like most of the people in his town, farmed for subsistence.

Trajean's house was tiny, rustic, but spotless. The floor was cement; as was true everywhere else in Brésillienne, there was no heat, no gas, no electricity, no running water. Trajean lit a couple of kerosene lamps; he offered us mushy tea, and we talked. He said affordable school would keep parents from sending their children away. At the only nearby school, the five teachers were paid $72 each per month. Each child's tuition was $5 per month. There were one hundred pupils, so if all paid, they would have a $140 annual surplus for administrative costs and materials. But few families could pay fully, and many tried to pay in yams or other noncash goods. The teachers never received full salaries.

The 1987 Haitian Constitution guaranteed free, universal schooling. If that were available, the percentage of families sending a child into slavery would drop from 95 to 60, Trajean said, the remainder seeing bondage as the only means to save their child from withering food insecurity. Knowing full well the horrors that might await in Port-au-Prince, one Brésillienne family nonetheless had allowed *courtiers* to take their daughter just a month earlier.

During the conversation, we ate startlingly large plates of lightly cooked yams topped with chunks of gristly pork. Less than a third of Brésillienne's families ate meat weekly, and none ate it daily, so this was a treat; but dehydration robbed me of my appetite. We settled in for the night. Serge was on the cement floor next to the table where we ate; Trajean insisted repeatedly that I take his foam mattress in the bedroom. His wife spooned her three children on the floor for warmth. Eventually, Trajean joined them. After he blew out the final candle, the darkness was absolute, and I fell sound asleep.

At 5 a.m., I woke to find that Litanne had been waiting for an hour by the embers of the fire outside. She was desperate to get her daughter back, and she thought she knew where she was. "I've heard she lives somewhere around Delmas," she said, "but I don't know where exactly she lives, what the number is."

Delmas is a long street, I warned her, and parts are dangerous. Camsease had relayed her approximate location through the messenger. I offered to pay for Litanne's trip to the city in one week's time. Though I doubted that we'd be able to find one little girl in a teeming mass of humanity, Litanne was confident.

Despite the omen of the tarantula, I left Brésillienne thinking that maybe making the trek here was not such a bad idea after all.

The symptoms of malaria would not appear for another week, but Port-au-Prince was sweltering, and I felt febrile. My conversation with Benavil left me with a predicament. I told him not to talk to any family without me. But still I felt as if someone had handed me the delicate life of a child. I had to decide whether to hand that life to fate, or to save a child I had never met.

As I sweated in the back of the tap-taps, I looked at little girls on the street and imagined the face of the one at the top of Benavil's list. She was somewhere in the mountains of La Selle, but soon she would belong to someone in the city. Perhaps her overseer would be a gentle soul who, though poor, would scrape together enough money to send her to school.

The odds were against this. Haiti has the highest rate of corporal punishment for children in the hemisphere, and the slaves are the whipping girls of the whipping boys. Studies showed that nearly every restavèk is beaten daily. Most girls are sexually abused by their male masters. Many of the capital's prostitutes are former child slaves, expelled from their masters' households after becoming pregnant or simply turning fifteen when, legally, they would have to be paid. The girl, whoever she was, would be owned entirely by someone, and that person could rape her, kill her, chop her into pieces, feed her to the pigs. Or that person could set her free.

I thought about all of the arguments for and against buying the child's freedom. There were practical considerations. Behind his smile, I knew that Benavil could be dangerous. After the February 2004 coup, thirtieth in the nation's history, Haiti averaged six to twelve kidnappings per day for ransom. Gangsters seized foreigners and demanded as much as a half million dollars. The family of Haitian journalist Jacques Roche, who had earlier reported on child slave labor, could not pay his ransom of $250,000 in a timely fashion. His kidnappers cut out his tongue, tortured him, and left him dead in his underwear in the middle of the street.

Aware of this ahead of my month in Haiti, I took out a kidnap and ransom insurance policy from Lloyd's of London. Still, men have guns here, and I knew from personal experience in Africa that slave traders are bestially cruel, as theirs is the most volatile commodity. These are not men to play games with. I thought I could solve this problem by having Benavil hand over the child I would buy at the Montana, a secure hotel, where UN officials stayed and where I had some acquaintants in the private military business who could bring greater force to bear if it came to that. But I wondered what would happen to the girl after I set her free. When the *New York Times* columnist Nicholas Kristof returned to visit a sex slave whose freedom he had bought for $203 a year earlier, he found that she had returned to the brothel, a slave also to her methamphetamine addiction. But drug addiction is not endemic to the Haitian countryside, and I could pay for at least one year in a good orphanage for the girl.

The potential for fraud was enormous. Assuming for a moment that Benavil smelled my humanitarian bluff, who is to say he would provide me with a girl genuinely poised to enter slavery? Perhaps he would give me the child of a friend of the family who was poor but not in danger, as a way for a *blanc* to pay for school. I thought of two journalists from the *Baltimore Sun* who in 1996 had bought what later were rumored to be false slaves, sold as a fund-raising scam for Sudanese rebels. One of the journalists, Gregory Kane, was sanguine about the possibility: "Do I have any regrets about being 'conned' and handing over $1,000 of *The Sun*'s money to the Sudanese People's Liberation Army, the southern group that has been fighting the government of Sudan forces for 19 years? Yes, I have several regrets. I regret we weren't able to give more money" to a group that, with adequate funding, might have taken out "O-Slimy bin Laden" and the "Islamic fundamentalist regime" in Khartoum.

Were Benavil to scam me, I would have no such justification except that I was helping a disadvantaged child, even if she were more fortunate than a restavèk. The case weakened.

As the evening rolled in, the air cooled, and so did my thinking. Journalists are not supposed to be activists; they are supposed to be objective and aloof. My grandfather, the editor of a small-town Connecticut newspaper for three decades, would have been appalled at the thought of a reporter becoming so intimately involved with a subject. But I also thought of Eddie Adams, who won the Pulitzer Prize for his 1968 photograph of the summary execution of a bound Vietcong prisoner. Would he have been wrong to remind the South Vietnamese general of the Geneva Conventions?

When the blackout came, I was getting to the heart of the issue. I couldn't overcome my instinct that no matter how just the cause, a human life should not be bought—even if it means that someone else may buy it instead. I established a principle for the rest of my work: I would give no money to slave traders; I would give no money to slavemasters. But I could not avoid getting involved with the lives of the slaves that I met.

In the case of Litanne's daughter, I was already involved with the life of a slave I had never met.

A week after traveling to Brésillienne, I waited with Serge for Litanne on the corner of Delmas 91. It was Sunday, and the large church across the street—next to the bullet-ridden Radio Haiti—vibrated with an ecstatic gospel choir, drums, and organ. Litanne arrived, escorted by Trajean. She had pulled back her hair with a black ribbon, and wore a yellow Sunday dress. We set out quickly to look for Camsease. Anxious, she walked with determination down Delmas until we hopped into a slow-rolling tap-tap.

After fifty blocks, we stepped out of the tap-tap. Litanne asked several times where we were, and I began to worry that she would never find her daughter. Then she got the scent, and we marched down Delmas 34. Young thugs crowded in, one aggressively asking for money. Like most side streets off Delmas, it was a moonscape of rocks, debris, garbage, and feces. Rusty car carcasses lined the roadside.

At the end, Litanne turned off toward a one-room cement house with a flat roof and rusty rebars jutting out at random angles. She knocked. Around the corner came Alette, an ursine, barefoot woman wearing a stretched green tunic—much different from when she had shown up in Brésillienne, Litanne said. Her unkempt hair shot off at improbable angles. Her face betrayed shock and immediate dismay to see us, and some fear. She recognized that three grown men represented *force majeure* and, as she had never paid for Camsease, she could not claim her as property. She managed a nervous smile.

The inside of the house looked like a prison cell, with water-stained cement walls, glassless windows, and a bare concrete floor. A shard of a mirror lodged in a crack was the only decoration. Alette offered the only chair to me, but I insisted that Litanne take it. I sat on the one bed, along with Trajean and Serge. Alette indicated a corner of the cement floor where Camsease slept; then she called to her.

Camsease appeared from behind a sheet hanging at the back of the house. She looked younger than her thirteen years. Expressionless, she glided over to her mother. "Are you coming to pick me up?" she asked in a soft voice. Her mother nodded, smiling, her eyes wet, and embraced her daughter for the first time in nearly three years.

"She's beautiful," Serge whispered to me.

"I didn't know you were coming," Alette said, flustered.

"Wash up," Litanne told Camsease. "We're going."

Camsease went back behind the sheet to change, and Alette rattled off a litany of excuses. "Things have been very hard for me over the last couple of years," she said. "My husband went to the Dominican Republic to find work and was killed."

Alette, forty-five, was originally from Jacmel but had been living in the capital for the last twenty years. She was an insurance regulator in the Aristide regime but had been out of work since the coup. Litanne was silent, but Alette continued.

"Look, I can't afford to send my own children to school," she said. "Things were better for me when I picked up Camsease."

Litanne sat silently, her fists clenched, but her face impassive.

"I dressed her," Alette said, "I gave her food."

Camsease emerged, wearing different clothes but empty-handed. Slaves, of course, own nothing. We left quickly. At the end of Delmas 34, Trajean bought Camsease some crackers, which she devoured. Litanne held her daughter's hand with a death grip.

Alette and her three children had controlled Camsease's every move. She was first awake in the house, an hour before dawn, and never went to school. Alette had lied about her inability to send her own children to school: dressed in their uniforms, they had gone every day. Camsease did all the work around the house. In the morning, she had to *jete pipi*, to clean out her mistress's chamberpot. Sometimes, she had to scrub Alette's feet. She was allowed to leave the house once a week, on Wednesdays, to run errands at the market. Although Alette's children were younger, they would beat her and call her *timoun bond*, slave child.

Camsease wolfed down lunch as I drew out details of her bondage. Litanne never took her eyes off of her daughter, as if to do so would mean losing her for another three years. After lunch, I asked Camsease what she wanted to be when she grew up.

"I want to learn how to read," she said, simply. I pushed her for a bolder goal.

"I want to be a doctor," she said, cracking a smile for the first time.

"She's going to eat a lot of yams tonight," said Serge.

Bill Nathan's tenth birthday came and went, and Bill himself did not notice. In 1994, he entered his eleventh year of life, and his third year of what slavery scholar Orlando Patterson terms "social death." Haitians have another term for restavèks who have absorbed their slave status—*zombifier*, zombified. Like the undead of the vodou tradition, the restavèks are assumed to have no will of their own, controlled entirely by those who granted them a second life.

Teanna, who had left no savings to her children when she died, had left them with important reserves of courage. But as Bill's memory of liberty faded, so too did his will to escape.

One day, Bill heard a knock at the Gils' gate. When he opened it, two men grabbed him. Sealon's elderly mother saw the abduction but could do nothing to stop it. As the two men led Bill away, they calmed his fears by saying that Sister Caroline had sent them. The men took Bill to Caroline's convent, where she fed him, bathed him, and gave him sandals. Caroline explained that neighbors had told her about the beatings. "If your mother were alive," she told Bill, "she never would have accepted that."

That afternoon, she sent Bill in a private car to St. Joseph's Home for Boys, a remarkable orphanage in Port-au-Prince run by an Iowan named Michael Geilenfeld. It was Bill's first night in a big city, but he was not scared. "I was happy," he said. "I felt like my mother was in that house."

Geilenfeld soon discovered Bill had a talent for drumming. He found funds for the boy to study the art in Gambia. In order to go, Bill needed a passport. In order to get a passport, Bill needed his birth certificate. For that, he would have to confront Sealon one last time. Four years after his rescue, Bill returned to the place of his enslavement. Hinche looked strange, and Bill got lost. But one of Sealon's children spotted him, and took Bill and his companions to the Gils' house.

"Oh! Look at you, you got big!" Sealon exclaimed with saccharine insincerity. Bill saw that a new little boy had taken his place, and that Sealon had forced the boy into the same spirit-crushing servitude she had imposed on him. Bill called the boy over.

"This is the same way I used to live in this place," he said. "Have hope: God is good."

Sealon treated the visitors like honored guests, offering them her children's bed, and ordering the restavèk to fetch them water. She asked Bill for money, and Bill gave her all he had. "For myself, when someone did something bad to me, I don't keep it," Bill later explained. "I don't do evil for evil. You do me bad, I do you good."

As he left, Bill stepped back when Sealon tried to embrace him. "I am no thief," he said simply, before turning to return to his new life.

———————

During my last week in Port-au-Prince, the Haitian National Police received a shipment of new uniforms. The hats were too big. Some officers were embarrassed and took them off; others stayed in uniform but tried not to move too much. The rims came down past their ears, and their eyes were barely visible.

Haiti was making baby steps toward stability. But the presidential elections that were scheduled for the following week had been canceled due to the persistent violence. The government was essentially nonexistent.

I saw Benavil again. He took me to his company's office, which sits a few blocks from where I had met him on the street, past Donald Duck Kindergarten, in the campaign headquarters of Haitian presidential candidate Dr. Emmanuel Justima. Benavil, who moonlights as Justima's head of security, proudly showed me off to the smartly dressed candidate, who introduced himself as "one of the most well educated Haitians in the world," and said that one of his campaign pledges was "greater rights for restavèks."

The problem of child slavery in Haiti has deep roots in society. And the problem has spread well beyond Haiti's borders. The day after my trip to Brésillienne, I took another motorcycle with a Belgian aid worker across the border to the Dominican Republic, where I visited four of the over three hundred sugar plantations. Although Haitian officials no longer offer their citizens at bulk rates to the sugar consortiums—as the dictator Baby Doc did—thousands of children are still trafficked to the Dominican Republic for plantation work, forced prostitution, and, of course, domestic servitude.

Unlike Sudanese chattel slaves or European sex-trafficking victims, Haiti's restavèks have no advocates with ready access to Washington. Historically, American response to Haitian slavery at worst has been encouragement, at best opportunistic condemnation. Most of the time, America averts its eyes. And in lieu of an enforced prohibition of the restavèk system, prosecutions for slave traffickers, and targeted aid for the source families, Haiti's slaves will do what they did for 400 years: survive, adjust, struggle.

And, occasionally, transcend.

In 2002, Bill Nathan performed at a concert in Toronto in front of a crowd of five thousand, including Pope John Paul II. He went on to perform for Brazil's President Lula, and to enthusiastic crowds at the Brooklyn Academy of Music, Harlem's Apollo Theater, and the Underground Railroad Freedom Center in Cincinnati. He never saw his sister after his rescue. He heard she had moved on from the family she used to "stay with," and was now living in the Dominican Republic. It saddened him to think of her.

On first meeting Bill, I was immediately struck by his calmness amid the abject chaos of Port-au-Prince. Where he got his strength to move on and to keep moving was beyond me. He would say it was God's will. Perhaps he had the same peculiarities that led Frederick Douglass or Harriet Tubman to defy great odds, seek their freedom, then help others. Bill was tough and street-smart enough to guide me past fifteen-year-olds toting M-1 rifles in Cité Soleil, but caring enough to nurse me back to health when malaria knocked me out for a week. He encouraged me to eat and rest. And he prayed for me.

"You need your strength, dear friend," he said. "Your journey is just beginning."

2

Genesis: A Drama in Three Acts

Waiting to meet America's antislavery czar for the first time, I heard his voice a minute before I saw him.

"Benjamin Skinner!" John Miller yelled from some recess of the cramped and colorless hallway of the Office to Monitor and Combat Trafficking in Persons in Washington, D.C. Miller stood six foot three. His body moved as if governed by its own law of physics, as if gravity affected him in a horizontal rather than vertical plane. His long arms and legs flailed as he approached. His auburn eyes glimmered, and a wide grin burrowed deep into his face. He was either possessed, or a politician—or a possessed politician.

"Benjamin Skinner!" he repeated, still shouting even as he laid a huge hand on my shoulder. "You're writing about the greatest human rights challenge of our generation!" In fact, at sixty-seven, Miller was more than a generation removed from me. And the challenge was a hell of a lot older than both of us.

He was not impolite, but never deferential. Throughout his three years in charge of American abolitionism, he'd received a lot of accolades. Different dignitaries gave him awards. Somewhere he had a pile of "grab 'n' grin" photos, as does every diplomat. But none hung in his unkempt office. There the only decorations were a framed quote from President Bush, an American flag, a Polish *Soldarinosc* poster, and cheap steel cabinets next to his desk. The office was in an ugly second-floor suite, at the end of a long, empty, unsecured hallway marked only with printouts reading "G/TIP," as the Trafficking in Persons office is known in American diplospeak. The building is seven long blocks from the State Department, but the distance did not bother Miller. G/TIP is only three blocks from the White House.

If your job is to fight global slavery, the least important thing is who is on your side in Washington. The most important thing is the height of the issue in the inbox of people that matter. Miller knew that most of the people that mattered did not sit in Foggy Bottom.

When I scheduled an interview with Miller after returning from Haiti, he insisted that we eat dinner. I was surprised. I had heard that, with more slaves in the world than at any point in human history, the man charged with freeing them had little patience for the niceties that befit his rank of ambassador-at-large. But when it furthered the cause of abolition, Miller would hold his pinky aloft and sip tea with the Queen of Sweden (whom he liked) or break *khubz* with the Crown Prince of Saudi Arabia (not so much).

Rain fell in sheets as we left his office. Miller did not own a car, but he shared his umbrella. He drilled me about Haiti, and particularly about Benavil Lebhom. He had spoken with over a thousand slaves and survivors of slavery but had never met a trafficker.

Preoccupied with the soaking of my one good suit, I failed to respond thoughtfully. At first I assumed that Miller, who was a head taller than me, was simply holding the umbrella askew. But he too was drenched, and I spotted the problem: while he had remembered to hold the umbrella aloft, he was too focused on the conversation to remember to open it.

We found an empty, fluorescent pizza place, where we talked for two hours. I tried to learn his own story, but he wanted to tell those of the slaves he had met. They animated him, he said. He had a lousy recall for details of his own life, but he remembered vividly the stories of survivors.

As he spoke, he leaned in to give me the "Lyndon Johnson treatment." His involved the actual laying on of hands: a reflection, possibly, of the practice of those he called his "constituents," the most fervent rank-and-file abolitionists, who tended to be devout Evangelical Christians. Whatever its origin, his lean now threatened to push my tray into my lap. A senior staffer had described how Miller, in his trademark thrashing, once smashed an entire shelf of what she called her "I-love-me photos" with important people. She jokingly said that Miller, who unlike most of his staff was Republican, had destroyed the pictures of Madeleine Albright on purpose.

He wore his standard outfit: button-down collar, a crisp pin-striped suit—but threadbare socks. As he talked, one of his navy suspender straps popped off, and he absentmindedly buttoned it halfway, only to have it pop off again and again. Once, in a pressurized bilateral meeting with foreign officials, he was so animated that he split his pants making a point. He didn't notice, but a staffer tried to cover up for him.

"Slavery has been around since the dawn of man. It's almost an eternal challenge. Yet at the same time, we're at the beginning of modern-day slavery," Miller said now. "We're approaching the end of the beginning, however, because we are starting to make some progress."

In a dozen meetings and conversations over several years, I have seen a glimmer of defeat cross his face only twice, despite the uphill battle he faced to get people within his own government to understand that slavery was slavery. The first glimmer came after a waitress, more than a little piqued that we were staying well past closing time, cleared his food before he was finished.

"Oh," he said meekly to no one in particular. "I think I lost my beer."

After the waitress kicked us out, we wandered around in the rain looking for an open Starbucks, which was a challenge. "In Seattle, you can find a Starbucks on every corner," Miller said. "It's great." Finally, we found one, and he kept debriefing me about Haiti, as much as I gathered stories from him. He wanted to know everything about the restavèks, and he took notes as I spoke. Then he explained the impossibility of pressuring the nonexistent Haitian government. When Starbucks closed, we talked in the shelter of a Metro station. He listed places that he wanted me to investigate if I could. Near midnight, he caught the Blue Line back to his apartment in Virginia.

His disarming candor made Miller a startlingly different breed of Bush administration appointee. He loved the media. He viewed it as an essential weapon of the new abolitionist movement, and he tended to speak without a filter. Chafing at clearance procedures, he often forewent them entirely, to the consternation of C Street bureaucrats.

In the fall of 2004, an HBO documentary team showed him what he described as "shattering" undercover footage of enslaved child camel jockeys in Dubai. The severely malnourished boys had been beaten, and one seven-year-old displayed his bruised posterior, where his trainer had sodomized him. The previous year, Miller's office, in its annual *Trafficking in Persons Report*, had upgraded the United Arab Emirates from Tier Three, where they could have faced sanctions, to Tier One, where Colin Powell singled them out for praise.

Miller "exploded" when he saw the video, a staffer recalled. But rather than indict HBO's Bernard Goldberg for what others might have defensively labeled "gotcha journalism," Miller blamed his own gullibility. "The UAE really sold the State Department a bill of goods," he said. "Of course, I'd made a mistake." The following year, Miller convinced Condoleezza Rice to relegate the UAE, a key Gulf ally, back to Tier Three. He had failed in many similar battles. "We're looked on as ogres," he said. "Everybody understands we're thorns within the department."

Deputy Secretary of State Richard Armitage once told Miller that an assistant secretary had praised his work cajoling foreign governments to pass and enforce antislavery laws. "If all the bureau chiefs start saying what a great job I'm doing," Miller responded, "fire me."

He has a long history of insolence. One freezing winter morning as a schoolchild, Miller saw a sylvan portrait of Puget Sound in a geography textbook at P.S. 6 in Manhattan. The caption described the area as "temperate," which Miller's fourth-grade teacher explained meant "not too hot, not too cold." That evening at dinner, the boy announced that he was moving to Puget Sound.

His parents were not impressed. Their world began and ended at the borders of the Upper East Side. Although they were liberal Jews— his father was just one generation removed from persecuted Latvian immigrants—they did not think much of America beyond the Hudson, and viewed the Soviet Union as "a fine country." They even railed against "evil" red-baiters like Richard Nixon. What they knew about Stalin, Miller later recalled, "could have been put in a thimble."

"Ridiculous," his father said of his son's westward yearning. "You'll forget all about it in a couple of weeks," added his mother.

Thirty-six years later, he was an anti-Communist Republican congressman representing Seattle. "If my parents had just said 'that's nice' and left it at that, I would have forgotten all about Puget Sound," he said.

He had been an outsider ever since he left home at age eighteen. Immediately after earning a law degree in 1964, John Ripin Miller ignored his mother's entreaties to take the bar in New York and instead moved to Olympia, then Seattle. While his grades had not distinguished him at Yale, his heavy Manhattan dialect distinguished him in Washington State, and not for the right reasons. He sent out over a hundred application letters. "I got one and a half offers: One firm made an offer, then withdrew it," he said.

After five years as an environmental lawyer, and a decade on the Seattle City Council, Miller was restless. In the early 1980s, he tried his hand as a baseball columnist, covering the Mariners for a year. His skill as a writer did not match his passion for the game. His time in local politics led to a job as a commentator on a local television station. But punditry was not his thing. Miller was a natural politician, but a rare sub-breed.

He thought more about what he did not know than about how to convince his constituents that he was omniscient.

While in his professional life he was adrift, in his personal life, Miller found his anchor. When he saw the young woman on a Seattle street, he nearly steered his car into traffic. He followed her at a distance until she walked into an office building. No pickup artist, Miller concocted a lame but passable excuse to get into her office, with one simple goal: to learn her name. He did more than that, and soon he and June Hamula were an item. "I had many quirks, but she tolerated them," Miller recalled with wonderment.

In 1984, the GOP congressman from his district retired, and a newly focused Miller made two major decisions: He asked June to marry him, and he decided to run for the open seat. Although many Republicans campaigned on Reagan's overwhelming popularity, Miller eschewed the trend. In campaign ads and stump speeches, he rarely mentioned the president.

On the night of his victory, he declared himself "a John Miller Republican, not a Ronald Reagan Republican." He stuck to that pledge, voting against Reagan's MX missile request, and working to rein in the president's wanton deficit spending. Of course, distancing himself from Reagan in liberal Seattle did not make Miller a profile in courage. But going to war against Boeing, the biggest employer in his district, could have ended his career. Concerned by stories of Chinese and Soviet forced labor camps, he drafted the "Miller Principles," a set of benchmarks the Chinese would have to meet to avoid sanctions. Miller dressed down Boeing executives, who had sold planes to China for over a decade, and voted against Most Favored Nation trading status.

While that move, and his support of the Nicaraguan contras, put Miller at odds with many in Seattle, his positions won the admiration of two rising Republican stars. Congressmen Chris Smith of New Jersey and Frank Wolf of Virginia were prayer partners and fierce Cold Warriors, small men with big hearts and outsized personalities.

But they, and Miller, also shared a passion for mucking up the Reagan administration's measured foreign policy. In the run-up to the 1986

Reykjavik Summit, Wolf called James A. Baker III, then Treasury Secretary, before a hearing on slave labor in the Soviet Union. When Baker resisted his demand to invoke the 1930 Tariff Act, prohibiting slave-produced imports, Wolf went purple with rage. "You have an obligation to bring a case!" Wolf shouted. "Those people have been in enforced labor camps for years—" "I'll decide what my obligation is, not you!" the normally unruffled Baker snapped, cutting Wolf off. "I don't come up here to get yelled at by you!"

Wolf and Smith found a fellow troublemaker in Miller. In the fall of 1991, shortly after Wolf and Smith visited Chinese prison labor camps, Miller spent three days with Nancy Pelosi in Beijing, criticizing Deng Xiaoping's human rights record, and visiting Tiananmen Square, where they laid white flowers to commemorate those that fell there.

But as Miller built alliances, June grew more isolated. After his first victory, Washington hadn't seemed so bad. June had sold her business in Seattle, and together they had found a Capitol Hill town house with enough green in the garden to make it feel like home. They even discussed adding a fountain, to remind them of Puget Sound.

Still, four increasingly competitive elections had soured June on life as a congressman's wife. During a ferocious campaign in 1988, Miller's opponent Reese Lindquist ran ads decrying his support of the contras, who had killed a twenty-eight-year-old Californian engineer the previous year. Miller's campaign got a call offering him an explosive if asymmetric response. The caller claimed he had evidence that, five years earlier, Lindquist, the Teachers Union president, had a sexual affair with a young boy in a university library.

"My God, if this comes out, can you imagine the effect on his wife?" June told her husband. The couple had just adopted a baby boy from the Seattle area. June couldn't stomach the idea of destroying another man's family just as they were starting their own. At her insistence, Miller decided not to air the charges. On January 5, 1993, Lindquist was sentenced to one year's probation for soliciting sex with a minor in a park. That same day, Miller retired from Congress, promising June that his D.C. days were over.

———————

The genesis of America's hidden war on modern-day slavery is a drama in three acts. But with John Miller out of public life during the Clinton years, the main protagonist was a hard-hitting neoconservative insider named Michael Horowitz. In five years, Horowitz and a core group of Evangelical activists pushed through laws that made global abolition a national foreign policy.

Like Miller, Horowitz was a New York Jew, but Horowitz's Bronx was a different world from Miller's Manhattan. "John was a sort of red-diaper baby, progressive, secular, Jewish liberal family," said Horowitz. "Mine was very different. Our focus was the synagogue and synagogue politics."

Short and bookish, Horowitz never met the tall, athletic Miller in school, although both men graduated from Yale Law in 1964. Miller was then the president of the Young Democrats, though both became Republicans later in life. Horowitz, who described his switch as "this contorted process akin to some gay coming out of the closet," moved harder right than Miller. While Miller was considering a centrist run for Congress, Horowitz was already honing his skills as a bureaucratic fighter in Reagan's Office of Management and Budget (OMB). He was a ferocious ideologue, leading the charge to defund the left by forbidding federal money for advocacy groups.

In 1985, Horowitz learned, through bitter experience, how to torpedo a career in a few short weeks. President Reagan had floated him as a possible federal judge, and a group of left-leaning groups, clearly insufficiently defunded, submitted a twenty-page memorandum to kill the nomination. The American Bar Association added its sense that Horowitz lacked "judicial temperament." Horowitz withdrew his name. His time in government over, he found refuge at the Hudson Institute, a conservative Washington think tank.

It was at Hudson that Horowitz staged Act I in the fight against modern-day slavery. The opening scenes, however, had little to do with slavery. His staunchest defenders in the Reagan administration were

Evangelical Christians. Now Horowitz moved, in a sense, to repay them by taking up an issue that most did not recognize as an issue: global Christian persecution. In 1996, he assembled a predominantly Evangelical coalition to push for the International Religious Freedom Act (IRFA), a law that made exterminating global religious persecution a goal of American foreign policy.

At first glance, Horowitz and the Evangelicals were odd bunkmates. The 16.4 million-strong Southern Baptist Convention (SBC), the largest Evangelical denomination in America, was at the time making efforts to save Jews through conversion. In 1997, the SBC shortcut the process with Horowitz by naming him one of the Top Ten Christians in its journal *Home Life*. Orthodox though he was, Horowitz took the designation as a compliment.

Horowitz found an ally in another ex-Republican White House official. Chuck Colson, the convicted Watergate conspirator–turned–born-again activist, was not a hard sell on what Horowitz called "Wilberforce issues." Like Colson, many in the Evangelical leadership placed the British parliamentarian and abolitionist William Wilberforce just below Christ in their pantheon of heroes. Colson quickly called together that leadership, who then relayed tales of overseas Christian martyrdom to the congregation via tens of thousands of churches across the country.

As the group coalesced, Horowitz met Colson's congressman, Frank Wolf. The Bronx Jew saw a reflection of his own piss-and-vinegar demeanor in the Virginian Evangelical, and convinced him to sponsor the religious persecution bill. Wolf, used to losing the Good Fight, was sure the secular elites in the State Department would kill it by labeling it one-sided. But Horowitz fought to keep it focused on anti-Christian persecution alone, believing that if the United States held countries accountable for "the Jews of the twenty-first century," then others would benefit.

Over Horowitz's objections to its enlargement, Congress expanded the bill to cover persecution of all religions—and the Senate unanimously approved the fuller legislation. Over Madeleine Albright's objections to some passages that would tie State's hands, President Clinton signed the act in 1998.

The IRFA was the first clean-cut foreign policy victory for the Christian Right. Though President Clinton was a Southern Baptist, the 1990s were the doldrums for signature Evangelical issues like school prayer and abortion. But, in the swift IRFA victory, Horowitz felt a strong wind of providence. Evangelicals were the largest single religious group in America. Soon, their foreign policy clout would match their size.

Act II, Scene I: On January 11, 1998, Horowitz read a front-page *New York Times* article about a lovely Ukrainian twenty-one-year-old named Irina. She was among the 800,000-strong post-Soviet exodus to Israel. Only she did not reach the Promised Land. A trafficker sold her into a brothel near Haifa, where she was beaten, raped, and finally rescued, only to be thrown into a desert prison for carrying forged documents.

Reading the story, Horowitz flashed back to a rainy night in 1965 when he saw a pimp smack a prostitute in a bar on the Upper West Side of Manhattan. More than anything he recalled his response: nothing. "At some very powerful level, when I'm dealing with the trafficking issue, it's *payback*," he said. "It's very fulfilling to me in a personal sense."

With his Rolodex of Evangelical leaders who abhorred the sin of prostitution, Horowitz had his troops; with the IRFA, he had his model legislation. And in the Clinton administration, he had a known adversary. The administration had begun to confront the emergent trafficking crisis. President Clinton spoke out in various minor international forums against trafficking, and Secretary of State Madeleine Albright discussed the problem with the female foreign ministers at the UN General Assembly. First Lady Hillary Clinton, deeply affected by meeting an HIV-positive sex slave during a 1994 trip to Thailand, was more robust in her speeches—and pressed her husband to act. To Horowitz, it was all window-dressing.

Though he claimed it was never his intention, Horowitz seized ownership of the trafficking issue for Republicans. He recruited Colson's old friend—and Miller's ex-colleague—Representative Chris Smith to sponsor legislation on sex trafficking. His knight in the Senate was Sam

Brownback, a deeply religious Kansan whose grandmother owned land where radical abolitionist John Brown once battled proslavery forces.

Despite the Republican branding, Horowitz also wooed some of the most reliably Democratic activists: feminist groups like Equality Now and the National Organization for Women. Evangelicals and feminists first shared a foxhole during the failed war on porn in the 1980s. Now Horowitz brought the two groups together again by branding trafficking "the great women's issue of our time."

Democrats, when they took a position, defined the issue more broadly. The late Senator Paul Wellstone of Minnesota sponsored legislation that would put the United States in the vanguard of abolishing all forms of slavery, including labor trafficking, forced domestic servitude, and debt bondage. Wellstone's staff studied modern-day slavery closely. They found that it required more than a robust enforcement of laws, that poverty was a central factor.

Horowitz disagreed. Vigorously. When I presented him with Wellstone's general approach, he shouted an expletive.

"That's the lie! That's the lie!" he yelled, slamming his desk and pointing at me. "The idea that you can sit back while these mafias are out there buying and selling women and say, 'Well, there's nothing much that I can do about these guys because there's poverty on the earth' is a moral cop-out and a lie."

I never had the chance to ask Wellstone for a response, as he died in a plane crash the year that I began to research this book. But his closest aide on the issue told me that the senator shared Horowitz's deep revulsion at sex slavery, and spoke of his desire to see every trafficker doing hard time. The single most moving experience for him as a senator, he once said, was meeting trafficked women from Russia, his father's birth country. It's just that Wellstone also learned that, sadly, sex slaves were far from the only ones in abominable bondage.

On November 2, 1999, Wellstone introduced a bill that did not prioritize the abolition of one form of slavery over another. Horowitz sought to scale it back to the mere issue of sex trafficking. "In our battle over the TVPA," Horowitz explained, " 'Less Is More' is the big, flashing neon sign. And if you can focus on a problem that galvanizes everybody, the ripple effects have enormous positive impacts on a whole lot of other reforms.

"If you want to end the enslavement of those in debt bondage in the brick factories in India, the best thing you can do is put all of the sex traffickers in jail, and just drive a stake right through the heart of that system," he continued. "The connection is these ripple effects, where if you succeed in taking out some people, you send a message to everybody else saying: 'You're next.'"

Horowitz wanted to define slavery narrowly, but at a January 2000 conference in Vienna, representatives from the President's Interagency Council on Women chaired by Hillary Clinton defined the issue a bit too narrowly. Arguing for international antitrafficking protocols to combat "forced prostitution," the officials—Horowitz contended—implied that "voluntary prostitution" was possible. To many conservative Christians and hard-line feminists, all prostitutes were slaves.

Seizing its chance to savage Hillary Clinton, who was absent from Vienna, and who condemned trafficking as "the dark underbelly of globalization," the Horowitz coalition pounced. Chuck Colson co-authored a January 10 *Wall Street Journal* op-ed entitled "The Clintons Shrug at Sex Trafficking," in which he claimed that the "actions in Vienna will be counted as yet one more shameful act committed by this deeply corrupt administration." Richard Land, head of the Southern Baptist Convention's political arm, followed suit with a damning editorial in the conservative *Washington Times*. Clinton, two months into her first Senate campaign, retreated from the issue.

Horowitz won the battle to sideline Hillary Clinton but lost his lonely fight to keep nonsex slavery out of the Trafficking Victims Protection Act of 2000. Wellstone and Brownback, who agreed on little else, hammered out a remarkably comprehensive agreement on the final definition of trafficking, which included those forced into domestic, agricultural, or other forms of labor, as well as prostitution.

In a rare policy loss for the administration's dominant trade experts, who had resisted a sanctions provision, President Clinton signed the full act on October 28, 2000. Under the new law, the State Department was to direct and sponsor programs to combat slavery. Critically, State was also to evaluate the abolitionist efforts of each nation with more than a hundred slaves—which included nearly every country on earth. Countries working hard toward abolition, and succeeding, were placed in Tier One; countries working hard but failing were placed in Tier Two; and countries making no effort at all were placed in Tier Three. If the president did not waive Tier Three countries ninety days after the report, the United States would initiate nontrade sanctions.

What mattered, of course, was implementation. And implementation depended on who wrote the State Department trafficking report, and who sat in the White House. The Supreme Court soon judged the rightful occupant of 1600 Pennsylvania Avenue. And before long, Horowitz would use his skill with the shiv to determine the rightful occupant of the antislavery office.

There was one instance of modern slavery that was already the subject of American Evangelical prayer. Actually, the reestablishment of chattel slavery in the carnage of the thirty-six-year-long Sudanese civil war was anything but "modern." And when word spread through the Bible Belt that Muslims were enslaving Christians, the stage was set for Michael Horowitz to direct Act III.

The north-south Sudanese war, not to be confused with the subsequent north-north genocide in Darfur, cost over 2 million lives and was at the time the longest and bloodiest civil war in African history. The principal combatants were southerners, mainly ethnic Dinka, who had rebelled against the northern Islamist government, mainly Arab, who then became the aggressors.

Though none of the militants were washed in the blood of the lamb, tales of Christian persecution enflamed American Evangelicals, who agitated for aid to the southern rebels, the Sudan People's Liberation Movement (SPLM). In fact, only 5 percent of Sudanese were Christian, but southern leaders inflated the proportion to encourage Western involvement. Religion, specifically Khartoum's declaration of Islamic law, might have sparked the 1983 southern revolt. But there were many causes, including a long history of violent Arab southward expansion, and conflicts over oil and water, both of which were concentrated in the underdeveloped south.

Neither water nor oil was the liquid that ginned up Evangelicals; it was blood. More specifically, it was the blood of Christian martyrs. Attempting to depopulate the rebel strongholds, the Islamic government armed Arab raiders to kill southern men, and enslave their women and children. Frank Wolf first heard stories of the raids during his 1989 trip to Kapoeta, a southern Sudanese village just over the border from Kenya. Four years later, Wolf confronted the Sudanese Ambassador to the United States with information from a classified State Department cable. "The government of Sudan's military trains are coming up with horses on them, unloading the horses, going out into the fields, robbing, raping, burning villages, putting people on trucks, exporting them to slavery," he said. "I'm talking about slavery as William Wilberforce would have talked about it back in the 1800s in Africa."

In 1995, Wolf met a front-line Christian activist named John Eibner, who not only bore firsthand witness to the plight of slaves in Sudan, but soon began paying intermediaries to secure their freedom through redemption. On March 22 of that year, Eibner testified in front of the House Committee on International Relations. As a speaker, Eibner had none of Wolf's electricity. But his content was charged. "The Government of Sudan's self-declared *jihad* against the peoples of these southern regions is tantamount to attempted genocide," Eibner said. He chronicled bombings, manipulation of humanitarian aid, religious persecution, and slave raids. He recited the testimony of child slaves, and called for a no-fly zone over southern Sudan.

"The crisis in Sudan is so severe that the policies of neutrality or appeasement cannot be options for the United States," Eibner said. "Failure to act will also give enormous encouragement to Iran and other subversive Islamicist forces throughout the world, and will bring great danger to the security of East Africa and the Middle East."

"We must isolate this regime in all international forums until it is forced to change its ways," Wolf concluded.

The Clinton administration was no coddler of Khartoum. Today, that fact is embodied in the twisted rubble of Omdurman's al-Shifa pharmaceutical plant, at which Clinton ordered six Tomahawk missiles aimed on August 20, 1998. The administration imposed broad sanctions on Khartoum, while becoming the world's biggest supplier of aid to the Dinka homeland in southern Sudan.

But Clinton's concern with Sudan then, and always, was terrorism. Frank Wolf had lobbied him about Sudanese slavery since 1993, but it was only a year after the al-Shifa strike that the president responded by appointing former Congressman Harry Johnston his envoy to Sudan. Clinton never met with him after the appointment. On December 6, 2000, a week before the U.S. Supreme Court ended the Florida recounts, Clinton finally decried "the scourge of slavery in Sudan."

The Horowitz coalition, with Eibner as a consultant, made sure that George W. Bush would not wait until the final month of his presidency to denounce Sudanese slavery. Some, like Eibner, called for measures to destabilize Khartoum. Most, like Horowitz, felt that slavery was a by-product of the war, and only a comprehensive peace agreement would end the slave raids.

Christian conservatives leaned hard on the new White House for a robust Sudan policy. In an October 2000 presidential debate, Governor Bush had implied that Africa would not be a priority in his administration. At a breakfast less than a month later the Reverend Franklin Graham, Bush's close spiritual adviser, urged him to save southern Sudan, where the pastor had established a hospital.

Chuck Colson, who had worked closely with Bush during his time in Austin, pleaded the cause of Sudanese Christians at a meeting immediately after the inaugural. Two months later, in mid-March 2001, Colson met for an hour with the president's top political adviser, Karl Rove, and explained that Evangelicals wanted him to make Sudan Bush's top priority in Africa.

Though not a particularly religious person, Rove was also not a dummy, and he agreed immediately. Not only Evangelicals but oil companies salivating at Sudan's estimated 262 million barrels of crude cared immensely about ending the war. Some neoconservatives even chimed in: the Islamist regime in Khartoum had sheltered Osama bin Laden, and sided with Saddam Hussein in the first Gulf War. Sudan, in other words, had it all: crucifixions, oil, and terrorism.

Once again, Horowitz was the angel in the whirlwind, directing the storm. This time, in addition to Wolf, Horowitz's knights were two congressmen who had visited Sudan in 1999 with Brownback: Colorado Republican Tom Tancredo and New Jersey Democrat Donald Payne. Payne, a member of the Congressional Black Caucus, helped Horowitz broaden the coalition to include African-American activists. Once again, Horowitz showed a deft ability to coalesce two groups that rarely found common cause.

In 2001, Tancredo and Payne drafted the Sudan Peace Act, calling on Khartoum to engage in good-faith negotiations with the SPLM, and calling on the U.S. president to investigate the claims of slavery. The House of Representatives passed the bill in June of that year; but Khartoum's antiterror cooperation after the attacks on 9/11, combined with a fight over a capital market sanctions provision in the act, meant that the bill languished in the Senate for over a year. In the meantime, on a sunny September morning in the Rose Garden, President Bush laid the groundwork for its implementation when he announced John C. Danforth, an Episcopal priest and former senator, as his envoy to the Sudanese peace negotiations.

Horowitz and Colson had pressed for an envoy, but they had no hand in the specific choice of "Saint Jack" Danforth, who once described himself as "a warrior doing battle for the Lord" when defending Clarence Thomas. Danforth also had strong convictions about Sudan. He first visited the country in 1984, was shocked by what he saw, and spoke out against subsequent Islamist regimes. The Horowitz coalition quickly agreed the plainspoken Missourian was an inspired appointment.

Finally, on October 21, 2002, in the shadow of a six-foot-five escaped Dinka slave, President Bush signed the Sudan Peace Act in the Roosevelt Room of the White House. The president would sit for several such photo ops with freed slaves during his administration. The task of freeing others fell to his appointees like Danforth and, eventually, John Miller. Their efforts would yield few Kodak moments.

While his Yale Law classmate was busy molesting the American foreign policy establishment with an overtly Evangelical agenda, John Miller was sleepless in Seattle. In the previous decade, he and his wife had settled into a quiet life. He chaired a think tank. He taught English at the local Yeshiva high school, and took in the occasional Mariners game on the weekend with his son, Rip. He even tried, and failed, to buy a farm team. It wasn't enough. Miller wanted a fight.

With the attacks of September 11, Miller sensed the time was right. An administration that had limped into office now seized a mandate to remake the world. Miller thought there might be a place for him, and after Rip decided to attend a boarding school on Vancouver Island, he called an ex-colleague and fellow neoconservative named Paula Dobriansky. Dobriansky and Miller shared mutual admiration from a decade earlier. In her capacity at the State Department's human rights bureau she had testified in front of his House International Relations Committee.

Miller asked Dobriansky, who then served as Under Secretary of State for Global Affairs, if he could be the U.S. representative to the UN Human Rights Commission. There was one problem: the United States had lost its seat on the commission in May 2001, partly due to the U.S. withdrawal from the International Criminal Court. Miller, it seemed, was out of luck.

Meanwhile, another program in Dobriansky's bureau, the fledgling human trafficking office, was off to a rocky start. Her choice to head that office, Ambassador Nancy Ely-Raphel, a former colleague at the human rights desk, had served under every president since Ford. But never in her long career had she faced the bare-knuckle politics of Michael Horowitz.

Ely-Raphel interpreted the law literally, and viewed her job as monitoring and combating all forms of slavery, not just sex trafficking. Her method was to push for change from within by leveraging her old alliances with regional bureau chiefs, in order to build a State Department culture that understood human trafficking. That, plus the fact that she had served in the Clinton administration, made her an "apparatchik" to Horowitz, who called her an "irretrievably disastrous choice." In a private meeting on March 11, 2002, he told her he planned to jugulate her career.

"I want to get rid of you," Horowitz said, according to Ely-Raphel. "And I will get rid of you."

Three months after that encounter, Ely-Raphel would have to present her office's most important product, the annual trafficking report. To compile that, she and her staff of three requested national trafficking data from 186 American embassies and consulates. Few Foreign Service officers had any notion what constituted "human trafficking," and only a handful of their host countries had policies to combat it. The information Ely-Raphel gathered was unsurprisingly shallow: she had hard numbers for only seven out of eighty-nine reviewed countries.

The Horowitz coalition clobbered Ely-Raphel over her first report, released in June 2002. Much of the criticism focused on Ely-Raphel's failure to sufficiently condemn countries like the Netherlands and Germany that had legalized prostitution. Colson's organization called it "an insult to women and children." In a *Washington Post* op-ed, Gary Haugen, a lawyer who headed the International Justice Mission, a large Evangelical antitrafficking group, called for a General Accounting Office investigation of Ely-Raphel's "whitewash."

Horowitz had someone close to the ambassador who was already sharpening the long knives. At his insistence, Dobriansky had named as Ely-Raphel's deputy a former antiporn crusader named Laura Lederer. Lederer, who had been his closest feminist collaborator during the formulation of the Trafficking Victims Protection Act, agreed passionately with Horowitz that sex trafficking should not be lumped with labor trafficking, and that American abolitionist efforts should focus on ending prostitution.

Two weeks after the release of the report, Ely-Raphel appeared before the House International Relations Committee to defend it. With Horowitz's encouragement, Lederer submitted questions, designed to embarrass Ely-Raphel, to Chris Smith. On principle, Smith did not ask the questions. But the ambassador knew she was finished. Horowitz, through Dobriansky, made sure of it.

"**What qualifications do** you have to head up a motor pool?" a friend asked, after John Miller reported Dobriansky's offer to take over the trafficking office. Miller, who knew almost nothing about modern slavery, was a bizarre and perfect choice. In a late October 2002 meeting with Michael Horowitz, Dobriansky floated Miller's name as someone who was looking to join the administration.

"Miller is a very dynamic personality," she recalled saying. "He would be very dogged." Horowitz did not remember Miller, and lobbied instead for Mark Lagon, a former aide to Jesse Helms. Also present at the meeting was Frank Wolf, who remembered Miller because he battled Boeing over China. "I always thought that was political suicide," Wolf told Horowitz and Dobriansky. "And now I think it was very courageous."

When Miller's name reached the White House, Karl Rove objected. He explained in an e-mail to Chuck Colson that Miller had endorsed John McCain in the 2000 election. "Karl looks at a person's track record carefully," said Richard Land, a friend of Rove since the early 1980s. "And Karl and the Bushes value loyalty very highly. It's very high in their pantheon of values." But the opinion of Wolf, who sat on the Appropriations Subcommittee for the State Department, carried weight. Backed by the Horowitz coalition, he overrode Rove's objection.

After Dobriansky called Miller at home to offer him the position, Horowitz followed up with thousands of pages of reading material, focusing mainly on sex trafficking. The issue felt immediate to Miller partly because the Seattle police had freed over a dozen Asian sex slaves just two months earlier. With June's blessing, he accepted Dobriansky's offer.

Miller crashed with Horowitz on his first night back in D.C. Before bed, he thought about his predecessor's sticky end. Miller knew that his learning curve would have to be steep, and his manner aggressive, in order to avoid her fate. Wolf had his back, so Miller could lean hard on top officials at State and, if necessary, he could make an end run to Congress. Outside of government, Evangelicals would make him or break him. He came in with preset Evangelical support, partly because in Seattle he had chaired the Discovery Institute, a local think tank that articulated the theory of intelligent design. Still, slavery was a new, massive challenge in a new, wartime Washington. Miller felt daunted.

In March 2003, Miller traveled to Bush's hometown. There, a small group called the Midland Ministerial Alliance asserted big influence on foreign policy. Its focus was Sudan, and it had hosted talks by a former slave named Francis Bok, and John Eibner, the slave redeemer. The same week as Miller's visit, the Alliance sent a letter to the Sudanese government warning that it should stop enslaving Christians or it would find itself in the dustbin of history. Specifically, it claimed the Islamist government was in "material breach" of the Sudan Peace Act, and warned that it would be "making a strategic error of historic proportions" if it did not cease its slave raids.

On his first evening in downtown Midland, the Alliance held a prayer service for Miller in the basement of the Petroleum Club. As members laid hands on him, closed their eyes, and called out to Jesus, Miller felt empowered but also awkward. Earlier, he had quoted Exodus, and now he worried that they mistook him for one of the Saved rather than one of the Chosen.

"Well, I think this is wonderful," he burst out. "This is the first time that I have had a whole group of Christians praying for this Jewish boy from New York!"

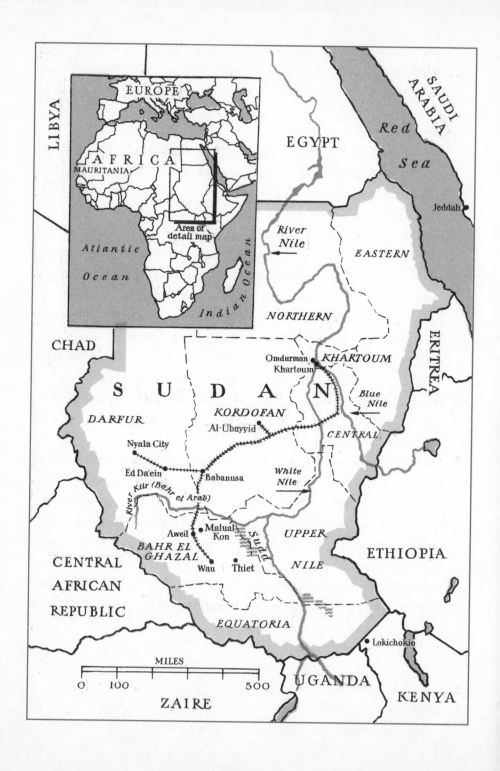

3

Those Whom Their Right Hands Possess

Muong Nyong Muong was born under a good sign in 1976, a rare moment of peace. His home, Bahr el Ghazal, was a front-line state in the civil war between Sudan's Arab north and predominantly Dinka south. Some Dinka parents used the specter of the Arabs ("Here come the camels!") the same way Western parents invoked the "monsters in the closet" to silence restless children at bedtime.

But, tired of war and enjoying a decade-long truce, Muong's father raised a strong boy, who would live peacefully even in a broken land. Muong's young life was filled with hard work, helping his mother and tending the family's few cattle. But he managed some insouciant pleasures like *atet*, Dinka hockey, in the hard-caked dirt of the eastern Sahel. Muong's favorite game was *alweth*, the local equivalent of hide-and-seek. Blindfolded, he had to find his brother, Garang, whose stifled laughter always gave him away.

The rare peace also bestowed a scarce blessing on Muong's childhood: hope. He looked forward to a ritual that would make Western adolescents cringe, but that to the Dinka signified initiation into manhood. Elders cut parallel lines into young men, usually at age fifteen, starting in the center of their foreheads and going to one ear, then the other. The cuts ran deep, leaving permanent, distinctive scars, even etchings in their skulls that would be visible long after death. The boys did not scream; they were proud, and by their silence they made their families proud.

Muong did not get that chance. In the mid-1980s, the civil war restarted, and a sandstorm of violence swept over Bahr el Ghazal, engulfing his family, and taking his father from him in 1987.

Though they lacked the formal markings of manhood, Muong and his brother Garang became the male elders in their family during the onset of a 1988 famine that killed 250,000 of their countrymen. With their mother, Aluat, the boys set out on foot, leaving their disintegrating village to seek work in the north across the River Kiir. On the second day of their journey, a lone *djellabah*-wearing *murahile*—an Arab militiaman—found them. The horseman, returning from raiding nearby villages, circled the family, shouted "*Abeed!*", and pointed his rifle at Aluat. Muong had never heard the word. He soon learned it well.

The stocky, light-skinned Arab dismounted and tackled Aluat. She fought back. Muong, stunned, looked on helplessly as the man threw his mother to the ground and beat her in the back with the butt of his rifle. Muong heard more horses coming, saw a cloud of dust rising, and grabbed his brother to flee. Before they made it to the brush, the other *murahileen*, towing several Dinka in ropes, cantered up and yelled at them in Arabic. Frozen with fear, the brothers saw their mother struggle to her feet and try to slip away in the confusion. Her captor cracked her head with his rifle, and she fell to the ground. Muong began to cry hysterically, as he thought that his mother, motionless, was dead.

"Are you crazy?" a captive shouted to Aluat, "Why are you resisting? Many others who have resisted have been shot—you don't want to die the same way." Tears and blood streaming down her face, Aluat rose again and, quietly, so as to calm her sons, allowed her hands to be tied to the caravan. Muong and Garang, unwilling to leave their mother, trailed close behind as the horsemen dragged the Dinka across the Kiir. In 1924, the British, Sudan's former colonial ruler, had established the river as a political boundary between north and south, between Bahr el Ghazal and Darfur. That same year, they formally abolished slavery in Sudan.

Muong's life as he knew it was over. He and his family were now *abeed*—slaves. They were the property of Adamoussa, the man who had beaten his mother. Adamoussa took them to serve in his home in southern Darfur, and Muong soon learned how to survive in his new world. In this world, he cultivated crops that he did not eat and carried loads of water that bowed his spine.

His new world was one in which he was worth less than the goats and cattle he tended. Adamoussa punctuated his sunup-to-sundown workday with beatings. All three in his family tended crops, but all three worked separately. Their only pay was table scraps and leftovers. "We had no rights," Muong explained, "but we had to work a lot." Adamoussa's wife made Aluat fetch firewood and perform domestic labor. At the end of each workday, Muong saw his family. That, to him, was a quiet blessing.

After a year in Darfur, Adamoussa moved his slaves with his family near to al-Ubayyid, a rail town in the northwest of the neighboring province, Kordofan. After the move, Adamoussa told Muong and his brother to refer to him as *abuya*: father.

Throughout their first five years of slavery, Adamoussa raped Aluat repeatedly, or, as she painfully recalled, "he used me in a 'sex way.'" Soon, his wife felt her status threatened. To maintain peace in his house, Adamoussa openly contemplated ridding it of Muong, Garang, and Aluat.

One evening, sensing their imminent destruction, the three slaves fled. They ran, then walked, for several miles into the parched Sahel until Aluat collapsed, exhausted. Garang knew that Adamoussa would soon follow, and urged them on. But as they rose, Muong felt a sharp sting in his ankle. At first he thought it was a scorpion or spider. Then he saw two puncture marks, and the skin around them turned blue and blotchy. In the darkness, Garang almost trod on the black-necked cobra that had bitten his brother. In two agonizing hours, Muong's foot inflated to four times its normal size. His head jerked back and forth as spasms drilled through his body.

Muong was terrified but thought that Adamoussa would kill all three if he found them there. He told his mother and brother to flee. They refused to leave him. Meanwhile, Adamoussa had charged off from camp on horseback. The militiaman had no dogs, but Muong claimed that he used witchcraft, specifically white shells from the Nile, which he threw on the ground to show him the way.

At dawn, Adamoussa found them. He tied all three to his horse and dragged them back to camp. There he beat Garang with the butt of his rifle until his eyes were swollen shut and he spewed blood. Adamoussa trained his rifle on Muong and Aluat. He told them he would shoot them if they fled again.

Two months after John Miller bowed his head in prayer with the ministers of Midland, I waited at 6 a.m. to fly out of Nairobi's tiny Wilson Airport to front-line southern Sudan. On this, my first trip to the country, I would travel with another icon of Evangelical America.

John Eibner, a Christian slave redeemer, stood in a corner of the hangar, communing with a seven-foot-tall member of the Dinka tribe. Southern Sudan has more Dinka than any other ethnic group and they formed the backbone of the rebel army, though this fellow was a civilian. The tribesman had to double over to hear the diminutive crusader, whose bouffant hairdo only slightly augmented his height. Eibner's blue eyes darted around as he spoke in hushed tones. He was gray-haired and unshaven, traits that lent a rugged air to otherwise delicate features.

He prepared to lead me on the same hermetically sealed tour he had given many breathless Americans. I would only see slavery in Sudan without a filter on two subsequent solo trips. It was on one of those that I learned the story of Muong.

But our second story begins with Eibner. I tell it because his is the story of how and why the United States came to bring an end to the Sudanese civil war. I also tell it because it reveals the lure and the danger of simple fixes for complex humanitarian problems.

Chattel slavery dates back more than 5,000 years in Sudan, long preceding even Islam, whose most sacred text instructs its followers how to treat "those whom their right hands possess." Yet before Eibner, Americans ignored slavery's recrudescence in Sudan's north-south war. Eibner alerted America by claiming to have bought back, or "redeemed," 85,000 slaves. I would find that the truth behind these redemptions was confounding.

Like Muong, thousands of Sudanese slaves have endured an absolute horror over the past two decades. After being captured in violent raids, they became brutalized property, raped, often mutilated, by masters intent on obliterating their cultural identities by smashing their humanity. The northern government of Sudan condoned their enslavement as a weapon of war against a fierce southern insurgency. The international community, to its shame, abandoned them. Finally, President Bush, at the behest of Evangelicals whom Eibner inspired, acted to prevent their further enslavement by brokering a deal to end the thirty-six-year-long war. It was a signature achievement for an administration that boasted few diplomatic successes.

But the peace deal had its critics, including Eibner. And Eibner himself had critics who, at the time I traveled with him, outnumbered his supporters.

Now, together, we set off from the verdant highlands of western Kenya to the scorched earth of Bahr el Ghazal, the region of southwestern Sudan most destroyed by civil war, famine, and slave raiding. There, in eight days, Eibner would buy over 3,000 slaves, in the hope they could be redeemed through money and, perhaps, Christ.

That might sound fanciful, even retrograde, but it made sense to John Eibner. For most of his life, he found himself part of religious institutions that were a step too slow for the times. The grandson of Hungarian immigrants, he was born in 1952 and raised Baptist in Valhalla, a small, affluent, largely Episcopalian community in Westchester County, New York. He graduated in 1974 from a now-defunct Christian school called Barrington College, at the time known more for its radio ministry than for its academics.

After graduate school, Eibner became the Hungarian specialist at London's Centre for the Study of Religion and Communism, which tracked persecuted Christians and assisted underground churches behind the Iron Curtain. The end of the Cold War rendered the Centre irrelevant. Eibner, a poorly funded crusader without a crusade, moved to Switzerland to work for a Swiss Reformed clergyman named Hans Jürg Stückelberger. In 1977, the reverend had founded Christian Solidarity International (CSI) to smuggle Bibles and broadcast an evangelical radio show to Eastern bloc countries. Eibner became Stückelberger's assistant, and early on established his own credentials as an adventurous Defender of the Faith, slipping under enemy radar in Azerbaijan to aid Christians in blockaded and war-torn Nagorno-Karabakh.

Sudan put CSI—and Eibner—on the map. A Sudanese Christian organization invited Eibner to visit Khartoum in August 1992, just as the Karabakh conflict wound down. Over the next three years, he visited Sudan six more times, and published urgent calls in the American Evangelical media for action to confront Christian persecution by the ruling Islamist regime. Word spread across the Bible Belt about a lone hero carrying the Cross in enemy territory. Khartoum banned him from Sudan.

In the summer of 1995, Eibner chartered a plane to an area of the south that Khartoum had redlined for foreign visitors, as it was a theater where their sponsored militias had displaced or killed one third of the population. Rebels there told Eibner that certain Dinka were buying back relatives—a transaction called "redemption"—from the Arab *baggara* tribesmen, nomadic cattle herders who were the mainstay of the slave raids. Stückelberger's "Christian duty," he said, was to free the enslaved Dinka. CSI began paying officials of the main rebel organization, the Sudan People's Liberation Movement (SPLM), to organize redemptions through Arab middlemen.

Eibner found an ally in a man named Charles Jacobs, who in 1994 had founded the American Anti-Slavery Group to decry slavery in Sudan and Mauritania. Jacobs, who called Eibner one of the "undiscovered holy men who hold up the world," worked feverishly to publicize the redemptions. Across America, abolitionist schoolchildren raised money to buy slaves out of bondage—and provided an irresistible human interest hook for news organizations.

"I thought it was good to give up my lunch money to free slaves," twelve-year-old Laquisha Gerald told an interviewer during her New Jersey school's May 2001 "Walk for Freedom." The story was an easy sell. *The Village Voice, Boston Globe, National Review, New York Times,* CBS Evening News, even Nickelodeon published paeans to Eibner. CBS dedicated an episode of the hit prime-time drama *Touched By an Angel* to the redemptions. The buybacks had their detractors, including UN bureaucrats, who in March 1999 argued the redemptions actually encouraged slave trafficking by making the slaves salable. Subsequently, UN officials ignored objections from Washington and abolished the word "slavery" to describe the practice in Sudan. Cowed by Khartoum, UN organs and agencies began referring only to "abduction."

Two weeks later, Eibner brought SPLM commander John Garang to address the UN Human Rights Commission in Geneva. Garang condemned "the genocidal character of this war, as manifested by *jihad,* slavery and other gross human rights violations by the Government of Sudan." Recognizing that Garang intended to speak for the SPLM and thus soil the UN's cherished neutrality, the commission's chairperson ordered him to step down from the podium.

For the rest of the war, Garang stayed mum about slavery. Relations between the embarrassed rebel leader and Eibner chilled, and later in 1999 Garang forbade several Sudanese expats from escorting CSI on redemptions. Meanwhile, the United Nations, whose unwillingness to recognize southern sovereignty aided northern aggression, booted Eibner. Over American objection, but with the support of such humanitarian avatars as Algeria, China, Cuba, Ethiopia, Pakistan, and Turkey, CSI lost its UN consultative status.

Eibner was unrepentant: "Knowing that tens of thousands of people are still enslaved and knowing that we can get them out, I couldn't live with myself and say, 'Sorry, I'm stopping because of some criticism from an ivory tower in London or New York.'"

UN condemnation helped turn CSI into a fund-raising juggernaut among conservative Americans. Five days after Garang's aborted Geneva speech, at half-time of the NCAA Final Four Championship game, the National Association of Basketball Coaches gave CSI a $100,000 check for redemptions. A Texas company donated $5,000. A homeless Alaskan pulled together $100. An impoverished elderly woman sent a dollar, along with a note saying it was "all I can afford."

Through Charles Jacobs and his American Anti-Slavery Group, Eibner raised millions. And through Michael Horowitz, he raised friends in Congress.

A few weeks after Eibner first set foot in their territory, SPLM units, which Khartoum had steadily rolled back since 1990, launched their version of the Tet offensive. They took out 7,000 government soldiers and demolished a mechanized division. The addition of tanks to the rebel arsenal was one reason for the turnaround.

The main reason for the new aggression, Eibner told a reporter, was "because they are no longer isolated." At the time, that might have been more hope than fact. But over the next few years, Eibner would work very hard to make it true.

Before I go any further with the parallel stories of Eibner and Muong, I need to step back and briefly explain the war that changed their lives, and the role that slavery played in it. The bloodshed had deep roots in the nation's tortured history. That history featured the efforts of the British, the former colonial governors, to stop the slave trade but not slavery. In 1956, independence in Sudan ignited long-simmering tensions between northerners who wanted one country under Arab rule, and southerners for whom that rule meant bondage.

The slave raids were more than a perverse explosion of old hatred.

They were a means of annihilating a race. It was not the first time in modern history that genocidaires had used slavery alongside mass murder for that purpose. Turks took slaves in the 1915 Armenian genocide. The Nazis enslaved 12 million. Two million died as slaves under the Khmer Rouge. But Khartoum's effort was the most prolonged slave raiding in the twentieth century.

Sadiq al-Mahdi, the Sudanese prime minister on whose watch the raids began in the mid-1980s, inherited a blueprint from his grandfather, the legendary Muhammad Ahmed, better known as the Mahdi. An austere nineteenth-century mystic who claimed descent from the Prophet, the Mahdi led the *baggara*—nomadic Arabs who herded cattle and, at the time, traded slaves—on a ferocious charge to topple the colonial government, enslaving thousands of southerners in the process. His followers coordinated a system wherein Arab horsemen raided southerners and rounded them up in thorn-fence camps known as *zaribas*. After the British ousted the Mahdists in Lord Kitchener's 1898 reconquest, some *zaribas* still held slaves, but the term mainly referred to cattle camps.

Al-Mahdi's followers, like those of his grandfather, filled the *zaribas* with human chattel once more. His immediate predecessor, Gaafar Nimeiri, had laid the groundwork by arming the militias as a means to quell the rebellion that John Garang had launched in 1983. Ending an eleven-year cease-fire in a war dating from Sudan's independence, Garang, a thirty-eight-year old Sudanese army officer, raised a rebel force to challenge Khartoum's claim to newly discovered oil and Nimeiri's declaration of Shari'a (or Islamic law). For Nimeiri, Garang's mutiny was a challenge to national unity. For al-Mahdi, it was also a challenge to Arab cultural supremacy.

Al-Mahdi's vision was fantasy, as there are no "pure" Arabs in Sudan. The *baggara* include such tribes as the Rizeigat, Zaghawa, and Misseriya. They are Muslim and Arab, but their dark skin testifies to the intermarriage that took place with the original African inhabitants of Kordofan and Darfur for centuries. Both groups are nomadic cattle herders; both groups are as poor as their southern neighbors. None of the groups defines themselves as "black," which in Sudanese Arabic means "slave." They prefer to call themselves *zurga*, which means "blue."

Nonetheless, al-Mahdi was masterful at promoting the defense of Arab culture against the mythical southern threat. John Garang lent credibility to his claims by calling for the "liberation" of the entire country. In response, officers from al-Mahdi's Popular Defense Force (PDF) began indoctrinating militias in the glory of martyrdom. Typically, their pupils weren't the martyrs. Dinka civilians with spears and hippopotamus-skin shields couldn't do much against the Kalashnikovs of the *murahileen* militiamen.

As al-Mahdi pressed southward, rumors of the resurgence of an ancient evil began to trickle out via international relief agencies. Most aid workers first heard the reports as they fed southerners during the massive 1988 famine. Locals had known about the raids for a while. In 1984, a young Dinka doctor, Priscilla Joseph, was treating refugees in Khartoum. "When they were coming, they would tell us that some of the people went missing," Joseph said. "By '86 it was clear there were abductions happening."

A picture of the raids began to coalesce. During the dry season, between November and April, *baggara* communities planned the raids, sorted out the division of booty prior to the attack, and prepared *zaribas* about five to seven hours' walk from the raided villages. The raiders set out before dawn, carried by government trucks to the River Kiir, from where they continued on horseback.

For the Dinka, the only early warning was the sound of hooves and a rising plume of dust. Those who could scatter, did. A Dinka aid worker for Save the Children–UK, an NGO that began work in Sudan in response to famine in 1950, spoke from experience to prepare me for a second trip to southern Sudan. "If you have a team that's on the ground during a raid, that's it," he said. "You just run for it. You run for the bushes and hide."

The raiding parties—consisting of as many as a thousand horsemen—shot escaping villagers in the back. Elderly men, unable to run but useless as slaves, were brained in front of their progeny. Raiders torched crops and *tukuls* (huts) as they left. They looted cattle, around which Dinka life revolves. And they looted women and children, whom they marched north, leaving the injured to die along the way. Through parched savannah, they gave the slaves no water. In the first news story on the subject, the *New York Times* recounted claims that "captives' hands were pierced and they were chained to each other to make escape virtually impossible."

Once the captives were hundreds of miles from home, their owners beat them into full submission. The *baggara* forced boys to tend goats or cattle in place of their own sons, many of whom had been drafted into the PDF. The militias compelled other Dinka children to fight their own relatives. *Murahileen* occasionally gang-raped young boys to erase their gender identities. The masters in the camps beat the children and forced them to sleep among the cattle. Sometimes the masters gave them scraps to eat; sometimes the slaves scrounged for maize around the camps. A master amputated the nose of an eleven-year-old boy who lost his cow. Another cut off his slave's arms when the boy attempted to run away. A herdsman nailed together the knees of one slave so that the boy would not try another escape. Dr. Joseph treated several young men who had their tendons cut. If they made it back to southern Sudan, they were helpless, as prosthetic limbs were unavailable. Using hot irons, masters branded some slaves to identify them should they flee.

Most of the slaves were women. And as was true during the zenith of the Ottoman Empire in the sixteenth century, most labored inside their masters' homes. Slave women's work included grinding millet, okra, and sesame, or fetching water from wells. The women's main use, however, was far more basic. Rape was common during and after the raids.

During the rule of al-Mahdi's grandfather, a young concubine could fetch seven times as much as a cow. Though oversupply had reduced their market value, they continued to be prized commodities. The *baggara* had lower birthrates than the Dinka, and the sexual conquest was often a conscious attempt to steal their wombs. Some masters cut uncircumcised women to make them "clean." After the ordeal, they returned the women to work the next morning. On occasion, masters even forced girl slaves to endure infibulations. Many masters and mistresses beat women who spoke to one another in Dinka. Many captives converted to Islam; some submitted to the Prophet by force.

The *baggara* masters, in other words, stamped out all semblance of Dinka culture among the slaves.

Before John Eibner, who justifiably credited himself with bringing slavery in Sudan to the world's attention, the story was barely a blip internationally. After a May 1986 *New York Times* piece, which the simultaneous Chernobyl meltdown buried on page seventeen, no newspaper mentioned the resurgence of slavery for a year. The *Times* itself was silent on the subject for nine years. Until CSI's involvement, only a handful of Western publications touched the story.

In 1987, a soft-spoken Kordofani linguist provided a sobering report of a slave raid, prompting the London-based Anti-Slavery Society to send investigators to Sudan. They were offered Dinka children for 40 Sudanese pounds, less than the cost at the time of an international postage stamp. At first, al-Mahdi agreed to cooperate with the society's investigation. Then al-Mahdi became irrelevant.

On June 30, 1989, the hard-line National Islamic Front (NIF) ousted al-Mahdi, whom they considered too weak for a war president. The new leader, Lieutenant General Omar al-Bashir, was Hitler to al-Mahdi's Hindenburg, a brutal operator with an extremist movement that replaced a project of national unity under Arabism with one of *jihad*.

After the National Salvation Revolution, the raiding policy hardened and spread. The National Popular Defense Act of 1989 codified the relationship between the *baggara* and the government, and the *murahileen* began enslaving other African Sudanese, particularly the Nuba and Shilluk. A military supply train ran eighty kilometers from Babanusa in Kordofan to the garrison town of Wau in Bahr el Ghazal. In 1992, the *baggara* began escorting the train. Ostensibly, they accompanied it to prevent rebel attacks. But up to 5,000 *murahileen* at a time, carving a wide corridor on either side of what came to be known as "the slave train," collected their fees in human flesh.

No longer willing to have infidels investigate slavery claims, the new regime expelled Anti-Slavery Society investigators. But Khartoum wasn't fussed when, in 1993, the UN Human Rights Commission appointed a special rapporteur for Sudan: The UN had received reports of slave raids since 1986 but the commission had never publicly condemned the practice.

The investigator, Gáspár Bíró, was not the average UN diplomat-with-blinders. Brutal totalitarian regimes did not easily intimidate Bíró, a second-generation Magyar who survived Nicolae Ceauşescu's anti-Hungarian policies in Romania. From his post in Sudan, Bíró submitted five reports in which he pulled no punches, blaming the NIF for sponsoring the raids, and decrying the misuse of Shari'a as a tool for prosecuting the brutal war.

In response, Khartoum attacked the messenger. In the *New York Times*, Sudan's Ambassador to the United States blasted Bíró's first report, saying it was "based upon hearsay and anecdotal evidence." He assured Americans that "slavery is against the fundamental teachings of Islam."

Unable to shame Bíró, Khartoum tried to scare him. The state-controlled media compared him to Salman Rushdie, and the government issued a circular entitled *Attack on Islam*. In it, the NIF said that Bíró's report contained "abusive, inconsiderate, blasphemous, and offensive remarks about the Islamic faith." Under Shari'a, blasphemy meant death.

Ahmed el-Mufti, a lawyer with the Sudanese Justice Ministry, was made the Hungarian's foil. El-Mufti, Sudan's internal human rights rapporteur, called the raids "tribal disputes," which Khartoum was addressing. At a UN meeting in New York, el-Mufti directly threatened Bíró. "We don't want to speculate about his fate if he is to continue offending the feelings of Muslims worldwide," el-Mufti said.

Meanwhile, the United Nations damned the slaves with faint interest. While the General Assembly approved resolutions expressing "deepest concern" about Bíró's findings, the Hungarian's UN colleagues became the tools of genocide. The World Food Programme had fed half a million Dinka every year since 1991. In 1998, al-Bashir's information minister, Brigadier el-Tayeb Ibrahim Mohammed Kheir—known as "Tayeb of the Iron Bar"—demanded that it cease flights to front-line Bahr el Ghazal. The resulting famine killed over 100,000 Dinka. Many crawled north, where raiders captured them.

Tayeb also increased aid to the *murahileen*. Under his guidance, the average raiding party grew from 400 to over 2,500. Their mandate was clear. The horsemen were to "wipe out" the rebels, Tayeb said, and kidnap, convert, and make "peaceful preachers" out of Dinka children. Bíró filed his final report in 1998. The following year, the most prolific year for slave raiding in the twentieth century, UN organizations ceased to speak of "slavery" in Sudan.

In 2001, Sudan replaced the United States on the UN Human Rights Commission.

On September 6, 2001, when President Bush appointed Senator Jack Danforth Special Envoy to Sudan, Khartoum reacted defiantly. The United States hitherto had shown no yen for tough diplomacy with Sudan. Assuming Danforth was another token, like Clinton's appointee Harry Johnston, to appease the Christian Right, al-Bashir saw no reason for pause. Slave raids, which al-Bashir blessed with his *Dar al Harb* versus *Dar al Islam* nonsense, crescendoed through the end of 2001.

Jack Danforth, it turns out, was not the sort of man to tiptoe around crimes against humanity; but he knew that the war was unwinnable, and soon found it was much less clear-cut than the black-and-white affair presented by Eibner and his ilk. He viewed his role as "catalytic" in the negotiations, and wanted all parties involved. He even met with Sadiq al-Mahdi, the ousted Sudanese leader who had fueled the slave raids. "When I went around and made calls to members of Congress at the early stages or even before I made my first trip," Danforth said, "they all made a point that there was no moral equivalence between the two sides. They saw this as leaning on the government. But I saw it as just trying to work something out."

One evening during his first of seven trips to Khartoum, Danforth sat with fifteen Christian and Muslim leaders at the dilapidated U.S. Embassy. The meeting seemed like a disaster. While white-robed Muslim clerics immediately assured the envoy that "everything's fine in our country," the Christians unloaded a litany of grievances. But afterward, leaders on both sides came up, wrung his hand, and thanked him for a "wonderful meeting." The two groups had never met before.

Danforth sought the same unvarnished dialogue at the peace talks in Kenya. Although the SPLM and Khartoum soon hammered out a cease-fire agreement, a northern representative told Danforth in St. Louis that they felt "damned if we do, damned if we don't." The Bush administration responded that good behavior would be rewarded with normalized relations. The allocation of $100 million annually to SPLM-controlled areas under the Sudan Peace Act, however, presaged the response for bad behavior.

Al-Bashir believed that a radical alternative American policy might kick in if he stonewalled. Bush's pastor Franklin Graham met with Danforth during the negotiations and privately tried to bring al-Bashir to Christ, but he also publicly clamored for military strikes against Khartoum. Eibner, who had pressed for the Sudan Peace Act, now felt that it wasn't enough. Negotiations, he noted shortly before our May 2003 trip, were not the answer. Regime change was. "The Bush administration would do well to look for alternatives to Khartoum's radical extremists," he wrote. "The United States will rue the day it imposes a paper peace agreement on Sudan with a terrorist, genocidal regime as its cornerstone."

Through all the bluster, Danforth recognized that one crime mattered to Evangelicals more than any other. "There is probably no issue other than civilian bombings that concerns Americans more than the continued existence of slavery," Danforth told the president. "The record is clear: the government arms and directs marauding raiders who operate in the south, destroying villages and abducting women and children to serve as chattel servants, herders and field hands."

Danforth, through remarkable persistence, got Khartoum to cop to what was essentially a no-contest plea to the charges. Publicly, al-Bashir continued calling reports of slavery "mere media propaganda." Privately, Khartoum's negotiators compromised by allowing an international investigation, provided that the Islamist government could maintain its public denials.

Our Cessna descended, and the slave redeemers and I landed in Loki-chokio, near the southern border with Sudan. Loki, as aid workers called it, was the command center for the world's largest relief operation, costing over a billion dollars a year to operate. It was also Kenya's second busiest airport, with the World Food Programme's thundering C-130 Hercules cargo planes taking off and landing every hour.

We then boarded another plane—a creaky, Soviet-era Antonov-28. The seats, folded cloth beach chairs, were nailed to plywood floorboards. The steaming cabin reeked of stale sweat and swirled with flies. The stench aggravated my dread: Fearing the Sudanese government would fulfill its pledge to shoot us down, Eibner earlier had asked that I "keep confidential the fact that you hope to travel with us."

Given that admonition, I was surprised by several unanticipated travel companions, including five giant mercenaries in military fatigues. Self-described "antiterror consultants," they gave tactical assistance to police forces, militaries, businesses, and governments in such places as Chechnya and the Middle East. They called themselves the Archangel Group. I asked the eldest Archangel what he was doing on a slave redemption trip. "God's work," John "Andy" Andersen barked as he spewed tobacco.

The presence of another unexpected group, Dinka refugees, was more understandable. Mechanized travel in southern Sudan—largely due to the dangers of mines and antiaircraft guns—was prohibitively expensive. Our charter cost $16,000. For penniless refugees, the only chance to move great distances quickly was to talk their way onto one of these "cowboy" planes, operating outside the UN mandate.

The plane was already well over the weight limit, and the chain-smoking Russian pilot tore out a seat in order to fit more luggage. A young refugee folded into a corner. The pilot, speaking no English, motioned for an unusually hefty Dinka man named Angelo to lean against the cabin door to balance out the weight. He took up the last of the floor space. The plane sputtered into roaring action, and as we careered forward, it seemed as if we were going to run out of runway.

"Angelo, we're going to have a problem!" said Eibner, panicking.

Angelo folded his hands and prayed. An ancient refugee with three yellow teeth burst into tears. With fifteen feet to spare, we cleared the treetops. The old man took out a thin gourd containing tobacco, sniffed it, and calmed down. Afterward, as saliva dribbled down his chin and chest, he chewed on a stalk of neem—a plant locals use to clean their teeth. The pilot unfolded a disturbingly simple topographical map.

I had researched Eibner but knew little about the Archangel Group. Through a mouthful of chew, Andersen bellowed out a few details about himself. A rhino of a man, Andersen was a Teddy Roosevelt for the twenty-first century, complete with flattop, ruddy complexion, handlebar mustache, and neckless, barreled torso. Born in a town of 250 people in northern California, he grew up in American warrior culture. "Been shootin' since I was knee-high to a grasshopper," he said. Now fifty-two, he had served as a Green Beret for over half his life. In that elite force, he had done it all, from fighting the Vietcong to delivering a stillborn baby. "I broke that kid in half," he said. "It felt like tearing apart a chicken. But I saved the mother."

He finally left the army with the rank of sergeant major to open a gun store in Colorado. Despite a tough demeanor, he claimed a warm relationship with a loving wife. "As long as you can still lay the pipe," he explained, "you can make the marriage work."

This was not Andersen's first trip to Sudan. Twenty years earlier, he visited the country during a training mission. In his career, Andersen trained armies in over fifty countries. The Special Forces, he laughed, were "glorified schoolteachers." But Andersen noticed something different in 1982, during the twilight of Sudan's dictator, Colonel Gaafar

Nimeiri. After the 1973 energy crisis, Chevron discovered oil in the south, and Washington began a less than beautiful friendship with Nimeiri, who served as a hedge against the Red Terror in neighboring Ethiopia. In 1980, only five countries in the world received more U.S. military aid than Sudan. During Ronald Reagan's first term, despite growing evidence of genocide in both Sudan and Ethiopia, the administration armed the non-Communist mass murderer against the Communist one.

"It was supposed to be training," Andersen said of the 1982 Khartoum trip. "But it was a resupply mission. We flew in heavy with C-130s, a Ranger battalion. We fired a lot of ammo, but a lot of it stayed there when we left."

The following year, Nimeiri used that ammo to initiate a brutal counterinsurgency. In 1985, his successor, Sadiq al-Mahdi, continued Nimeiri's pogroms and began arming the *murahileen* horsemen of the million or so *baggara* Arabs who bordered the Dinka to the north. Al-Mahdi's defense minister, *baggara* himself, organized his brethren to raid southern border villages and seize their own payment therein. For some, the payment took human form.

Now Andersen was back to battle an evil that he inadvertently helped unleash. "I joined the Special Forces to help free the oppressed, '*de oppresso liber*,'" he said, quoting the Green Beret motto, "and that's what I'm doing here."

To Andersen's right sat Archangel's president, John Giduck. He was also a former Green Beret and had stories from eight conflicts and the 82nd Airborne tattoos to prove it. The forty-four-year-old Russian American looked every inch the protégé of his elder, right down to the handlebar mustache, flattop haircut, and barrel chest. Giduck also closely mirrored Andersen in his social views, which he articulated with a Rush Limbaugh inflection, spitting out disdainful words such as "Muhzzlims" and emphasizing the last word of every sentence. "AIDS," he said on the flight, "did have the positive effect of overpopulation *control*."

A July 2001 issue of *Penthouse* brought the mercenaries to the Christian slave redeemers. In it, Giduck read a detailed account of John Eibner's work. Moved, he shared the magazine with his Archangel brothers, who agreed that using their skills to fight slavery sounded better than glorified schoolteaching. Giduck tracked down Eibner, and in February 2003, he attended a redemption.

The rest of Archangel sat behind us, including Darron, a tattoo-covered veteran of the world's most elite military unit, the British SAS; and Yuri, a hulking Ukrainian with his blood type tattooed in Cyrillic on his left lat—a sign that he had been a commando in the rarefied *Spetsnaz*, Soviet Special Forces. Largely silent save for a few utterances in broken English, Yuri's combat-hardened glare from under his cowboy hat said enough.

In stark contrast to the mercenaries, Gunnar Wiebalck, Eibner's sidekick, projected the sunny ease of a contented soul. Typically New German in his polite and deferential manner, Gunnar's beatific smile expressed his happiness to be in what he viewed as a Christian paradise. "This is a virgin land," he said, looking up from his treatise on the Bible to gaze out of the porthole.

"The real Soudan, known to the statesman and the explorer," Winston Churchill wrote in 1902, "lies far to the south—moist, undulating, and exuberant." From 10,000 feet, the White Nile, bracketed by green, was dusty brown. It drained into the world's largest swamp, the *Sudd*, meaning "barrier," in Arabic. For centuries the Sudd protected southern Sudan. In 1840, at the behest of the Egyptian viceroy, a naval expedition broke through. Slave raiders soon followed.

The Dinka call the period "the time when the world was spoiled."

Three hours into the four-hour flight between Loki and Bahr el Ghazal, we made a rough landing on a dirt airstrip in a village called Thiet. Eibner explained there was a SPLM summit involving the rebel leader John Garang.

On disembarking, the 130-degree heat felt like a Kevlar blanket. Hundreds of Dinka lined the airstrip. Women wore colorful dress. Men wore ragged SPLM uniforms and plastic flip-flops. Children were in loose-fitting fatigues and held AK-47 and PKM rifles. For front-line Dinka, the lone ambassador of the modern world is the assault rifle. A boy of ten who may never wield a TV remote is already expert at stripping and firing a Kalashnikov.

The market price for the guns was greater than the price for the children themselves. In 1986, an AK-47 cost ten cows, or about $1,000. By 2001, a glut of guns (and dearth of cows) shrank the cost to two cows, or about $86 along the Sudan-Uganda border. The child market was more volatile. In early 1987, after al-Mahdi began his counterinsurgency, a Dinka boy cost $90. By 1990, as supply swelled, the price fell to $15. At the time of my visit, CSI had agreed to pay $33 per slave.

Garang had left, but his number two, Salva Kiir Mayardit, embraced Eibner on the airstrip. Kiir, perhaps six foot eight, wore a beard, bush hat, military fatigues, and Nike high-tops. He carried a cane, and was followed by a retinue of armed guards. A legend among the Bahr el Ghazal Dinka, Kiir's daring victory over long odds and government troops in a battle near the Ethiopian border in 1984 brought waves of recruits to the SPLM. Despite his title, he was a critic of Garang, and observers feared that criticism augured another internecine "Emma's War," which in 1991 cost tens of thousands of lives.

Commander Paul Malong Awan, chief of staff of the SPLM's third front, also embraced Eibner. Balding, Malong wore a neat goatee, garish gold jewelry, and a crucifix. In the shade, he removed his aviator sunglasses to reveal an icy stare. Shot twice in the leg while fighting in the Upper Nile in 1984, he was shot again while fighting in the Blue Nile at the time of the first slave raids in 1985. In total, he had eight war wounds. He now commanded five brigades, each with 1,200 troops, and maintained forty wives. As Malong was the warlord (Eibner preferred "peacelord") who controlled the area that included our destination, Eibner brought him along with us.

We soon descended into Malual Kon, ground zero for the slave raids. Villagers scattered out of the path of the plane, the same kind the Sudanese government used regularly and recently on bombing runs. After a low pass to scare off cattle, we landed on a 450-meter clearing. Here endemic guinea worm, measles, whooping cough, polio, river blindness, leprosy, kala-azar disease, and tuberculosis joined forces with Khartoum to savage the village residents. Malual Kon was a three-and-a-half-hour walk from the nearest clinic. There were six working bore holes, and with no medicine, diarrhea was deadly. Add the searing heat, and a case of the runs could kill within a week. The villagers survived only by the grace of God and the World Food Programme (WFP), and most died by age forty-two.

A crowd gathered after we landed, smiling broadly at the sight of rare white *khawajas*. The odor of dung fires punctuated the overwhelming heat. Historically, each family had a cattle base, centered around mud, stick, and grass huts known as *tukuls*. Dinka sometimes washed in cow urine, as water was scarce. The practice was effective, according to the German explorer Georg Schweinfurth; nineteenth-century Dinka were "rarely troubled with vermin or fleas which everywhere else, like desolation and slavery, seem invariably to have followed the track of Islam."

Most in the crowd were half-naked—sensibly so, given the heat. Some wore handouts promoting JUST TWO DROPS of polio vaccination or WFP. Others sported prized T-shirts bearing the faces of American rap stars such as Tupac. Dinka are the world's tallest people, and their long, lean shape, height, and deep black color lent the assembly an almost ghostly, imperial aspect. Many had bloodshot eyes. The irises of others bled into their scleras, signifying anemia or malaria, as common here as the flu. Most were barefoot, though the soldiers wore flip-flops.

Several of Malong's men escorted us past a plainclothes guard with an AKS-74 assault rifle, into a reed-fenced *baay*, a circular compound around the largest tree in the village. Trees here are rare, exceptional, blessed. Their roots are sprawling; their canopies are flat and expansive; their shade is elemental to community. On the way in, a young man challenged Andersen to grapple in a Dinka passion: wrestling. His friends laughed skittishly at Andersen's bulk, and goaded the brave soul. Andersen ignored him.

Inside the compound, I drank water from a fuel barrel. Despite the charcoal filter on my water bottle, it tasted like jet fuel. Dehydration would be a constant companion during my first month in southern Sudan. In this first week, I lost twenty pounds, and eventually repaired to Kenya vomiting and enflamed with dengue fever.

The central tree housed several cobras. Schweinfurth observed that Dinka revered snakes, treated them like pets, and considered it criminal to kill them. He recalled restless nights listening to the creatures slithering in the roof of his *tukul*. My neighbors were less fond of them, but snakes were omnipresent nonetheless. I later grew accustomed to the snakes and lizards in my *tukul*. But scorpions, perched on a mosquito net inches above my face, always raised my heart rate. Like the Dinka, I developed a taste for termites, though I preferred mine roasted, sans wings.

On this, my first night in Sudan, the darkness overwhelmed me. Without electricity for miles, there was no ambient light save for the moon and stars. Now it was cloudy, as we had landed at the end of the dry season, and *habub* sandstorms would soon roll in. I fumbled for my headlamp.

"Do you wanna get shot?" asked an invisible Giduck. "Turn off the light. Let your eyes adjust."

I did as ordered and followed the sound of American voices to the tree. Eibner was always deliberate when he spoke. He said that as *jihad* was essential to Islam, an Islamic state could never be peaceful. For the moment, southern Sudan was "pure," and a low AIDS rate was evidence. But once the impending peace deal broke down, which he felt was inevitable, southern Sudan would become Gomorrah, if not Hell.

Eibner turned to Andersen: "Would it be possible to mount heavy machine guns on a Honda?"

"Sure," Andersen responded. "If you mount them sidesaddle."

"Communications is key," said Giduck. "CB radios are needed."

"This would be no problem," concluded Andersen.

Later, I asked Eibner if he thought talking war at a time when peace negotiations were bearing fruit seemed perverse. The government and the rebels both use UN-sponsored humanitarian groups as instruments of policy, Eibner said. Either way, neutrality is jettisoned. He preferred that CSI be on the side of "the good guys." I asked if mass slave buy-backs, one of which we were to perform the next morning, were the best way to tackle the slave trade. Critics had said that the redemptions were mere fronts for SPLM fund-raising, and involved no follow-up aid to the theoretically "redeemed."

"Some of the ways in which we do things," Eibner responded, "are not the ideal way in an ideal world."

In the 1990s, the number of slaves in Sudan was a volatile subject. Mainline human rights groups like Anti-Slavery International estimated 14,000. SPLM officials in Bahr el Ghazal began keeping records in 1988, but had no concrete numbers. One official, the Civil Commissioner of the most raided county, Aweil West, said 200,000. Although the commissioner had no documentation to back that claim, CSI adopted his figure and publicized it in its appeals. Up until the Danforth initiative, the government said that the number was zero.

John Ryle, a British researcher co-opted by the State Department as the Danforth negotiations progressed, found a solution: make a list of the abducted. While elegantly simple in concept, the idea, which he conceived with a Loyola Marymount professor, Jok Madut Jok, was exceedingly hard to execute.

Ryle was arguably the only man outside Sudan who could pull it off. A dashing, Oxford-educated journalist-cum-academic, Ryle had always been an adventurist, beginning with mountaineering expeditions in his father's rucksack at the age of two. Once in Pakistan's wild western province of Baluchistan—where bin Laden has been rumored to hide—Ryle arm-wrestled the local champion, a one-eyed giant named Tariq. It was called a draw.

In addition to his bold soul, Ryle had several skills that made him ideal to compile the list. First among these was that he was, as one local aid worker put it, "more Dinka than the Dinka." Ryle had spent years living in the south, first in the 1970s when much of the territory was still unmapped. He learned the language, and the locals gave him a Dinka name, Mawurnyin, because of his resemblance to a certain type of bull. For the cattle-worshipping Dinka, it was a sign of great respect.

An avid cyclist, Ryle's passion also was indispensable in compiling the list. Southern Sudanese roads were impassable by vehicle in the rainy season. In part this was because the plashy trails, normally haphazard, frequently dissolved entirely into mud. In part it was because the rains unearthed land mines. Southern Sudan had 2 million such mines; and northern Bahr el Ghazal had the densest cluster. At one point during my second visit, a day before I was to travel in an SUV, an exploded land mine left its driver and two passengers in critical condition.

Ryle and Madut led fifty Dinka tracers out to interview those left behind, who might remember somebody taken in the raids. Over eighteen months, they covered an area the size of New Mexico on foot and by bike. Their work was painstaking, as I found out firsthand. After meeting with Ryle in New York and Nairobi, I arranged to interview a recently returned slave with one of his tracers during my second visit to Bahr el Ghazal. We mounted ancient Chinese Phoenix bicycles, which often ground to a halt in the mud. We rode past a decrepit, Soviet-era, twin-turret T-55 tank tagged in Arabic, past cows and people bathing in the same newly formed pools. Barking dogs trailed us, as did gleeful, screaming kids ("*Khawajas* ride bicycles!") and the occasional grinning rebel with a Kalashnikov strapped to the crossbar of his bike. I ran out of water (the tracer didn't need any), but boiling hot, sickeningly sweet red tea—the only item for sale at several markets—sustained me on the return leg. It was 115 degrees Fahrenheit, and we biked twenty-six miles.

With such an effort needed to interview one woman, the final list of over 11,000 names was astonishing. No mere soulless rendering, the list contained myriad details about the missing. Ryle called it "a baseline of fact." The tracers missed many. Children were born in captivity. Some had been kidnapped while in the north. Relatives had forgotten after twenty years. Often, the *murahileen* left no survivors to tell the tale. "But Khartoum can't say the issue is finished anymore," said Ryle.

As Ryle's tracers quietly fanned out across the savannah, John Eibner presented 500 ragged slaves to me and Archangel at the first redemption of our trip. The women sat under a giant tree, impassive save for the occasional, languorous attempt to clear away biting flies clustered around the eyes of their naked, dusty children. Eibner spoke neither Dinka nor Arabic, so an SPLM operative translated. Nonetheless, his introduction seemed lost on the predominantly animist women.

"When you remember this day," he said, "remember that we have come and we've met you because there are many people around the world who have cared about you, who have prayed for you, and God has heard your cries, and He has seen your tears."

The mercenaries, looking wilted in the 120-degree heat, stood in the background. At the foot of an adjacent hill, built up over the years by an impressive amount of cow dung, sat three cross-faced Arab *djellabahs*, so-named for their white cotton neck-to-foot gowns. Arabs first acquired the moniker in the nineteenth century when they took slaves to market. These traders, Eibner said, were here to do the reverse.

Eibner's redemptions, like Ryle's list, were elegantly simple in concept. The retrieving *djellabahs* went to northern cattle camps where slaves were held, and secured their release. They then transported them to the south, where CSI bought their freedom.

One fawning *Boston Globe* reporter labeled Eibner's work "the Sudanese version of the Underground Railroad." His numbers started small. On CSI's initial expeditions, Eibner redeemed around 100 per trip. As their funding exploded, so did the numbers of slaves. Between 1998 and 1999, they redeemed over 15,000 slaves. Over the next two years, the organization paid for nearly 44,000. On our trip alone, CSI bought the freedom of 3,782. The total for eight years stood at 84,792.

The numbers were staggering. And some said, too good to be true. In July 1999, Richard Miniter, writing in the *Atlantic Monthly*, claimed that corrupt SPLM officials used false slaves to scam hard currency from duped redeemers and, by extension, their widening base of donors. That month, the Sudanese Christian group that had originally invited Eibner denounced redemptions. In an open letter the following year, Aleu

Ayieny Aleu, a wounded SPLM commander, said that other officers had ordered his relative, an SPLM captain, to pose as a retriever. Two years later, Karl Vick, Nairobi correspondent for *The Washington Post*, wrote a front-page exposé of "prevalent fraud" surrounding the redemptions. But the coup de grâce came when CBS, which previously had aired a glowing profile of Eibner, interviewed a defector from CSI's ranks.

"It's a show. It's a circus. It's—it's a staged event," said Jim Jacobsen, a fund-raiser and Washington representative of CSI since the start of the redemptions.

"We ran two stories about, quote, 'slave redemptions' on the *CBS Evening News*," intoned Dan Rather. "Were we had?"

"Yes," said Jacobsen.

"Were we taken?"

"Yes."

Eibner took the criticisms as only the latest examples of the liberal media's systematic persecution of international Christian initiatives. Nonetheless, the stories angered him. "Some writer sits on his fat ass in Nairobi and pretends to know about our work," an uncharacteristically exercised Eibner said, referring to Vick. None of the skeptical journalists had traveled with him, Eibner said, and those "independent" journalists and researchers who had, approved of the redemptions. He claimed that the *Washington Post* story was a rehash of Internet rumors of Garang's Bor Dinka faction of the SPLM, which opposed Malong and Kiir's Bahr el Ghazal faction.

Charles Jacobs, who had built the American Anti-Slavery Group around the redemptions as much as he had built Eibner through publicity campaigns, stood pat: "You can tell the difference between the villagers who are free and the slave kids," said Jacobs, shortly after his first visit to Sudan in 2001. "I mean, the slave kids are sickly and frightened, and you can simply tell." Jacobs had previously spun criticism into fund-raising gold, and he again condemned the "well-paid U.N. bureaucrats [who] drank Perrier in plush conference rooms," while Eibner strode into the lion's den to free the slaves. "UNICEF pays the raiders," wrote Jacobs. "CSI pays the redeemers."

But this time, the United Nations was the least of the critics. Two of Eibner's most prominent collaborators, British baroness Caroline Cox and Canadian televangelist Cal Bombay, broke away from CSI. The principal author of the Sudan Peace Act, Tom Tancredo of Colorado, had been Eibner's most vocal defender in Congress. Now even he wavered. "Even if it is accurate that some of the folks being redeemed really aren't slaves and then you say to yourself, 'Well, okay, let's say half of them aren't.' All that means is that you're paying double the amount for those that are and I'd, in a way I'd say that's acceptable," Tancredo said. "And I don't know whether I'm just rationalizing because you're hoping against hope that what you're doing is the Lord's Work in reality."

But for the presidential aspirant Tancredo, Eibner had become damaged goods. "You never know if he's motivated by anything even more sinister than ego," Tancredo said. "If there's anything that's preventing him doing this the right way it's the fact that his ego is involved."

"We see a very clear marginalization of CSI," acknowledged Eibner. "Why is CSI the leper?"

Eibner was particularly scornful of John Ryle, whose ongoing research he saw as an attempt to discredit him. "Oh, *he* speaks Dinka," Eibner, who had never met Ryle, said acidulously. "*He* went to Oxford."

While Khartoum claimed that the SPLM manipulated the list, Eibner claimed Khartoum had a hand in it. Ryle's numbers made Khartoum look bad. They made Eibner look fraudulent, as he claimed to have redeemed nearly eight times the number that Ryle had catalogued as missing in the first place.

They weren't the only troubling numbers. CSI's money trail over the past decade is opaque at best. Eibner's colleague Gunnar said that KPMG International audited the tax-exempt organization annually. The skeleton balance sheet that he referred me to simply listed CSI's goals (with no mention of redemption) and showed that they had twenty employees and an annual income of 6.5 million Swiss francs (about $5 million).

Independent investigation showed where much of that income came from—90 percent was from private individuals—and more tellingly, where it went. The devil was in the exchange. Eibner, "for security reasons," kept secret his exchange practices, although he said that once he lugged a bag of Sudanese dinars from London. "One has to take into account that southern Sudan is not a part of Sudan," explained Eibner. "They have their own currency and currencies, they don't have a bank, local customs. One cannot work with an official bank with a bank rate that you would get in Khartoum."

Instead, Eibner exchanged redemption money with notoriously corrupt SPLM representatives. For example, a Canadian journalist in 1997 recorded that Eibner exchanged a total of $25,000 for 14,700,000 Sudanese pounds. At 1997 rates, Eibner should have received 39,393,500 Sudanese pounds, but instead the SPLM official netted 24,693,500 Sudanese pounds (or $15,671.05). The point is moot because he was exchanging U.S. dollars for Sudanese pounds, a non-backed, non-traded currency. (Eibner claimed that he had "never handled a Sudanese pound," although he appeared in several photographs handling duffle bags full of them.) In other words, he was buying a stack of paper for $25,000. In total, Eibner gave $3 to $4 million to SPLM officials. Up until the time of our visit, that represented one of the largest single sources of hard currency for the rebel movement.

The larger question was exactly how the rebels spent their windfall. The per capita GDP for all of Sudan was $412. South Sudan's GDP was probably less than half of that. Four million dollars could sow the seeds of prosperity for a generation of Dinka—or reap the whirlwind.

Karl Vick cited a claim by one of Eibner's SPLM bursars, Justin Yaac, that the money went to buy "26 Toyota Land Cruisers, more than 7,000 uniforms, plus fuel—all purchased for the war effort." He went on to report that much of the money went to Malong, "whose wealth is quantified in wives." Subsequently, Yaac told me that "the dollars they get are very, very useful to the local population who have no access to hard currency."

Others close to Malong, who was instrumental in the redemptions from the beginning, said that Eibner gave the warlord high-tech communications equipment, including his first satellite phone (Eibner acknowledged that CSI kept such a phone "in the field," but avoided details). In 2000, a report commissioned by the Canadian government cited claims that the redemption money was spent to "buy arms and ammunition, and even to build a power base in opposition to John Garang."

One of several SPLM officials that Eibner kept on his payroll simply pointed to his new jeans when I asked how the money was spent. "I'd rather the money went to buy jeans for an SPLA official than to an Arab slaveholder!" Eibner said, when I told him of the officer's gesture.

Buying new jeans for rebels or funding the polygamy of warlords was not, perhaps, what Evangelical Sunday School children had in mind when they emptied their coin jars. But Eibner might still be justified if the redemptions were otherwise bona fide.

"Even if, in the worst case, seventy-five percent of the people are not slaves," Eibner said, "I would feel good about the twenty-five percent who were freed."

What I saw at the redemptions made even 25 percent seem optimistic.

Eibner ended his opening soliloquy by telling the assembled that he was going to ask some questions to verify their identities. "Nobody should be afraid, nobody should be too shy, there's no shame. If there's any shame, it belongs to people who've done terrible things to you."

He and Gunnar proceeded to conduct, through SPLM interpreters, interviews with approximately ten out of the five hundred women, comparing their answers to forms already filled out on their behalf. On several occasions boys referred to themselves as servants ("*khadim*") rather than slaves ("*abd*"). The translators always used the word "slave." Earlier, Vick had reported that a Dinka-speaking Italian priest who was present for a redemption observed the translators simply feed the redeemers stories of enslavement, regardless what the "slaves" said.

I noticed several inconsistencies—particularly on the issue of religion—between the forms and the women's answers. I asked Eibner how many discrepancies would be too many and cause him to reject a clearly falsified slave. "I haven't thought about a certain percentage and I don't think that one can look at it like that," he said. "There are certain inconsistencies that can be easily explained because of the illiteracy of the people who are being interviewed."

Eibner showed no interest in truly verifying whether or not the slaves were genuine, though he collected as many horror stories as he could. At one point he asked the group if anyone had scars that revealed the brutal abuse of their captivity. Four women came forward, one dutifully lifting her shirt so that Gunnar might photograph her broken flesh. The lines of questioning tended to focus on the issues of forced Islamicization and rape—"Were you raped? Were you gang-raped? By how many men?"

Despite Eibner's admonition to be unashamed, for a woman, supposedly held in a conservative Muslim environment for years, such questions coming from a group of men—strangers and peers alike—seemed a harsh welcome to freedom. If, indeed, this was an emancipation at all. Many of the women were probably enslaved at some point. But I saw no evidence beyond the SPLM translators' words to prove that they had come back through redemption. None of the redeemed had been in the south for less than three months by the time of this event, which made me wonder what authority motivated them to show up and meet us. In part, the answer came in the form of a number of large WFP food sacks that, an SPLM official said, were for the assembled women, but only if they performed at the redemption.

The numbers at the first buyback were conceivably manageable; at the second redemption, they were impossibly large. Chaos reigned, but Eibner seemed more focused on what I was seeing than on bringing order. At yet another redemption, several of the retrievers said that they never paid for any of the Dinka they had brought back. I later heard from aid workers based in the areas through which the retrievers supposedly had taken the slaves. None of them had noticed any kind of massive Arab-guided movements of Dinka.

The redemptions were a macabre song-and-dance show. As a vehicle for SPLM fund-raising, at least, they were an enormous success.

After perfunctory ululations and a warm benediction delivered by a sweet-faced preacher called Santino, Eibner gave the retrievers filthy Sudanese pounds—or perhaps dinars—in fifteen stacks, each with a rubber band and a handwritten "1,000,000." Although the bills were of various denominations, the retrievers did not count the money. As the crowd sang a paean in Dinka to Commander Malong, and a hymn in mimicked English to a higher power ("We Are for the Lord!"), the redeemers and I loaded ourselves into an SPLM truck. Our driver, a bearded and frequently stoned soldier in a green robe, sat facing an upside-down speedometer, below the scrawled words CROSS OF JESUS.

En route back to Malual Kon, thirty people crammed into the back of the truck. Kalashnikovs clinked together on broken floorboards as we bounced over the porous dirt road. I sat on an enormous tire in the flatbed between the pastor, Andersen, and a retriever wearing a *djellabah*. It was a tight squeeze. I was facing backward. An SPLM irregular clutching an AK-S faced me about six inches away so that after big bumps I got a smelly armpit in my face or a knee dangerously near my crotch. The rebel had a small afro, mirrored aviator sunglasses, a filthy blue tank top, shorts, and flip-flops. Periodically, he shoved Santino's head into me just before branches with two-inch thorns snapped by his face. "My savior," the pastor said, smiling widely at the irony of his statement. Two monkeys and a chimp bounded beside the truck. Locusts the size of sparrows whirred out of trees as we passed.

We stopped in a local market where *baggara* on camelback came to sell everything from greasy goat heads to jelly sandals and Osama bin Laden T-shirts. Few Dinka could afford any of it, but they could barter. Since the dissolution of a local truce in 1990, raiders had burned the market down three or four times. But after Malong moved his base of operations to nearby Malual Kon in January 2001, the raiders stayed away. Now the place had become something of a hopeful vision for Sudan: despite cultural and economic disparities, Dinka and Arabs spoke the common language of trade.

As we idled, a huge crowd surrounded the truck. A man with blood-shot eyes and breath reeking of the mouth-numbing local drink *sika*, stumbled up and grabbed me. In Dinka, he said there are three types of people: black, red, and white. "Black people are good," he said, "red people are bad, and whites can help."

A small, contorted, mentally handicapped man squeezed on board. "The village idiot," said Andersen. As we drove off, he started bark-ing like a dog, to the amusement of all of the Dinka except the pas-tor. The barking morphed to braying like a donkey and finally praying like a *muezzin*. When his call-to-prayer in pidgin Arabic began, the retriever—presumably the only Muslim on the truck—turned to shoot him a stern, threatening look as the others stifled giggles. The *Adhan* morphed into laughter, the Arab turned back, and the truck erupted in hysterics.

That evening, we paid a "courtesy call" to Commander Malong in his bomb-damaged and carefully guarded compound, the only mortar-based structure for miles around. He gave us a feast, complete with goat, flatbread, chilled soda, and steamed milk. Malong was quiet, but char-ismatic. He had helped to convince the American civil rights leader Al Sharpton, attending a redemption in 2001, to speak out against Khar-toum. To break the ice with the mercenaries, Malong tried the universal language of firearms, emerging from his house with what I mistakenly assumed to be a sawed-off shotgun.

"A blooper!" Andersen and Giduck cried in nostalgic unison, cor-rectly identifying a Vietnam-era M-79 single-shot grenade launcher.

Archangel and Malong pulled their chairs together. Giduck later explained they shared tactical advice—including scaling out routes to Khartoum—for two hours. "I will fight one hundred years," said Malong, who was more encouraged by the three-month-old rebellion in Darfur than Danforth's impending peace deal in Kenya. "We will keep fighting as long as it takes to achieve our objectives, or we are defeated."

Eibner was clear on Malong's objectives: "To liberate the people, and with regards to the government of Sudan, to remove it."

"The bureaucrats"—he curled his lips when he said the word—"seem to think that constructive engagement is the policy" for dealing with Islamists. "This is not how these people think."

On the morning of May 26, 2004, a sandstorm—what Khartoumers call a *habub*, or "phenomenon"—encased the Sudanese capital in dust, casting the city in ghostly sepia tones. But that day, events in Kenya cut through Khartoum's gloom. Southern and northern negotiators signed a protocol that ended what had been Africa's longest and bloodiest war. "The people of Sudan can now hope for a new future of peace and prosperity," Colin Powell said after the signing. That evening, celebrants waved the rebel flag for the first time in Khartoum. People were upbeat, particularly the Dinka. But I heard no wild ululating.

The average southerner in the north knew to celebrate softly. The average Khartoumer, no less relieved at the end of the war, was unconscious of Arab responsibility for the carnage. He lived in ignorance, often willful, that the practice of slavery still continued in his country. One Sudanese friend conceded he had heard rumors "from outside sources" of the existence of slavery in Darfur and Kordofan.

Pressed by the impending release of the Danforth report, al-Bashir finally announced that "we are determined to end intertribal abductions once and for all." The regime's public relations hatchetman, Ahmed el-Mufti, stepped up a program they called the Committee for the Eradication of the Abduction of Women and Children (CEAWC). Al-Bashir first agreed to form CEAWC in 1999, at the height of the slave raiding, as a compromise once UN organs agreed to avoid referring to Sudanese "slavery." Since then, while Khartoum's militias enslaved thousands, al-Bashir and el-Mufti sent a handful of them home. It was a humanitarian showcase, but an empty one.

Ryle's list highlighted CEAWC's failings, and challenged el-Mufti to make 11,000 names disappear. When I visited el-Mufti in Khartoum, he foreshadowed the government's response. Chain-smoking in a sharkskin suit that was almost as shiny as his office, el-Mufti had his presentation down pat. Over an ornamental Q'aran standing on his desk, he acknowledged only "abduction" as part of "tribal conflict," and said that prosecuting slavemasters was unfeasible. "The country is very large," he said, "and the abductors might resist." He blamed a lack of funding for the halting liberation, but claimed CEAWC had returned 700 in four years.

El-Mufti said that the government was about to cleave the problem by returning 5,000 Dinka. In my notes, I wrote "500," assuming he had tripped on the translation. He meant, to my shock, 5,000. "This cannot be an open-ended thing," the minister of finance had told him earlier. "Give us a year," he responded, and CEAWC would erase the embarrassment by returning 800 abductees per month.

In Washington, Khartoum's returns left John Miller perplexed. "You have this paradox in Sudan," he said. "They have these terrible human rights abuses, at the same time CEAWC has reunited seven thousand slaves with their families." His Trafficking in Persons office upgraded Sudan to Tier Two in its 2005 report. Eibner decried the upgrade, called for an independent commission, and labeled CEAWC's efforts "a fiasco." One hundred and nine members of Congress signed a letter to Condoleezza Rice calling the upgrade part of "a policy of appeasement." Then Eibner, strangely, claimed credit for CEAWC's results. Then he called them insufficient.

The government returned many of the Dinka by force. CEAWC had seized—en masse and without warning—Dinka women and children off northern streets or from northern camps. Some had gone willingly, if hesitantly. Many women actively resisted.

The women's resistance underscored one of most confounding aspects of slavery in Sudan: As was often true with slaves throughout Islamic history, many had effectively negotiated the terms of their bondage. Some had transcended the violence of their original abductions through the decades. Some had married, acquired property, fallen in love; or what they believed to be love. Most feared return to the devastated south, where many no longer had relatives. A boy, born in the north, had been "retrieved" while his mother was away. Many forcibly returned women pleaded to be allowed to go back north. Some made the dangerous journey back on their own.

"If I have a way," a boy ripped from the arms of his grandmother in the north told an aid worker, "I will go back to my grandmother."

For some Dinka leaders, CEAWC was a way to return women to the depopulated south. For Khartoum, it was a quick and very dirty way to bury Ryle's list, which CEAWC never used to cross-check against the returnees. Neither group seemed particularly interested in tracking down real slaves.

Shortly after the final peace agreement ended the war, CEAWC ended the returns. For its *2006 Trafficking in Persons Report*, the State Department placed the new Government of National Unity in Tier Three for its inaction. But now Miller's office had no leverage on the issue. Meanwhile, in thousands of starkly isolated *baggara* strongholds, like that where Adamoussa held Muong and his family, thousands toiled against their will in violent bondage.

On my trips to Sudan without Eibner, the dark crystal of slavery revealed more sides and more angles. As I fanned out on foot and on bicycle and found verifiable survivors of slavery, they always said what they really needed: food, bore holes, clothing—ultimately, paved roads, health facilities. And CSI, at least when I traveled with them, wasn't in the development aid business. They were in the "salvation" business. But emancipation often meant the freedom to starve.

One morning as I rested in my *tukul*, word came over the CB radio that government forces had attacked ten villages in the eastern Upper Nile, taking over a dozen into slavery. That same morning, another government entity, CEAWC, was scheduled to bring back roughly the same number—four women, four girls, and one boy—to the south. That day, I would witness the dramatic return.

When the freed slaves appeared from a UN Cessna which had flown them from Khartoum, they wore colorful head-to-toe *tobes*—a Muslim tradition in a Dinka land. In stark contrast with CSI's half-naked and dust-covered "redeemed," they were modest, demure, and sweet-smelling. After shedding their shyness, the children goofed around like the kids that they were. The girls wore pink and yellow frilly dresses, which didn't stay clean after they began rolling in the dirt.

We boarded a truck and drove for two hours while the women—Achok, Awein, Aman, and Arek—took in their new old world. Sometimes they cried softly, sometimes they clapped and laughed. Achok, the eldest at forty-five, laughed a lot. The largest woman sat regally impassive, breastfeeding a newborn. They spoke about how long the journey had been, and how long they were in the north. For Achok, it had been twenty years. For all of them, it had been an odyssey of pain, but ultimately some accommodation as well. Several had borne their master's children. They were nervous about returning home.

"In the north," said Achok, "people said that it is very bad here, that there is no food, and that even the foxes eat people."

Awein, forty-two, began to recognize her surroundings. "Oh, I remember that tree," she said, as we passed a particularly big and shady tree and thorns raked our truck. "I remember these thorns!"

Achok looked confused when we passed a clearing. "Wasn't there a school there?" she asked.

A minute later, we drove by a bombed-out brick skeleton where a school used to stand. Fewer than 25 percent of the south's children were in school; here the figure was closer to zero.

Our first stop was supposed to be Achok's family. We were arriving a day ahead of schedule and there was no one but a few children at her old homestead. None were old enough to remember her from the time *murahileen* horsemen seized her. A girl pointed at Achok.

"What's your name?"

"Ngong," she said. The girl beamed.

"That's my family name," she said, adding that everyone was at the market. We drove on.

As we pulled in to the Mangar Angwei market, which smelled like marijuana and peanuts, a huge crowd gathered. There was some confusion, concern. The first person to approach the truck was a screaming old madman, and I realized that many people in the market were either drunk or stoned.

Then a man who recognized the women climbed aboard, overjoyed. One of the returnees, the little boy in a *djellabah*, snuck in behind, scared, trying to climb down. Others recognized the women and approached them, crying and wailing.

The locals hugged Aman and Achok ferociously, and passed them around among their relatives and the village elders. The returnees' flowing silk *abaya* robes stood out against the rags of the others, but learned or forced cultural differences melted away in a matter of a few tearful seconds. Villagers held their new, screaming babies aloft. Relatives passed a water bowl through the crowd, and everyone spat in it before dumping the contents on Achok's head in a traditional Dinka welcome gesture. Many danced and ululated in exultation.

Aman's brother came and reached up to the truck, crying. He took my hand and appeared to thank me in Dinka. Quivering, he pointed to his heart. I pointed to Chol Changath, a local aid worker who had coordinated the return for Save the Children. The little boy in the *djellabah* began dancing with the rest.

As the truck pulled out of the market, the grim silence of the two remaining women, Awein and Arek, contrasted sharply with the mayhem behind us. We found what used to be their village. War and drought had smashed it beyond recognition. The town was once a hub of activity before government troops killed the local chief. Now there were no services here.

The returned women, unrecognized, cast their eyes down. Locals milled about, more interested in the sack of sorghum Chol had provided than with the newcomers. Awein choked back tears. Not, I thought, tears of joy.

For Muong and his family, there was no redemption. No cloaked middleman ever emerged to broker his release. No UN Cessna swung low to carry him home. He never heard the name "Eibner," nor "Bush" for that matter. At least, throughout his years in bondage, his family stayed intact. But in order for Muong to survive, he would soon have to continue his odyssey alone.

After their first escape attempt, life had become harsher for his family. "Beatings all the time," recalled Muong. Adamoussa continued to rape his mother, and soon Muong had a new half sister.

In 1998, after Aluat bore Adamoussa a second girl, she became overwhelmed with dread that the shifting family structure might spell the end for her sons. It was not uncommon for the *baggara* to rid their homes of their male slaves as they came of age and began to pose a physical threat. Sometimes, they would cast the young men out onto the street; other times, slaves awoke to find the masters had slashed male slaves' throats. Aluat told her sons they should save themselves and escape. Muong knew she meant it.

Several months later, while minding the cattle, Muong saw his opportunity and bolted into the tall grass. His lungs burning in the heat, he slowed to a trot but kept going until nightfall. He never said good-bye to his mother.

Muong wandered across the barren, rolling plain. He survived by avoiding camel camps and begging from anyone not in a *djellabah*—the white robe worn by the *baggara* Arabs. After two weeks, he came to a Dinka settlement in neighboring Darfur. A Dinka elder told him about CEAWC, which the government had just formed as a sop to international pressure. He gave it a shot, hoping the committee would help free his family from bondage. But he feared that he was too late, that his escape had prompted Adamoussa to shoot his mother and brother.

"My heart was never at peace after I left," he said.

For three years, Muong worked through the Dinka elders in Darfur to lobby CEAWC to help his family flee Adamoussa's grasp. For three years, local officials in Kordofan did not respond. In 2002, war politics once again changed the lives of Muong and his family—this time for the better. Danforth's initiative had gathered steam as Khartoum was eager to show good faith in the peace negotiations. CEAWC provided

Muong with an armed police truck. After a tense January 2003 standoff in which Adamoussa threatened to kill himself and the girls—whom he insisted were his property—Muong won the freedom of his entire family.

Adamoussa would find them if they stayed in Kordofan, so the family made the dangerous trek southward. It took eighteen days of hard travel, but finally Muong, his three younger sisters, his mother, and Garang made it back to Bahr el Ghazal. There, they found that their former home—a mud, stick, and grass *tukul*—and their entire hamlet had been obliterated in a 1992 *murahileen* raid. They had to fight for the barest essentials in a drought-stricken and war-torn land. But there were a few survivors who helped them rebuild. And, for the first time in fifteen years, they were free.

"It was a *long* walk," said Muong. "But I'm home."

Much of the bondage that persists in Sudan is a mystery. A good deal of it looks like the kind of horror dutifully recited during CSI redemptions. Forcing someone to work for no pay under threat of violence is a barbaric crime against humanity. But the decision matrix for slaves in Sudan is a difficult one, and escape is frequently a terrifying option.

Sudan and Mauritania are the only two countries where racialized chattel slavery persists. They are also the two poorest countries in the Arab world. This is no coincidence.

As I found out in Haiti, radical underdevelopment led some families, even among those who had escaped the raids, to surrender their weakest members to a more secure future, even if the price of that security was forced work, bound by violence. Dinka historians told of a precolonial system whereby parents could use their children as collateral to raise credit, in essence renting them out until they could repay the debt. At the time of the 1988 famine, Dinka parents pawned their children to the *baggara* for $100 apiece. The alternative would be to witness starvation slowly kill their progeny. In the rare instances when they tried to reclaim them, they had to pay twice the original price.

Adult Dinka also fled violence and famine to the north, offering their services in exchange for food. Many times, they worked for people unwilling to release them after they fed them.

A tragically large number fell into that trap. Sudan had more domestic refugees than any other country in the world: 4.5 million. The United Nations, in a typically clinical designation, referred to these as "internally displaced persons," or IDPs. The term did not begin to describe the trauma of a young man who, upon seeing his mother raped, his father shot, and his grandfather brained, ran from his village, found others running from their villages, and sought to survive wherever he and they could, and however they could, in the vast country.

The 2005 peace deal between the SPLM and Khartoum brought waves of optimism for southerners in the north. The Dinka might never return to a time when influence was measured in the number of cattle, but for a few shining moments, it seemed as if they might be able to return to a place where it was no longer measured in guns. As many as 1.4 million refugees were expected to return to the south. And each day for the first two months after the peace deal, about 400 Dinka came back to the area around Malual Kon. As was true after manumitted slaves returned south during the British colonial period, many found a hard landing.

When I met him in a friend's dusty homestead, Muong wore a plastic cross around his neck, a sign of his recent conversion to Christianity. He had declined Islam when he was Adamoussa's slave, though many others in his position would have declared there was no God but Allah. Despite CSI assertions to the contrary, most Dinka conversions to Islam were at least somewhat voluntary: acculturation was the only way to survive and move forward in an intolerant north. In contrast, Muong had accepted Christ precisely because he wanted to erase his time in the north as much as possible. But Jesus had not given Muong or his family a home of their own yet, and they struggled for food on a daily basis.

Denied the scars of Dinka manhood, Muong bore the scars of Adamoussa's wrath on his back and arms—and in his head. When Muong learned I was his age, he lamented his illiteracy. "It is too late: instead of books, I was given beatings," he said as his voice broke, an unusual occurrence for a Dinka man, particularly when he is talking to a stranger. "I assume you come from a place where there is an idea that humans have rights," he added, regaining his composure and kicking at an ashy firepit. "Why does no one care about our slavery here?"

It was a fair question, and all the more poignant after the peace deal. Despite his hardship, Muong was one of the lucky ones—thousands still languished in bondage. But Khartoum's main response continued to be denial that slavery existed in Sudan, and detention of investigators who claimed otherwise.

Meanwhile, another horror had emerged during my first trip to Sudan. The genocide in Darfur—which involved the arming of different regional militias, the displacement of millions, small-scale slave raiding, short-term sex slavery, and massive of amounts of bonded labor and forced child soldiering—showed the extent to which hate still poisoned the national leaders.

But, to end the civil war, Danforth's initiative harnessed a feeling that transcended racist politics. To the average Sudanese, northern or southern, it mattered less that their neighbor was black or brown, "red" or "blue," than that an eviscerating and hopeless conflict bled all of them white.

Over 2 million Sudanese had died in the war between north and south. Since 1983, Khartoum had spent a million dollars a day on defense. Scores of young Khartoumers killed themselves rather than face conscription and the savage conflict in the south. Despite decades of war, the government of Sudan held no POWs at the time of the armistice. Militias summarily killed or enslaved surrendering Dinka men and boys. A generation of Dinka, Nuba, and Nuer barely survived to carry on their people.

Six months after signing the Comprehensive Peace Agreement that made him Sudan's vice president, John Garang died when his Russian M1-172 helicopter crashed in southern Sudan. Salva Kiir, as the peace agreement mandated, replaced Garang as vice president. In an April 10, 2006, speech to the new Parliament in Juba, Kiir said that the government "remains deeply committed to the retrieval of Southern Sudanese women and children abducted and enslaved in Northern Sudan."

John Eibner followed Kiir's speech with an Easter appeal to President Bush, asking him to verify that Khartoum was freeing slaves. Discredited in the eyes of all but those who viewed redemption as a revealed truth, CSI fought to put Sudanese slavery back in the spotlight.

But Eibner's was once again a lonely struggle. Internationally, there was never serious discussion about charging those who orchestrated the slave raids with war crimes. Within Sudan, there was never a single prosecution at any level of a slave taker or slaveholder. Slave raiding was a weapon of war. Now, a shattered country remains where thousands are still forced to work, for no pay, under threat of violence. Slavery, once the sword of genocide, has turned into the blunt plowshare of economy. Hardly the vision set forth in the Book of Isaiah.

Eibner's vigilante humanitarianism faded. The international community offered no robust response to Sudanese crimes against humanity. And Sudan continued to fulfill Isaiah's later, darker prophecy (18:1–2):

Woe to the land shadowing with wings, which is beyond the
rivers of Eth-i-o'pi-a: That sendeth ambassadors by the sea,
even in vessels of bulrushes upon the waters, saying,
Go, ye swift messengers, to a nation scattered and peeled, to a
people terrible from their beginning hitherto. . . .

4

A Moral Law That Stands
Above Men and Nations

It didn't seem like a fair fight. In 2003, John Miller's first year in charge of the trafficking office, he had a budget of $10 million. His nemeses—pimps, traffickers, and slave-masters—reaped as much as $32 billion annually from the flesh of slaves. But Miller, a born guerrilla, relished asymmetric warfare.

Miller's first task was to learn his subject. He came into the job with a somewhat hazy vision of slavery, thinking it was just an extreme form of poverty. The Michael Horowitz coalition sharpened his view by giving him graphic reports of young Asian and European girls who endured grotesque abuse at the hands of traffickers. Many left bondage only when they became HIV-positive.

His second task was to show the world what slavery really meant. Most people thought of it as a metaphor for underpaid and over-worked wage laborers. Merriam-Webster's first definition of the word is "drudgery; toil." The recording artist Prince scrawled the word "slave" across his face to protest a binding contract that paid him $10-million advances per album. Activists would claim a worker in an Indonesian shoe factory received a "slave wage" of $1.25 per hour. Few knew the horror that the word, properly used, connoted.

In 1785, the British abolitionist Thomas Clarkson faced a similar challenge of educating a population that didn't want to learn. Researching slavery for a Latin essay competition, he interviewed eyewitnesses to the trade. The horrors they described broke his heart, but he knew that alone, a twenty-five-year-old Cambridge student couldn't do much. Two years later, he met William Wilberforce, a rising star in Parliament who had recently undergone an evangelical transformation. Wilberforce's speeches, informed by Clarkson's research, launched the campaign that ended the slave trade.

Miller needed a Wilberforce. In fact, Miller needed a Super-Wilberforce. Clarkson had to convince some 600 MPs that slavery was wrong. Miller had to convince the world that it even existed.

In Frank Wolf, Sam Brownback, Chris Smith, and Donald Payne, he had committed congressional backers who gave impassioned speeches. But Miller knew they would be lost on all but a few colleagues and the odd C-SPAN junky. The Horowitz coalition helped, but with no legislative fight to mobilize around, the Evangelicals had begun their drift back to signature social issues like abortion and gays.

Officially, as senior adviser to the Secretary of State, Miller had the ear of the highest-ranking member of the cabinet. But just getting his bosses to call the evil by its true name was an ordeal. When Colin Powell rolled out the first TIP report, in 2001, he never used the word "slavery," nor did Miller's immediate boss, Paula Dobriansky. During the release of the following report, compiled by Miller's predecessor, Powell cautiously employed the phrase "modern form of slavery" just once.

The first time Miller prepared a speech for Powell, he included "slavery" prominently. Dobriansky redlined the word. "We don't use that term," she said.

Miller's was an old challenge. "Slavery has been fruitful in giving itself names. It has been called 'the peculiar institution,' 'the social system,' and the 'impediment,'" said Frederick Douglass in a speech in 1865 after Congress passed the Thirteenth Amendment. "It has been called a great many names, and it will call itself by yet another name; and you and I and all of us had better wait and see what new form this old monster will assume, in what new skin this old snake will come forth."

To the modern State Department, slavery was "trafficking." But to Miller, "trafficking" was a euphemism. Some bureaucrats, ironically, believed that adopting the term "slavery" would trivialize the suffering of African Americans like Douglass. Others were cautious about using the loaded term with countries that had never received a formal American apology for the transatlantic slave trade. Trafficking, as defined by the United Nations, was not a crime against humanity. Slavery, like genocide, was. As such, it would require a robust response. Miller had long known that the term "robust response" made the pinstripes curl on the suits of State Department bureaucrats.

Dobriansky compromised and approved "modern-day slavery." But in the wrangling, Miller could see that he would not find his Super-Wilberforce at the State Department.

On the evening of February 5, 2003, Miller met Michael Gerson. They were both attending a dinner at the Washington Hilton hosted by Chuck Colson, the convicted Watergate conspirator turned Evangelical power broker. Colson was giving his organization's William Wilberforce Award to Sam Brownback, the Senate cosponsor of the Trafficking Victims Protection Act. Gerson was an odd character. A petite man with a floppy haircut and small hands, his most defining feature was a pair of horn-rimmed Armani spectacles. He didn't look like a crusader. But if moved, Gerson could provide the megaphone that Miller needed.

Gerson was the most powerful man that nobody knew, because he wrote the public script for the man that everyone knew. He was President Bush's handpicked speechwriter and one of his most trusted aides. On his dog-eared yellow notepads, he scrawled much of the States of the Union, the inaugural addresses, the post-9/11 call to arms. He was damn good. Even Bush critics—thoughtful ones, anyway—compared him to Ted

Sorenson, President Kennedy's legendary wordsmith. "Michael Gerson is so gifted," wrote *The American Prospect* editor Robert Kuttner, a liberal, "that he could make a trained monkey sound like Thomas Jefferson."

Inside the White House, he had another reputation: the last man fighting to prevent the "compassion" of the president's "compassionate conservatism" from being pulverized in the crucible of war. Like Miller and Horowitz, Gerson was a reformed Democrat: his mother was a Kennedy supporter and he had been enamored with Jimmy Carter, principally for the overt faith of the thirty-ninth president and his commitment to human rights. Gerson lobbied hard for those people who had no lobbyist, and he once described his friend Bono the same way. One morning, arguing for $15 billion to combat AIDS, he struck other key advisers dumb when he told Bush that "history will judge us severely if we don't do this."

That year's State of the Union address was behind him, but Gerson, who served on the White House Iraq Group, had plenty of items competing for his attention. Miller, as only Miller could, leaned on him and eventually got a meeting.

Like Miller, Gerson was a Starbucks addict, but his time was short, so they met for breakfast in the White House Mess. Horowitz had briefed Miller beforehand, explaining Gerson's deep and animating Evangelical faith. Gerson saw himself as the heir to the mission of his "godly heroes," like Wilberforce, who he said was "the model of Evangelical social involvement." Twenty years earlier, Gerson had studied Wilberforce's struggle closely when he ghostwrote a chapter on him for Colson's book, *Kingdoms in Conflict*.

The pale thirty-eight-year-old across from him did not look like Miller's Super-Wilberforce. But in Gerson's words, which even in casual conversation flowed and resounded like the president's finest orations, Miller heard someone who might speak for the slaves.

After that breakfast with Miller, Gerson quietly sold the political value of the abolitionist agenda to doubters inside the White House. The march to war in Iraq was not the only thing that dominated his time in the spring of 2003. Having achieved a razor-thin victory in 2000, Gerson's boss was already gearing up for the most competitive reelection ever involving a wartime incumbent.

In his windowless office two doors down from the president, Gerson explained to me his deep convictions about fighting contemporary slavery, both for reasons of national security and because he felt the calling of his faith. But he acknowledged that, while September 11 made it impossible to be harmless as a dove, he often had to be wise as a serpent to get trafficking into his boss's speeches. "Mike is the one always wondering how we can achieve liberal goals with conservative means," Karl Rove once said in backhanded praise of Gerson.

Miller did not have to convince Gerson that slavery fit the president's agenda; Rove, who had tried to kill Miller's appointment, and whose leanings were much more libertarian, was beyond his reach. After their first breakfast, the antislavery czar talked with Gerson regularly, but Miller met Rove only once, for a total of ten seconds, at a White House picnic. Gerson later claimed that he and Rove saw eye-to-eye on Wilberforce issues. Insiders said that while Rove may have had sympathy for Gerson's agenda, his game was politics, and slaves didn't vote.

Without Rove, who with Vice President Dick Cheney was the most influential of the dozen people to vet each speech, slavery would be no more than what Bush called a "cram-in," and a brief one, no matter how much the president personally cared about the issue.

Chuck Colson and Southern Baptist Convention policy chief Richard Land, to whom Governor Bush had confided in 1999 that "God wants me to be President," worked to sell Rove on the idea that if Bush wanted to be president again, God, and the congregation, wanted to see human trafficking high on his agenda. In 2000, white Evangelicals accounted for 40 percent of Bush's total votes, but millions never came to the polls. Slavery might not be an issue that turned purple voters red, but it could galvanize the faithful and get them into the booth. Rove saw their logic.

Gerson knew that Evangelicals were not the only portion of the electorate impassioned by slavery talk. On July 8, 2003, Bush stood at the windswept harbor of the notorious slavetrading island of Gorée in Senegal. It was his first visit to Africa and though he stopped short of offering the first presidential apology for "one of the greatest crimes of history," he delivered a brief but soul-searching speech under the scalding midday sun. It was vintage Gerson.

"Christian men and women became blind to the clearest commands of their faith and added hypocrisy to injustice," said the president. "A republic founded on equality for all became a prison for millions."

Immediately afterward, the Bush-Cheney '04 listserv sent supporters the Gorée address under the headline: "President Affirms Shared Values of Americans and Africans, Vows to Work Together." At the top of the e-mail was an unsubtle "Donate Now" link. In spite of that, Colin Powell dismissed a reporter in South Africa who questioned the motives behind the speech: "It was designed to deal with real problems facing people in need in Africa," he said.

I asked Gerson, who once introduced a freed Sudanese slave to the president, why he and his fellow speechwriters did not use the speech to address contemporary slavery. Senegal bordered Mauritania, where antislavery organizations estimated that Arab White Moors held as many as 100,000 Afro-Mauritanians as chattel slaves. Gerson admitted that Africa was not the intended audience; the African-American electorate was. "I'll give you the honest reason," he said, contradicting Powell. "The honest reason is that much of the speech was directed more at an American audience, and had to do with race relations in our country."

As Election Day neared, the president began to address contemporary slavery head-on. Speaking to a trafficking conference in Tampa, Florida, Bush quickly pivoted to Cuba, a magnet for sex tourists, and one of five countries that regularly endured sanctions under the TVPA. The president held that those sanctions would "hasten the day when no Cuban child is exploited to finance a failed revolution." Though the forty-year-old embargo made those sanctions superfluous, the Miami base could never get enough Castro-spanking.

The Gorée and Tampa speeches both targeted specific ethnic groups in the electorate, but Gerson geared all antitrafficking statements first and foremost toward Evangelicals. He used religious language judiciously. But given the deep faith that he shared with his boss, his description of slavery's transcendent horror was understandably a bit more saturated with Christian apologetics. Gerson scoffed at the idea that he wrote "coded messages" to the faithful. But if the allusions fired up the base, he wouldn't weep.

That fall, in the Royal Banqueting Hall at Whitehall Palace in London, the president referred to T. S. Eliot's "Choruses from 'The Rock,'" and praised William Wilberforce. Bush also lauded the efforts of the Royal Navy, which lost 2,000 sailors while freeing 160,000 slaves in the nineteenth century. That history was a reminder that Gerson's rousing speeches would amount to nothing unless followed by, in the State Department's least favorite phrase, "robust response."

The British antislavery fleet peaked at thirty-six ships; John Miller had a staff of thirteen people. Firing up sympathetic constituencies was a baby step. Next, Miller needed the president to rouse the conscience of the world.

During the first week of September 2003, Gerson met in the Oval Office with the president, chief of staff Andrew Card, national security adviser Condoleezza Rice, and her deputy, Stephen Hadley. Gerson had been angling for a major address about human trafficking since he met Miller, and the forthcoming UN General Assembly in New York presented a perfect venue.

Gerson had won support for slavery talk by convincing Rove it would shore up the domestic base in the ongoing campaign. Now he argued that addressing the topic would assuage rising international discontent over Iraq by showing that, as he later put it, "we have a broader concern than just going after terrorist groups."

Two weeks earlier, a bomb at the Canal Hotel in Baghdad had killed twenty-two UN employees and aid workers, including Kofi Annan's special envoy Sérgio Vieira de Mello. The attack, which Al Qaeda operative Abu Musab al-Zarqawi claimed was his handiwork, was followed by another the day before Bush was to speak at the General Assembly. The attacks led to the withdrawal of the United Nations' international staff from Iraq, and aggravated the sense that the United States had rushed to war without sufficient UN approval.

Gerson now suggested that, while most of the speech would have to be an Iraq sales job, this was a chance to confront world leaders on the issue of trafficking. But the motivation was strategic as well as altruistic. "I think there was a real desire and a concern to match this with a kind of soft power strategy," said Gerson.

Partly because the issue appealed to his faith, the president immediately wanted human trafficking in the speech, and not just as a "cram-in." He also had a lot of questions. How many slaves are there? Where are they? Who are they?

Gerson called John Miller on his cell phone as he walked down G Street and told him the boss wanted numbers and ideas, as soon as possible. As the scribe and his six writers bent over the words of the speech, Miller and his staff fed them suggestions. Gerson used some of the data, specifically the high-end estimates for the total number of international trafficking victims. But he used none of Miller's verbiage. "What we submitted was so prosaic," Miller later admitted. "I mean, I'm embarrassed, given what emerged in the speech, which was so moving."

On September 23, Bush became the first world leader to call on the General Assembly to fight modern-day slavery. In theory, abolition was a priority for everyone in the chamber. Since World War I, the international community had agreed to over a dozen conventions and resolutions, including the Universal Declaration of Human Rights of 1948, which banned slavery and the slave trade. In practice, the calcified UN could only bring itself to denounce "virtual slavery," "trafficking," or "abduction," for fear of offending member states by calling the crime by its true name. The end result was the greatest number of slaves in human history.

For most of those in the audience, including millions watching on TV, this was the first time they had heard of American efforts to combat human trafficking. Most of the president's speech concerned terrorism, AIDS, and of course Iraq. But Gerson held the final fifth for slavery. Substantially, Bush pledged an extra $50 million to combat trafficking. While the American budget for human trafficking was less than 0.3 percent of the budget for drug trafficking, the new allocation represented the most significant expenditure on abolition since Reconstruction.

"We must show new energy in fighting back an old evil," the president said. "Nearly two centuries after the abolition of the transatlantic slave trade, and more than a century after slavery was officially ended in its last strongholds, the trade in human beings for any purpose must not be allowed to thrive in our time."

But Bush only detailed his concern about the trade in human beings for one purpose: sex. With Jack Danforth eyeing a resolution in Sudan, Evangelicals had shifted their focus to prostitution, and so had the president. He touted a law he had recently signed that criminalized international child-sex tourism for American citizens, and encouraged other nations to pass similar legislation.

"The victims of the sex trade see little of life before they see the very worst of life: an underground of brutality and fear," he said, as world leaders shifted uncomfortably in their seats. "Those who patronize this industry debase themselves and they deepen the misery of others."

Bush drew a just line when he proscribed "voluntary" child prostitution, which, shockingly, some nations still considered legitimate if distasteful. But he made no mention of child slaves in other industries like the restavèks of Haiti. Was a girl who was raped by her master less violated if her body was sold first into domestic labor? He made no mention of slaves taken in war. Was Muong's mother less raped by her master because she was never sold into commercial sex? And he made no mention of the millions of slaves who languished in generational debt bondage on the Asian subcontinent. Yet, despite making no mention of these, the great numerical majority of slaves worldwide, Bush purported to speak for all of those in bondage.

"The founding documents of the United Nations and the founding documents of America stand in the same tradition," the president concluded. "Both assert that human beings should never be reduced to objects of power or commerce, because their dignity is inherent. Both recognize a moral law that stands above men and nations."

It was a stirring sentiment, and Bush made history when he expressed it. But his narrow focus left many wondering if he felt that one type of slave had more inherent dignity than another.

With 600 words, the president had dropped a rock in a pool. There were no ripples. To many abroad, particularly in Europe, the speech was more bizarre proselytizing from a man with a messianic complex. Four days after the address, Bush pressured Russian president Vladimir Putin to act against trafficking during a bilateral summit at Camp David. Few other world leaders so much as sniffed.

"We ought to be raising holy hell with those countries that are allowing this to go on," railed Dan Burton, a senior Republican on the House International Relations Committee. Instead, "when the President talked about this issue in the United Nations, it was viewed as almost a distraction." The American media barely touched the slavery references, and some television networks cut away from the remarks after he finished addressing Iraq.

In 2004, 78 percent of Evangelicals voted for Bush. The 43,000 Southern Baptist churches were the base of the base, and one of them even expelled parishioners who admitted to voting for the president's opponent, Senator John Kerry. But trafficking did not prompt their votes. They supported Bush on the basis of his advocacy of a constitutional amendment to ban gay marriage, his opposition to embryonic stem cell research, and other "core" positions of the Christian Right. As a political tool, slavery talk was tried and found wanting.

On the morning of December 16, 2004, Gerson had a heart attack. Two coronary stents later, he was back on the job, but in a different role. He would still help the president shape his message, but he was no longer his chief speechwriter. From then on, though Bush referred to it in a half-dozen lower-profile speeches, trafficking was, in the president's deathless prose, a "cram-in." In his 2004 General Assembly address, Bush devoted just three sentences to contemporary slavery. In 2005 and 2006, he did not mention the crime at all. Despite Gerson's best efforts, the president's Super-Wilberforce moment was just that: a moment.

After 2003, the spotlight faded. From then on, John Miller would fight a hidden war. But low profile did not mean low intensity. And underfunded did not mean cheap. On a personal level, at least, his struggle for the slaves would cost him a great deal.

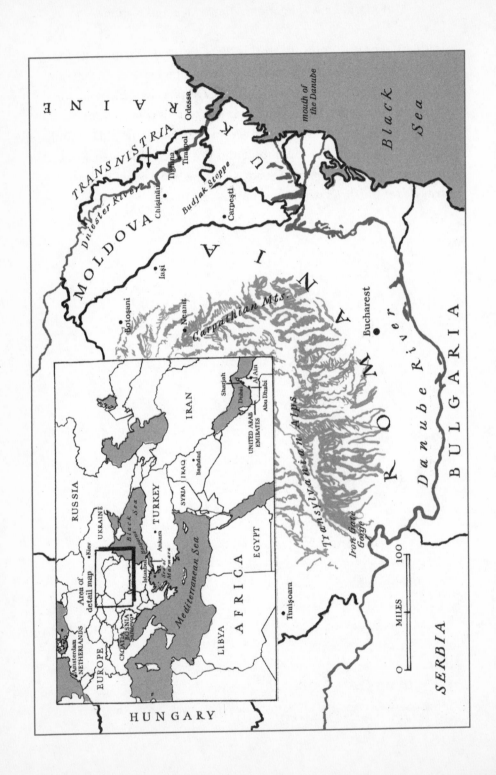

5

A Nation Within a Nation

Our first three weeks together had been tense. Now Tatiana was, as our landlady said, *volcanica*.

I had met her on a blustery February day in Amsterdam, a world away from the sweltering June air of the crumbling Bucharest apartment we now inhabited. Tatiana was a vision in pink, and her words bore an intensity that her pixyish looks belied. I had asked her to accompany me here because she had a distinctive skill. In many brothels, free prostitutes worked alongside women in bondage. To the johns, to the police—even to most aid workers—they were indistinguishable. To Tatiana, the slaves were unmistakable.

Tatiana knew them because once she was one of them. She survived, got free, and instead of retreating from the world as others did, she went right at the traffickers, testifying in their prosecution. Later, she founded Atalantas, an organization that reached trafficked women by placing stickers on bathroom mirrors of brothels, slipping them contact information in lipstick containers, letting slaves know they were not alone. Like Bill Nathan in Port-au-Prince, Tatiana had a transcendent courage that enabled her to regain her freedom, and then risk her life to help others do the same. But whereas Bill embodied quiet determination, Tatiana was ferociously defiant.

Now she was in full fight mode. I had dug a little too deep in an interview, and asked too many questions about her family. Quivering with rage, chain-smoking, she accused me of bringing her to Romania under false pretenses, of using her to justify Bush administration policies on sex trafficking—policies that from years of working in the field she saw as profoundly flawed.

"You don't understand!" she yelled. "You will never understand! You can't understand! John Miller will never understand! He offers these statistics. He issues these reports. What does he know?"

She was right. There was no way that I could understand what it meant to be a slave. I said that I hoped to get closer by going undercover, by listening to slaves and slave traders. She said I would expose her name, her family, and her nationality. I pledged that I wouldn't. She threatened to fly back to Amsterdam the next day. I offered to pay for the trip. She refused my offer and said that she would cut off cooperation with me entirely. "I'm so stupid to have trusted you," she said.

I was about to infiltrate a local slave market in one of Bucharest's most violent zones and was to meet confederates to whom I would entrust my life. I was late. And I was tense. I lost my cool and slapped the table to try to pause her invective long enough to defend myself.

The sound, the motion—or maybe the unconscious flash of anger across my face—smashed into Tatiana like a sledgehammer to the solar plexus. She sucked in all her breath and curled into a ball, hyperventilating between sobs.

"No violence!" she screamed. "Oh my God, I'm suffocating!"

Never before had I felt so thoroughly feared. A woman who had been a five-foot pillar of strength when I met her was now trembling, struggling for air in terror. In me, in that moment of disquiet, Tatiana had seen the fiendish apparition of her former slavemaster.

Mortified, I apologized. But I quickly realized there was nothing I could say to take away the threat that my very presence posed. I apologized again and hurried into the street.

During one month in Romania, I met a man who made over a million dollars by selling human beings. I met another who agreed to trade a young woman to me for a used car. But during the course of one day, I saw the true price of slavery.

My argument with Tatiana left me shaken by self-doubt and concerned for her well-being. But I had to get in character. I set out toward the Intercontinental Hotel to meet the men who would guide my descent into a Romani, or Gypsy, slave brothel. Between our apartment and the Intercontinental lay the gleaming, dense, and heavily fortified U.S. Embassy. In front, a crowd of about a hundred had gathered, as they did every weekday morning. Next door, a convenience store advertised "VIZA USA" pictures. *Vis* means "dream" in Romanian.

Romanians do not consider smoking a vice, and a thin haze crowned the gaggle. A man emerged from the store, desperately tearing the plastic from a carton of Pall Malls. Romanians do consider prostitution a vice, and an illegal one. Nonetheless, telltale red-on-black neon signs advertised the subterranean Diva and Pussycat nightclubs a few doors down. In the evenings, foreigners paid $30 for nude lap dances on red leather wraparound sofas, segmented by office cubicle walls. The cost of sex was negotiable; the freedom of the women was suspect.

Across the street stood the twenty-two-story Intercontinental. When Romania's former Communist dictator Nicolae Ceauşescu oversaw its construction, this was Bucharest's tallest building. Like the hotel, Ceauşescu's ghost—perforated though it was—still loomed over the city. After taking power in 1967, the ex-shoemaker replaced a fifth of the capital's glorious single-family town houses with drab tenement blocks as part of a bizarre and brutal reformation of Romania into a "systematized" utopia.

The Intercontinental was an exception to Ceauşescu-era construction, its design meant to lure foreign cash rather than crush local spirit. In the weeks after Ceauşescu's execution in 1989, Western investors, doctors, journalists, and aid workers flooded the hotel, which became the first point of contact between Western capitalists and a new, distinctly Romanian breed of capitalism.

Back then, black marketeers swindled guests on money exchanges or hawked suspect Danubian caviar for a fraction of the market price. Paying entry fees to the Kalashnikov-wielding guards, half-dressed prostitutes poured into the hotel, dialing Westerners' rooms at random, knocking on their doors at all hours. In theory, in Ceauşescu's utopia, prostitution had not existed, and thus there was no need to ban it. In practice, the dictator's secret police, the Securitate, managed the trade by confining it to certain areas, and collecting information from prostitutes to blackmail visitors. When the secret police dissolved, the women worked for themselves. Some did, at least.

On our first night in Romania, Tatiana and I had gone to the McDonald's on Nicolae Bălcescu Boulevard. The street was downtown Bucharest's main drag and, for a five-block stretch beginning at the Intercontinental, ground zero for international sex tourists. We sat in a well-lit patio in front of the restaurant. Families and lovers enjoyed Western cuisine. Meanwhile, tourists, Westerners among them, pulled up in foreign cars and SUVs to enjoy Romanian women.

A tubby Romani man, directing the girls from nearby, wore flip-flops and tight shorts that bunched around his crotch. *"Poliţia!"* he yelled at one point, sending the girls skittering on their stilettos into the darkness, like newborn foals fleeing a fire. When the police drove past, the girls reemerged, with the pimp close behind. "He wants to make everyone understand that 'these are my girls, and if you want to be with them, you have to negotiate with me,'" Tatiana said.

Several nights later, on my own, I shadowed a vice bust in the same neighborhood. Four policemen jumped out of two cars. The pimps stayed hidden, and the girls scattered to side streets. The officers corralled three prostitutes and gave them tickets. The pimps would pay the fines and deepen the girls' debt bondage accordingly. For third offenses, the girls would go to jail. The police knew that the pimps were nearby, but they would not look for them. I asked one officer if he had been trained about human trafficking. "We know about human trafficking," he said, "but this is just a prostitution bust."

Around a dark corner, a lone woman, perhaps twenty, with black hair and an hourglass figure, cowered behind a car. Across the street, a man motioned toward me. The woman stepped out of the shadows.

"Sex? Fifty Euros," she asked in strained English.

I explained I was a writer, and asked if I could talk to her pimp across the street.

"Sex? Fifty Euros," she replied, eying my McDonald's bag.

I gave my French fries to her and she immediately shoved the entire contents into her mouth. She was starving. When she had finished, I asked her again if I could talk to her pimp.

"Sex? Fifty Euros."

I relayed the story to Tatiana the next morning. She said that the girl was enslaved. How did she know? "You just *know*," said Tatiana, exasperated.

It wasn't what I knew that was important, I told her. It was what I could prove.

Waiting in the Intercontinental, I admired the upgrades to the lobby since the Stalinist era. It had become a classic business meeting point—black leather chairs, green marble columns, floor-length mirrors, well-oiled revolving doors. Romanians sucked down their last cigarettes before their invariably nonsmoking American counterparts arrived. Eyes searched for new business or diplomatic contacts. "I'll be wearing a black suit with a red tie," several would have said.

The language here was English. The currency was the Euro. Ceauşescu prohibited his people from holding more than $7 in foreign currency. But today, although the hotel's store accepted lei, it wouldn't for long. Shortly before my visit, the Romanian central bank knocked off four zeros from the lei, only to phase it out entirely in four years. It was not the only evidence of a herky-jerky economy.

Polite, neatly dressed doormen had replaced gun-toting thugs, and prostitutes in Lurex were swapped for girls in neon halter tops distributing World Cup–themed advertising materials. But the oldest profession was still in business here. As the clock registered 9 a.m., a middle-aged, portly South Asian man emerged from the elevator bank escorting two young, raven-haired girls to a taxi. The girls wore stilettos, hip-hugging jeans, midriff-baring shirts without bras, fiercely arched eyebrows, and heavy makeup. This was standard summertime wear for young Bucharesti women. But there was little doubt as to the nature of their threesome.

Petrică Răchită and Alexandru arrived. Petrică, thirty, was a hard-nosed, no-bullshit journalist with deep contacts in both the underworld and the police. He was not a talker, but in the month that I would spend traveling with him, I saw up close that he was a natural democrat, the brave embodiment of a new young Romania. Though forced to wave Ceaușescu's banners in parades as a child, he was disgusted with the past. Yet he, along with a small, vibrant segment of his countrymen, radiated hope that they could change their country.

Alexandru, his cousin, was a fresh-faced twenty-one-year-old agriculture student, who spoke excellent English and would be my translator. As Alexandru smoked and wired me for sound, Petrică drained a tumbler of Scotch and explained he wouldn't be able to go into the slave sale with me. This was a surprise, though I knew that Petrică's colleagues had been threatened and attacked for writing about police corruption. Recently, in the area of our investigation, Petrică had tangled with the new Romanian special police, the *mascați*. The masked shock troops had an ugly record of unchecked violence, including summary executions.

As Petrică spoke, I put two spoonfuls of sugar in my coffee. "Careful of that," said Alexandru, taking the cigarette out of his mouth for a moment. "Diabetes."

Driving east, we passed an onion-domed Orthodox church with a Byzantine cross, and Petrică, an ordained priest, crossed himself. Despite its wrenching history, or because of it, downtown Bucharest still rumbled with decrepit grandeur. Flaking Belle Epoque buildings retained elaborate balconies, decorative guardrails, rusted steel, and green glass awnings reminiscent of a Jeunet and Caro film.

Centered in the first traffic circle was an enormous gray clock, engraved with the words ROMANIA and EUROPA, and surrounded by an island of purple and white poppies. The clock confidently counted down the 186 days left to Romania's supposed accession to the European Union on January 1, 2007. But accession was not a fait accompli; European parliamentarians warned that problems such as human trafficking might delay the process.

Millions of Romanians had preempted the European vote with one of their own, using their feet. "Fuck Romania," one young woman had said to me, using a word that represented approximately 10 percent of her English vocabulary. She had been sold in Western Europe, horribly abused as a prostitute, and wound up in a Romanian shelter, where I met her. Despite her ordeal, she couldn't wait to leave again, and was headed to Cyprus.

The "Fuck Romania" phenomenon was the dark competitor to Petrică's optimism. It was not new. Fourteen days after Ceauşescu's army shot him, the new Foreign Ministry lifted all travel restrictions for Romanians. For many in the second poorest country in Europe, emigration was the only option.

Those who stayed were rewarded with a tanking economy. Aid poured in, but by 1993, the inflation rate hit 300 percent. Ceauşescu had obsessed over the external debt, even rationing heating oil while his subjects froze; solvency was more complicated in a non-command economy rife with corruption. Citing insufficient economic reforms, the International Monetary Fund suspended loans. Many investors and

aid organizations pulled out as well. By 2000, over a third of the population of Romania—and of Eastern Europe as a whole—had fallen below
the poverty line. Alcoholism, always a problem in a country with the
second highest rate of alcohol consumption in the world, became epidemic. Infant and maternal mortality rocketed. Life expectancy plum-
meted. Families disintegrated.

Generally, those who sought a better life beyond the Danube weren't
the poorest of the poor. They may have said, "Fuck Romania!" but their
$3.5 billion in annual remittances, along with strengthened demand
from EU export markets, pulled the country out of recession in 2000.

Some did not find prosperity abroad. Tens of thousands became
slaves. Even as the Foreign Ministry officially lifted travel restrictions
in January 1990, the first networks were trafficking women into prostitution in Istanbul. Smugglers sold young men into bonded labor on
Spanish farms. Begging rings trafficked Romani children to Italy.

The Roma are Europe's largest minority, and Romania's poorest ethnic
group. Their history, since they emigrated from India some twelve centuries ago, has been one of slavery and resistance. Early Romanian elites
favored Romani girls as concubines. In 1836, a German named Eremiten
von Gauting was en route to Constantinople when he intervened in the
sale, for two gold coins, of a lovely fifteen-year-old Gypsy girl.

"I went up to the barbarian man and told him that I would buy her
back, but he was very rich and laughed at my offer of 50 gold coins.
He bragged that he had bought her for his pleasure," von Gauting
recounted. The buyer offered to sell the German one of his 500 other
Gypsies, but von Gauting instead went to the authorities.

"Gipsies are our property and we can do with them what we like," the
police told the visitor.

In the twentieth century, Ceaușescu's social engineering, which was
supposed to uplift the Roma, instead had the opposite effect. The dictator banned contraception and abortion for all Romanians, and compelled women to produce at least four children. Those women who
had twelve would be named "Heroes of the Republic" and given a gold
medal, free train transport, and an all-expense-paid vacation. Though

their infants normally went unregistered, the Roma had the highest birthrates in Europe.

The only reward that Romani families received for their patriotic breeding was destitution. In the 1960s, many lived five to a room, some at twice that concentration. One third of all Romani mothers saw their children die, and two thirds lived in poverty. Most parents were unemployed, and their life expectancy was a fraction of their non-Romani countrymen. When Romania's GDP per capita inched back after 2000, they benefited not at all.

In the nineteenth century, a British visitor called the Roma "a nation within a nation." They still were. Four out of five children in Romania's notorious orphanages had been Romani. But under EU pressure, the government closed the orphanages and banned international adoptions. The options for unwanted children were few. Orphanages dumped thousands in unprepared hospital wards. Babies became scarred by neglect in row upon row of caged cribs. Nurses sometimes tied together the hands of mentally disabled children so they would not injure themselves. Others wound up in an even deeper abyss.

Petrică pushed east through late rush-hour traffic, past shiny seven-series BMWs and beat-up, two-stroke East German Trabants. Most Romanians, with a healthy distaste for products turned out under communism, believed that the Trabants were made of pressed cardboard. The right rear window of Petrică's dented Opel station wagon was, in fact, cardboard, and a water bottle full of motor oil rolled around the rear floorboards.

We passed several sex shops, one called "Amsterdam XXX," bearing the subheading "*We Make Sex Fun.*" Posters still hung for a two-week-old 50 Cent hip-hop concert, sponsored by MTV, a company that simultaneously ran an antitrafficking campaign. The signs featured the self-identified "P.I.M.P." wearing jewelry over a bulletproof vest. Petrică steered across the Dâmbovița River, into which jumped three street kids, holding hands.

At one point, a young boy in rags darted between cars to wash windshields, passing his earnings to a large Gypsy woman waiting on the street corner. Along the arteries that lead into the city, several solitary handicapped kids begged at heavily trafficked intersections.

Petrică veered around the Parliament House, known under Ceaușescu as the *Casa Poporolui*, or People's House. The original name was a grotesque distortion, just like the structure itself, that symbolized the rapacious regime. The self-declared "Genius of the Carpathians," in an effort to emulate his idol Kim Il Sung, built the world's third-largest building with 1,000 rooms, 1 million cubic meters of Transylvanian marble, and close to 1 million metric tons of steel, bronze, and glass. Meanwhile, his people could not buy fresh meat. Now the palace stood as a metaphor for Romania itself: magnificent from afar, but far from magnificent. Nearly half of the building's interior was still under construction.

In front of a black strip club by the J.W. Marriott Hotel, Petrică stopped, explaining that was as far as he could go because the *mascați* had blown his cover during a prior investigation. Now his car, as well as his face, might trigger a violent reaction from the brothel owners. Ion, an underworld contact of his, would guide Alexandru and me from here.

A minute later, Ion pulled up, slouched behind the wheel of his late-model Opel, beautifully customized with leather interior and a crackling bass tube.* He didn't say a word, but smiled and, as was the custom in Bucharest, parked on the sidewalk. Ion was a *haiduc*, a term loosely translated as "brigand," but there is no direct English equivalent for the big-hearted, Robin Hood–type thief that it connotes. Romania has always maintained an easy attitude toward petty crime. Thanks to the battalions of computer engineers left unemployed after communism, Ion's racket, credit card fraud, was a well-staffed industry.

Petrică turned to me with a final word of advice before he disappeared. "Speak low, but not too low," he said. "Some Gypsies speak English, but even if they don't, they will be suspicious if you whisper. Any problem, call me. I call the police."

---

* I have changed Ion's name.

We were about to enter an area of Bucharest untouched by Western antitrafficking efforts. I did not know who I would be negotiating to buy, but I guessed that she was an unregistered aftershock of the recent explosion of internal migrants who made Bucharest Europe's most densely populated city. Some found their fortunes here. Others, invisible, were slaves.

Ion drove to the Gara de Nord rail terminus. During the 1990s, as the orphanages closed, more than a thousand children made their home in cardboard boxes near heating vents in this station. In 1998, Bucharest officials purged the kids, but pedophiles already had staked out the area. Older children, who kept the visitors' money, pimped younger children, who received candy and glue. The kids lived in the sewers, and serviced the clients in grotty apartments or at the nearby Hotel Ibis, well known to middle-class Romanian men and budget-conscious sex tourists.

We crossed the street to a public park, where homeless men and women slept on benches. Two filthy, glassy-eyed boys approached to beg. They peeked out above the plastic bags they held to their faces as they huffed Aurolac, a paint thinner that quickly numbed the hunger pangs in their stomach while it slowly destroyed the cells of their brains and livers. One boy had burns on his forehead, perhaps from where the caustic smear had touched his skin.

For two cigarettes, a boy slurred out the place to purchase a girl. We got back in the car and Ion drove around the corner to Şoseaua Orhideelor, in the *quartier* Basarab, one of the most loathed ghettos in Bucharest. In this area, Ceauşescu had forcibly resettled the lowest in society, the Roma, in the mansions of the highest in society, wealthy foreigners, who subsequently went back to their home countries. The government still owned 90 percent of the buildings here, but planned to demolish many to build an overpass.

We got out in front of a ramshackle nineteenth-century town house situated between a shoe store and a tire repair shop. Alexandru was uneasy; this was a new line of work for him.

A Romani woman with a hatchet face jumped up from a folding chair in front of the building. From her hair color, she might have been in her mid-thirties. From her permanently frantic expression, wiry frame, and rotting teeth, she might have been in her mid-eighties.

"Florin!" she shouted.

Around the corner came a Gypsy, short and, like his partner, wild-eyed and aggressive. Florin's nose was smashed, his arms lithe and muscled; but his hands were stocky and short, making his fists perfect spheres. He had a receding hairline, an underbite, stubble. He wore a yellow watch, shorts, and an unbuttoned navy blue shirt. Scattered on his arms and left thigh were dark green jailhouse tattoos. Though his entire torso was emblazoned with a faded multicolored dragon, he was known as a *peşte*, a fish—Romanian street slang for pimp.

There was no phatic communion, no "How are you?" no "*Cu plaçere*," not even a hello.

"I want to buy a girl," I explained through Alexandru.

"How much are you offering?" Florin responded, deadpan.

"That depends on what the girls look like," I said. "Can we come inside?"

Through a banged-up sheet-metal gate, we stepped onto a courtyard of crumbling, exposed brick that reeked of mold. Squealing toddlers played in the muck on the ground. A large woman with a baby on her chest sprawled on a mangled sofa in front of a single-story annex.

"Gagicuţe!" Florin shouted.

From the annex emerged a frightened-looking young Romani girl in hotpants and a tank top.

"The most I can give you her for is one week," said Florin.

"I'm thinking more long-term," I said.

"Two weeks?"

"I want to buy a girl *outright*," I explained. "How much would that be, and what's the cost basis? How much would you be making other-wise?"

Florin shook his head.

"Not possible?" I asked.

"Not more than a month. And for a month is a lot of money—a thousand Euros."

"I want to buy her for good," I said.

"No. Just for rent. For a week, okay. One week, two weeks, tops. You won't find a girl to buy anywhere in Bucharest. For her, not more than a month and a half."

"How old is she?"

"Twenty," said Florin, surely overstating her age by at least four years.

"I'm looking for someone a bit younger," I said.

"We also have a blonde," the hatchet-faced woman interjected.

"In a room upstairs. But just for an hour—or two, three, four, or five. But just here, just here in the room. She knows how to do a good job. She is good," said Florin.

"They don't seem very eager to sell her," Alexandru explained quietly. "They say they'll be losing money."

"I want to find out how much money," I said.

The hatchet-faced woman led us into the back of the shoe store, up cement stairs to a landing, where she told us to wait. The toilet green walls cast all in a sickly hue. In keeping with the toilet motif, the place smelled of feces and dead mice. Clear plastic tubes ran sewage along the sides of the stairwell, expelling it onto the concrete courtyard below. Maybe it was just the normal choke of an average, fetid urban cave in Bucharest, but it seemed there was some miasma here, wet and pungent. If, as Cicero said, slavery was death, then this was a charnelhouse.

Then, a scream from above us. A fat woman with orange hair pulled back in a gold loop emerged and talked fast.

"She doesn't want to come," she said. "She's scared, she thinks you're going to beat her or sell her again."

The fat woman went back upstairs. "Make her come out!" she yelled.

We walked to the second floor, where two women shouted into a darkened room. A third woman emerged, clutching the girl.

She had bleached, rust-colored hair. Her head was shrunken, her nose flattened against her face. Mascara ran from pools of tears around deep-set eyes, cast downward at her bare feet with widely spread toes. Her hastily applied makeup could not conceal the evidence of Down syndrome. Lipstick was smeared beyond the boundaries of her parted mouth. Her flesh rolled out of the tight yellow tank top and shorts. Her captor held her left arm so tightly as to hunch her shoulder. Below her right bicep were no less than ten deep, angry red slashes, raised, some freshly scabbed.

I had been in a dozen seedy brothels on three continents, but I had never seen anyone in such a condition. I remembered that I was wearing a wire, that I had to keep in character. But what would my "character" do when confronted with such a creature? Should I be enjoying myself? I tried to smile. I looked at Alexandru and Ion's faces, which betrayed sheer horror.

"Do you like her?" one of the women asked.

"Can I talk to her?" I asked. "How old is she?"

"Twenty-eight," the woman said on the girl's behalf.

"What type of price are we talking about?"

Her captor asked if she would go with me. The girl mumbled something, which Alexandru couldn't make out exactly, about being hit.

"She said yes," the woman said.

"I think she's really scared," Alexandru said. "She doesn't want to come."

"Okay, why don't we go talk to the guy about price, then," I said, as we turned to leave that place.

Downstairs, Florin was locked in an argument with his partner. I couldn't make out the words, but I heard *cașcaval*—a term that I knew meant "cheddar" or "cash."

"There is nobody that will give you a girl for as much time as I will," he said. "For two months, two thousand Euros."

"What are the rules?" I asked.

"No rules. Whatever you want to do. Two months."

"Two thousand Euros? I don't understand, because you wouldn't be making two thousand off her in two months. That seems high."

"That's not a lot. For one night, I make two hundred Euros off her."

Lying to *gadje*, or outsiders, is a Romani tradition. Later, police deduced that each of Florin's customers, probably locals, paid the *peşte* around 10 Euros. They also surmised that the girl was raped five to twenty times per night. Florin's estimate was therefore feasible, if high-end.

"Tell me a bit more about the girl. I want to know more about the product that I'm buying," I said.

"She's very clean. A very nice girl—you won't have any problems with her. Whatever you say, she will do. Anything you want."

"Two thousand seems like a lot," I said.

"No, for two months that's very inexpensive!" The whiff of a big sale woke him up. "The girl is very nice, she is not doing drugs. She is good at what she is doing."

"How about something else?" I proposed. "A trade. A motorcycle—I can see that being about the value."

"A car, maybe. Not a motorcycle. A good car."

"A Dacia?" I proposed, offering the local make.

Florin's eyes lit up.

"But only if I'm buying the girl for three months," I added. "And the car will come with fifty thousand kilometers." The car I'd described, I figured, might cost 1,500 Euros from the right chop shop.

"Okay," Florin said, revealing a stained grin for the first time.

"I've got to call around," I said. "Could I leave the country with her?"

"What if you leave me with my eyes in the sun?" he asked, employing a Gypsy expression for being stood up. "I don't know if you'd be back with her. I need a deposit. But I can get a Romanian passport for her."

I shook his hand and we returned to the car. As we pulled out, Ion turned off the music. We all slumped. Finally, Alexandru broke the silence.

"What the fuck was that?"

Still dazed, I didn't respond.

"A blonde, huh?" he said. "Oh, yeah. Britney Spears."

It was off-color, offensive. But I laughed. The alternative was to cry.

Beginning in the 1990s, human trafficking metastasized faster than any other form of slave-trading in history. As many as 2 million people left their homes and entered bondage every year. Some crossed international borders; many did not. Human beings surpassed guns as the second most lucrative commodity for crime syndicates of all sizes, netting around $10 billion annually.

Thanks to that meteoric growth, American abolitionist efforts dwelled on trafficking. Meanwhile, contemporary slavery as a whole received a sliver of the concern it deserved. Thanks to the Horowitz coalition, sex slaves dominated Washington's antislavery bandwidth. Meanwhile, fewer than half of all trafficking victims were forced into commercial sex work.

But when Florin agreed to trade a severely handicapped young woman—who had repeatedly tried to kill herself to escape unyielding rape and torture—for a used car, I understood the Bush administration's single-mindedness. It was a wave of nausea, and a wave of clarity.

Earlier on, like many of my fourth estate colleagues, I thought of government-issue stories of sex trafficking as prurient hype for consumption by salivating Christian conservatives. Sloppy Bush administration prognostications did not help. Following the 2004 tsunami, John Miller warned of an impending surge in child selling. In the run-up to the 2006 World Cup, Chris Smith and the Southern Baptist Convention reported that traffickers were about to sell 40,000 women to brothels and mobile rape units in Germany, where prostitution was legal.

At first, breathless reporters uncritically repeated the omens. Then the predictions proved false. While one TIP official said, justifiably, that "we helped prevent" the upsurges through the publicity campaigns, Miller was embarrassed, and mainstream news organizations felt burned.

Undaunted by skeptical editors, a few journalists kept reporting the horrors. In England, 200 years after abolition, slave traders still held auctions in public places, including a coffee shop in the arrivals hall of Gatwick Airport, where a Serb pimp won a bidding war for two tearful Lithuanian teenagers. Traffickers shot dead four Romanian girls when they refused to have sex with horses. In Rome, a pimp forced a Romanian slave into freezing water on each night that she failed to earn enough. Women from Romania's estranged sister, Moldova, fared just as badly, and in greater numbers. *Time* magazine reported in 2001 that "when Marina, a 25-year-old from Chisinau was met in Budapest by a stocky Bosnian calling himself Ivo, he told her she was too ugly for prostitution and might have to be sold by the kilogram for her organs." Others languished in underground cages, some not seeing daylight for months on end.

Albanian networks that took women through Western routes via the former Yugoslavia paraded their merchandise in nude auctions, where buyers prodded the women like cattle. Some slaves taken eastward through Ukraine had been beheaded or buried alive or mutilated beyond recognition. Victims in the reports were sometimes abducted, occasionally blackmailed with homemade pornography, often tricked, always coerced by violence. Pimps never allowed them to refuse a customer. Many suffered gang rapes, forced abortions, HIV.

While skeptics still discounted the stories as exaggerated and suspiciously monolithic, the Christian media often treated them as revealed truths. With Horowitz fanning the flames, President Bush had his mandate to move against the new slave traders.

Tatiana's road to slavery was not an unusual one, but her family was unusually close. In her words, she had "wonderful parents," and lived as traditional, quiet, and discreetly Orthodox an existence as was possible in her transitioning Eastern European country.* Growing up, she heard little about the West, but government propaganda about capitalism did not diminish her interest in learning more. She was a willful student, competing on equal footing with boys in her class, and aspiring to be a journalist when she grew up.

Then, she said, "the difficulties began." Her family was dearly affected like most of their countrymen by economic chaos after the fall of communism. Overnight, life savings evaporated as families saw their bank accounts devalued by a factor of 100 or more. In 1989, there were 14 million poor people in Eastern Europe; a decade later, the number was 147 million. Public services fell apart, including the police force. Into the breach rushed local mafias. "If you start a business, you get a knock on the door from someone that says if you want protection, you have to pay," she said.

Still, Tatiana studied hard, and at twenty-one, she was accepted into a university program in history and archeology. Adding to the hope of the moment, she met a young man, Luben, while out one evening with her friends. They soon became an item. Though she wasn't interested in marriage at the time, and was not the type to be swept off her feet, he impressed her. He was gallant with her parents, even bringing flowers to her mother.

"He was nice, charming, a gentleman—let's say, the perfect guy," she said. "But that was his job."

At the time, however, Luben's job was not entirely clear. She knew it involved frequent travel to Germany and The Netherlands, and that his company paid well enough for him to afford a flashy car and multicourse dinners in the capital. But Tatiana was raised to be independent, and what really interested her were not shiny things but academic achievement.

Tatiana's own job at a cell phone store ended when the branch closed, and all of a sudden she had no means of financing her education. Luben,

---

*At her request, I have changed the names of Tatiana's family, friends, and traffickers, and concealed the name of her home country.

who had been dating her for six months, mentioned that he knew of an au pair position in Amsterdam. A year minding the children of a Dutch family, he said, would yield enough money for her entire university education.

For her mother, Luben's offer was a red flag. She had seen U.S.-sponsored posters and billboards warning about human trafficking. But Tatiana's strong personality won out, and in late spring 2002, she and Luben prepared to drive west.

There were two immediate complications. First, Luben's car had broken down. Tatiana asked her friend Sasha if he would drive them, knowing that he had to go to Germany anyway. He agreed, but could go only as far as Frankfurt.

The second complication was that Tatiana, like so many people from Eastern European countries where movement had been severely curtailed under communism, had no passport. For Luben, this wasn't a problem. Twenty million passports went missing every year, and only a quarter of those were registered in police databases. Luben got a third-country passport for her, replacing the original owner's picture with Tatiana's.

As Tatiana put the last bags in Sasha's car, her mother gave her a brochure from the antitrafficking NGO La Strada. It warned of "the loverboy phenomenon" of young men tricking their girlfriends out of the country, then selling them into prostitution.

"If anything happens," she told her daughter, "just call me."

Tatiana, angry at her parents for treating her like a child, crumpled up the brochure and tossed it out the window as she drove away.

The next evening, the three arrived at the Frankfurt train station, where Sasha would send them on alone. When Luben was in the bathroom, Sasha told Tatiana that something about Luben made him uneasy. Tatiana thanked him for the ride, but dismissed his concern.

On the train to Amsterdam, Luben was tense and distant. By the time they got to Central Station, he wasn't saying a word. As they got off the train, they were met by a beefy fellow named Anton. At first Luben and Anton walked ahead, huddled in close discussion. Then Luben told Tatiana to wait in the main hall by the ticketing offices. He asked to borrow her cell phone as his was not getting reception. As she waited, she was transfixed by the new smells, clean streets, new fashions, and signs in English and Dutch, neither of which she spoke. Then Anton came back, alone, and handed Tatiana her phone.

"I've paid a lot of money to bring you here," he said.

Tatiana's heart dropped into her stomach. He explained he had paid $3,000 to cover restaurants, transportation, the passport—even the flowers that Luben gave to her mother.

"Where is Luben?" she asked.

"Oh, don't worry," Anton said. "He's just gone ahead but he'll meet us at the flat."

Her mind raced, and she immediately thought to call her friend in Frankfurt. She looked at her cell's phone book, and saw it had been deleted.

Anton drove her to his apartment in central Amsterdam. It was May and the tulips were in bloom. Locals peered from low, flat houseboats in the canals; others looked down from exposed brick buildings adorned with the red-and-black "XXX" shield of the city. White with fear, Tatiana saw none of it. Anton led her into the apartment, where she met two other Eastern European girls. Now there was no doubt what had happened.

"You have to pay," Anton explained to her. "That's the rules. The only way you can give me back my money is by working on the street. I own you. I'm the boss now."

"I was sold like a piece of meat," she later recalled.

She reached again for her cell phone to call her parents, whose number of course she knew.

"If you call your parents or if you try to leave," said Anton, "it will be your family who suffers."

Anton gave her a bottle of vodka, locked her in the apartment with the other girls, and left. Terrified, Tatiana shut herself in the bathroom and tearfully drank the entire bottle while sitting in the shower.

Luben's job was complete. Tatiana's dream, over the course of an hour, had evolved into a symphony of pain. This was the opening movement.

Worldwide, most sex slaves, like the girls in Florin's Basarab brothel, are below government radar. Sometimes they are illegal aliens, worried about deportation, and kept as a subculture within a subculture. Such was the case with the Nigerian trafficking victims I interviewed in Amsterdam's largely West African Bijlmer district. Sometimes the lost victims have been in the same land for centuries, but form a nation within a nation.

"It is difficult to enforce the law in Romani communities," said Alina Albu, one of Romania's most successful antitrafficking prosecutors. Like Petrică Răchită, she was young, passionate about her country, and dedicated to justice despite personal risk. But Albu was also frank about the shortcomings of the Romanian legal effort. Although the number of Romani traffickers had exploded in the last five years, there were no Romani police officers specialized to work with their own communities. Romani slave traders were a distinctively brutal and evasive lot, as Albu explained when I told her about Florin. "They have *their* law. The victims don't cooperate. The traffickers are more violent than Romanian traffickers because it's in their culture, their blood."

Say the police raided Florin's brothel and took the girls to a shelter. He could have them back in a day if he maintained he was the primary caregiver, and the mentally handicapped girl, clearly traumatized, failed to testify. Under the Romanian system, no testimony meant no prosecution, even with the evidence that I had on my wire. "If I don't have a victim to present in front of the judge," Albu said, "I don't have a case."

Getting victims to testify was the most daunting obstacle to nailing slave dealers. The problems started on contact, when local police treated prostitutes like low-level criminals, not victims. A woman who was raped and enslaved by a man she initially trusted was then asked to trust a detective she had never met before. Add to the problem that, for decades, the Romanian police were the most odious element of a vile state. Add, too, that the justice system in Romania is one where prosecutors are "objective" investigators and not, as in the American system, advocates seeking to justify the state's interest in the criminal activity of the accused. Add that pimps told victims that if they talked to police, they or their families would be killed. Add that shamed clients, whose role was never punished, rarely testify even as witnesses.

The sum of those circumstances revealed just how remarkable it was that Albu was able to win any convictions at all. She credited American pressure for forcing national leaders to confront the problem: trafficking was made illegal only after the TIP office put Romania in Tier Three. Since then, American trainers—FBI agents and Justice Department attachés—provided guidance. But Albu herself derived her tenacity from a personal calling.

"I have a daughter," she said.

The day after the Basarab investigation, Alexandru, Petrică, and I drove ten miles south of Bucharest to interview Florian Costache, a top trafficker for Nuţu Cămătaru, the biggest fish hauled in by Alina Albu's colleagues. I had seen low-scale woman selling up close. Now I wanted to interview a man who had made millions off the trade. But Cămătaru, who was held in the same jail, would not talk: twelve days earlier, his lawyer had been sentenced to thirteen years for embezzling nearly half a million dollars from the Bucharest city government.

Past a barren field strewn with rocks and garbage lay Jilava maximum-security prison. Originally designed as a garrison for 500 soldiers, the prison was now a heaving mass of over 3,000 inmates, petty criminals and serial killers among them. Shards of glass and rusty wire topped the bare cement walls; armed guards looked down from towers. The guards had a reputation for sadism, and had recently beaten a teenage Romani prisoner to death. Extended *mascaţi* rampages swiftly ended several hunger strikes for better treatment.

In Romanian, *jilava* means "wet place," and anyone who smelled the prison in summertime would understand why. It was built on a rotting swamp, and the cells featured moldy walls and slimy floors. Prisoners shared their cages with rats, mice, and cockroaches. From them they got lice and scabies. Rampant overcrowding meant that prisoners, often awaiting trial, had to share beds with other inmates. From them they got different diseases.

Receiving us was a sweaty guard with a perfect V-tan to midchest, where evidently he ended his buttoning procedure every morning. He led us past the first sentry into a rocky courtyard. There, two lame and mangy dogs scavenged. The guard, a chatty fellow, was nostalgic for Ceaușescu's rule, under which the prison received its last upgrade. I asked him about the social order. Not surprisingly, the pedophiles— including several foreign sex tourists—occupied the bottom level.

"We're an Orthodox country: they have it hard in here," he said with a grin. "They become girls."

"Who's on top?"

"Cămătaru."

Nuțu and Sile Cămătaru were the noms de guerre of Ion and Vasile Balint, the most prolific Romanian slave traders since the Ottoman period. Like all great crime bosses, the Cămătarii were not born into power; they took it. The brothers were Romani, which made them minorities in Romania, but not in their neighborhood, *quartier* Ferentari, locally known as Ghetoulanda—Ghettoland. Ceaușescu's monolithic apartment blocks were everywhere in Ferentari. Most were unheated, and many were charred after residents tried to warm themselves using traditional Gypsy methods. There was scant public transport, and taxis refused to go to the neighborhood. Stealing was a popular way to survive. Selling drugs and women was a common way to get out.

Blessed with ursine size, the Cămătarii dominated local kids in adolescent turf wars. As teenagers, they became dedicated bodybuilders, and learned to break kneecaps from their mother, Smaranda Stoica, known affectionately in the neighborhood as "Mimi the Moneylender." But it was a stint with the French Foreign Legion that exposed the brothers to the money they could make by selling Romanian women, reputed to be among the most beautiful on the continent. As legionnaires, they and other big-name human traffickers like Serb Milorad Lukovic closely studied the nexus of sex, money, and violence. Upon return to Romania, they had the skills and the knowledge to build an empire. Critically, they also had the brutality.

Drawing from a $30 million loan-sharking war chest and well-formed criminal architecture, the brothers seized control of a rival's drug business, and grew his relatively modest sex trade into an operation that moved hundreds of slaves per year to Western Europe. On the street, the brothers, who sent women to France, Italy, Spain, and beyond, became known as the fathers of Romanian trafficking—an image they cultivated. But they were not alone.

The Romanian slave trade, successful a venture as it was, had a thousand fathers. I was about to meet one of them.

"They have fast hands," the guard said as he checked my bag one last time. "Don't give them any pens or any sharp objects. Careful with batteries. If they approach you, do not touch them. If they attempt to give you anything, do not accept it. Good luck." He flashed a grin from behind bulletproof glass, and opened the door. We walked past the last of the Kalashnikov-wielding guards to a large rusted metal gate. Prisoners shouted from their cells on the other side.

Ceauşescu transformed Jilava into the most frightening place in Romania. He stuffed as many as eighty inmates into each cell, some kept twenty feet below the ground. Many never saw daylight. Of his 400,000 political prisoners, the most prominent were held here. There were some exceptions, but most of the prisoners today were of the violent variety.

The gate rumbled open, and we walked into the filthy main yard. An inmate threw a chunk of bread at us from his cell. Another lowered a tied sack to his subjacent neighbor. A guard led us into a room arranged like a school guidance counselor's office, only with padded doors.

Florian Costache strutted in. Swarthy, with long black hair pulled back in a ponytail and shaved on the sides, he had a trim goatee and a jutting, cocksure underbite. His build and bearing were those of a bantamweight boxer, and he rolled up his tight black T-shirt to display razor-blade tattoos. Despite his swagger, or because of it, it didn't take long to get Costache talking. He had been an able recruiter of young women, breaking their wills and selling them above market value. In the process, he became one of the top earners for the Cămătaru clan. "I know Nuțu Cămătaru," he boasted. "He's a friend of mine."

Born in 1975, Costache grew up in Bulgaria, Hungary, and Romania. Like many Roma, his family didn't have much use for national boundaries. His parents were flower sellers, hence his given name. "They didn't steal," he volunteered, assuming I held the widespread stereotype about his people.

The family business, not surprisingly, was an insecure one, particularly in the economic devastation after the revolution. He had a strong distaste for the drug trade, he said, so, in 1993, he taught himself how to sell the next most lucrative commodity. "Dealing women was a way to make easy money, and the risks weren't high," he said. "I could have stole, but I didn't."

At first, he was just pimping, and not selling girls outright. He had good instincts for the business, talking to neighbors and relatives to find girls who had family problems, including many orphans. Most of his girls were fifteen or sixteen. One was twenty-four, but she was harder to control. The youngest was fourteen and a half. "But she was tall," he said.

The girls came from Botoșani, an economically depressed county in the northeast, pressed against Moldova. In a place where young people sold their kidneys for $3,000, and where nearly every family was touched by alcoholism and domestic abuse, it wasn't hard to find desperate recruits.

Costache put most of his girls in clubs or on the streets of downtown Bucharest. Although some traffickers resorted to outright abduction, Costache, like most, relied on a soft approach followed by a hard reality.

"We would take the girls from Botoșani to Bucharest with the promise of jobs as waitresses or similar jobs. And we did in fact have a little bistro in Bucharest and the girls would wait the tables. But we also had them provide sex to the customers."

At first, girls would resist. Some girls probably knew they were going to be prostitutes, though Costache did not acknowledge this. "When I told them they had to be whores, I said that the alternative was to go home. No one wanted to do that. I told them that in a couple of weeks, they would have a better life than they had ever dreamed. Nice clothes, earrings. You have to be a little smart, you see, and then eventually they won't *want* to leave. You can just *take them.*"

None signed up to be slaves, but that's what they became. And no one ever escaped. In Botoşani, and neighboring Neamt, he would, as the Sudanese expression goes, "use a slave to catch a slave," sending back broken-in girls to recruit those who were several years after them in school.

Was he like a father figure to the girls? "No," he said. "More like a boyfriend." He trained the girls himself, he said. He raped them, even getting one pregnant. "Sometimes the girls are scared. There were girls that didn't like to give oral sex," he said. "So I taught them."

How much of the money that they earned did the girls keep? "None. These girls didn't even want money," he claimed. "I gave them a bit when they needed it. But I gave them a place to stay, clothes, food, condoms, protection."

Did girls ever give him problems? "A couple."

How did he solve those problems? He grinned broadly and raised his fist.

In 1995, he walked into a police setup. It was the first, and last, time he escorted a girl to a client. "All of a sudden there were *mascaţi* everywhere."

Because trafficking was not then a crime, and Costache was still small time, he received a seven-month sentence for pimping. At twenty, he considered jail a rite of manhood, one that earned him the respect of his peers.

While Costache was in prison, a sea change occurred in the Romanian underworld. The Cămătarii consolidated their hold over their illicit enterprises. Smaller gangs were unwilling to cede the lucrative markets, and while battles occurred in other parts of Bucharest, *quartier* Ferentari became a war zone.

When Costache was released, he shrewdly decided to support the brothers. He sold his most beautiful girls to the sister of Nuţu and Sile, Angela Stoica, who managed the trafficking operations. Costache rose quickly in the clan, eventually reaching to "second, third, maybe fourth from the top," he said.

Costache, with the blessing of the Cămătarii, began to expand internationally as well. At the time, three in four Romanian sex slaves were trafficked west through Timişoara, over the Transylvanian Alps, then west across the Danube at the Iron Gate gorge to Serbia, a country that the Canadian journalist Victor Malarek called "the breaking grounds" for trafficked women. Costache blazed his own northwestern trail. He never had problems acquiring forged passports and visas for the women, and border police always facilitated the traffic for a fee. "The business took off at the end of 1996," he said. "We expanded operations into Hungary, where I have relatives." In Budapest, a larger Russian organized crime (ROC) group purchased the women at wholesale, prices varying according to looks and experience. From there, the Russians sold the women to one of hundreds of ROC affiliates operating in nearly sixty countries. Often the girls would be sold five or six times. Slavery is the dark side of commercial sex—a $100 billion global industry—and Costache's women wound up in some far-flung corners. Some went to Amsterdam, others to Israel. ROC cells in Vladivostok channeled women to Japan and South Korea's mammoth sex markets.

Beginning in 1997, for the first time in his life, Costache had money up to his eyeballs. Still, he had even bigger plans to expand operations to the final points of sale, where truly massive profits happened.

A destination-point pimp could earn twenty times what he paid for a girl when he put her on the street and forced her to endure upward of fifteen clients per night. Provided the girl was not physically brutalized to the point of ruining her beauty, the pimp could then sell her again for an even greater price because he had trained her and broken her spirit, saving future buyers the hassle. A 2003 study in The Netherlands found that, on average, a single sex slave earned her pimp $250,000 per year.

Costache rolled his mammoth profits into a pirate radio station, then a Web site, which allowed men from all over the world to book his girls. The first international customers were Asian. Soon, the main clients were German and Italian. In Bucharest, a good girl made Costache $200 on an average night. He prided himself on customer service, making sure that the women who worked for him did exactly what the clients wanted. Once or twice a girl stole a client's expensive cell phone. Costache always made sure he got it back, and punished the girl.

In addition to the international auctions, Costache sold girls outright in Bucharest. Around the Intercontinental, he sold several girls for $2,000 apiece to local pimps. Occasionally, clients tried to buy the girls. One German was particularly insistent. But Costache sold them only to professionals.

Why did the clients want to buy the girls? "They liked them," he said with a smile. "But you never know exactly."

Meanwhile, from their Ferentari hedquarters, the brothers forged a *Pax Cămătaru* in the Romanian underworld. Petty criminals quickly learned to yield them tribute. If a carjacker stole a truck with thirty laptops, he gave the Cămătarii five. If Costache captured a transcendentally beautiful "dime bitch," he knew to sell her to Angela Stoica rather than his Russian buyers. Another big business of the Cămătarii was money laundering. Costache's money was easy to wash: all of his girls' earnings went to him under the table. Unlike in the drug trade, where a big sale might yield half a million dollars that then had to be buried, Costache's income was widely spread and hard to trace.

The money laundering was strictly precautionary. During those halcyon days, Costache worried little about getting caught. "There wasn't so much police then," he explained. "I wasn't afraid of them, anyway. I could trust my bitches. To arrest me, they need a lot of evidence. They would have to catch me in the act."

The Cămătarii rolled Costache's profits from the flesh trade into drugs, arms, or into what their ROC counterparts referred to as *matryoshka* companies, legitimate businesses which, like the Russian dolls they were named after, concealed entity after entity. But the Cămătarii themselves, who by 2003 were worth over $50 million, were not interested in keeping a low profile. They drove around Bucharest in special-edition Humvees. On the grounds of their enormous alabaster villa, they had an unlicensed zoo, extravagant gardens, and a race course.

To the *haiduc*-obsessed Romanian media, they were constant gossip fodder. Tabloids reported on one comely young conquest after another, Nuțu finally proposing to a full-bosomed blond actress.

To other Romanian criminals, they were icons. And targets. In 1998, low-level domestic warfare erupted again between the Cămătarii—who now had 500 soldiers—and rival gangs. Costache explained that Romanian trafficking became a chess game. Sometimes, the knights would meet for combat with knives and bats. Mostly, however, the action took place at the pawn level. Rival gangs abducted several of his women off the street. If a girl had been a good earner, he would pay to get her back or he would kidnap a girl from the abductor in retaliation. Sometimes the police arrested girls on behalf of Costache or his enemies. Targeting pimps would constitute an escalation, so both police and rival gangs captured only women, which sent a message, but was essentially a property seizure.

Around the same time, similar contests broke out all over Europe, particularly in the Balkans, where the presence of UN peacekeepers meant tremendous profits. One Albanian syndicate came up with a novel solution: they tattooed the slaves with their brand in order to deter theft of the women.

In 2001, Costache probed deeper into the billion-dollar Japanese market by sending managers to handle destination-point prostitution rackets. Once again, he found himself in the right place at the right time. After intense negotiation with a blunt John Miller, the Japanese government had nearly halved the number of entertainer visas—which Miller called "a sick joke"—issued to poor Filipina women. The *yakuza*—the Japanese mob—scrambled to maintain control of the brothels, but Costache and the ROC syndicates—whose girls were considered exotic in Japan—quickly filled the void.

For the Cămătaru clan, these were flush times. "I always had money," Costache said. "I always had girls. I earned a fortune and had nice cars. I had a great house, nice boats."

But the clan also had an enemy who had been planning their destruction for years.

Western diplomats credited an American initiative for the fall of the Cămătarii. Housed on the tenth floor of the gigantic Parliament building, the Southeast European Cooperation Initiative (SECI) began with a half-million-dollar American grant and was a favorite program of John Miller. Twice a year, Interpol, American, and Western European observers met with national police officials from ten countries in the region, to coordinate operations against human traffickers.

In September 2002, SECI launched "Operation Mirage," an effort to smash regional trafficking networks. It was billed as the modern equivalent of the nineteenth-century British naval operations that freed tens of thousands of slaves. In place of slave ships, the national forces raided discothèques, motels, saunas, street corners, weak border points, and, of course, brothels, massage parlors, and nightclubs. Operation Mirage was the crown jewel of American antislavery efforts. In June 2003, John Miller's boss, Paula Dobriansky, announced that in Albania, the United States would "support a variety of hard-hitting programs, including the Delta Force, a rapid reaction unit to intercept traffickers."

It all looked great on paper. But when it came to freeing slaves, Operation Mirage lived down to its name. Investigators interviewed 13,000 women and children and identified 831 sex traffickers; but with no clarity as to what constituted a slave, they assisted only 63 victims. In Romania, the state-funded shelters were normally empty. Many of the freed slaves were simply sent home. Although USAID funded some efforts to warn villagers about trafficking, no organization or government body provided the kind of hands-on economic and psychological rehabilitation necessary to deter retrafficking among returnees.

Operation Mirage closed certain slave routes, and U.S. pressure may have spurred intangible, almost atmospheric shifts in the way traffickers asserted their ownership. Costache even claimed that he began treating the girls more humanely as a result of the 2001 law banning trafficking. "Now it wasn't so much like slavery, like forced work," he said, smiling cryptically. "It was more of, I guess you could say, a partnership." But Costache credited someone other than John Miller—whom he had never heard of—with bringing down Nuțu and Sile Cămătaru.

That someone was Fane Spoitoru, a former godfather whose dismemberment of a police officer led to his own fall and the Cămătaru rise. Spoitoru fled into exile after the attack and in 1997, a Romanian court convicted him in absentia. Finally expelled from his sanctuary in Canada on July 22, 2000, police seized Spoitoru upon his return to Bucharest.

After serving a short sentence, Spoitoru went back to business with help from high-level officials who owed him favors and money. He wanted to run Bucharest again, and that meant liquidating the Cămătarii.

On January 7, 2002, the brothers hosted a poker game and invited some high-rolling whales, including former presidential candidate Gigi Becali, who was into the Cămătarii for more than $2 million. Alcohol flowed, but this was business, and Nuțu stayed sober enough to notice when his security cameras caught two Moldovans placing grenades under his car. Nuțu blamed a Spoitoru associate. Ion Pitulescu, the police chief who had resigned after Spoitoru was furloughed, called the resulting violence "the Third World War."

Cămătaru soldiers hit back hard, beating up street-level rivals and kidnapping Spoitoru-owned women off the streets. In February 2003, in response to the escalating violence—and, some said, to aid the more highly connected Spoitoru—Bucharest officials ordered police to build a case against the Cămătarii. Alina Albu's colleague Marian Sîntion directed the investigation. He used the Romanian equivalent of the RICO Act to tap Cămătaru communications. But it was a defiant slave who finally brought down the empire. Sîntion convinced a brave young woman to testify about her decade-long bondage after being abducted off the streets at age sixteen.

In 2005, the *mascaţi* swooped down on Costache and the Cămătarii. In all, the police netted thirty-two people, mainly pimps and traffickers.

The brothers' trial was a barn burner, as they laid out police at all levels who were on their payroll. Nuţu Cămătaru received nine years—his brother Sile got fifteen—for a wide range of charges, including extortion, rape, human trafficking, confinement, and assault. Their mother was sentenced to five years. Costache received three years, the average sentence for the dozens of human traffickers now serving time in Romanian jails. "I got convicted unfairly," complained Costache. "I mean, I'm guilty. But I got convicted with testimony of witnesses that I didn't even know."

Ion Clamparu, the Cămătarii's biggest trafficking partner in Western Europe, was never caught. But Alina Albu's team collared seven of his lieutenants over the course of two years. In 2005, Spanish police moved in to arrest Clamparu, who had sold hundreds of women, at his home. Unbeknownst to them, he had been tipped off, and as they waited for the order to move in, he shuffled out in his slippers and robe. He bought a newspaper from a nearby stand. Then he got in a car. Then he was gone.

When the police raided his home, they found DVDs of the three *Godfather* movies. "At least he was serious about his work," said Albu.

Tatiana woke up with a miserable hangover one misty Amsterdam morning in late May 2002. The misery outlasted the hangover. This was her first day in slavery.

At 6 p.m. that evening, Anton returned, unlocked the apartment, and took her to her new workplace. Because she was one of an estimated 150,000 illegal aliens in the Netherlands, she could not work in the regulated clubs or in red light districts. Instead, he drove her to a desolate, waterfront *tippelzone*, one of several taxpayer-funded areas that in 1997 the Amsterdam City Council had zoned to contain streetwalkers.

There she saw a menagerie of some eighty prostitutes, including crack-addled Dutch women, strutting transsexuals, and dozens of trembling illegal Eastern Europeans. All waited in designated bus shelters where businessmen, students, even city councilmen drove up and rented their bodies.

Anton pulled over to a small store with a shower for the women. He bought her condoms, and told her what to do. If a car pulled up, she was to say, "Twenty-five Euros," and get in. The client would then drive her to an area of the parking lot subdivided by screens. There she was to have sex with him. Not more than fifteen minutes, Anton told her. And no talking to the clients or the other girls. "If somebody asks you something personal," he said, "you only name the price."

For every hour of every day, Tatiana was on call for Anton's escort service. Each evening in the *tippelzone*, he forced her to have sex with as many as fifteen clients. "You feel miserable, you feel dirty," she said. Some clients were Dutch, others were foreign. Some were connected with the network that enslaved her. In those instances, her blood ran cold. "You have no idea if it's just for training or whatever," she said.

Anton intimidated her, he contained her physically. But he never broke her will. "I'm gonna get out," she told herself.

Once, during an escort call to a hotel, a client—whether out of discomfort or pity—did not rape her. He gave her money nonetheless, as he knew her pimp would demand it. "I feel sorry for you," he said. "Let's just talk and have a drink."

"Okay, there are still human beings out there," Tatiana thought. "That's pretty much like heaven compared to where I have to go next."

Tatiana regularly saw police come through the *tippelzone*. Officers in the Amsterdam antitrafficking vice units were allowed to purchase sex from prostitutes, as long as they did so out of uniform, and not in their own jurisdiction. In Tatiana's case, they just nodded at her falsified passport, and moved on. "I found it ridiculous," she said.

The other girls in the *tippelzone* explained what would happen if she told the police that she was a slave. They would deport her to her home country. "If I got out at the airport there," she said, "the traffickers' friends would be my escorts." A girl from Tatiana's country escaped with the help of a client. When her traffickers found her at home, they killed her. There was no investigation by the police. "Case closed," Tatiana said.

In Strasbourg, France, late in the evening on May 15, 2006, Romanian interior minister Vasile Blaga assured the European Parliament that his country had secured its borders, and was arresting human traffickers in droves. Eight months later, the EU rewarded Blaga's countrymen by letting them into the club. The United States, which had lobbied hard for Romania's accession, could point to Operation Mirage and Romanian antislavery diligence as reasons for getting in.

Meanwhile, from prison, the Cămătarii continued to pull the levers of their criminal ventures. But because their money was thinly spread, new rivals commandeered those ventures one by one. "Now Gypsy singers give their protection money to other people," said Marian Sîntion, who successfully prosecuted the brothers.

Regional initiatives had hardened Romania's western border, making less attractive the most common trafficking route. But new Middle Passages emerged, as they always do.

Sex trafficking is a hydra. Close one big brothel, and two smaller ones open elsewhere. Close those two, and traffickers start an escort service. Arrest or kill slave traders along one route, and they pour over another one where officials are more corrupt. Clean up the border police, and traffickers shift to the hundreds of miles of tattered, unguarded green borders that crisscross Europe. Smash a mafia-run network, and thirty neighborhood-level operations take its place.

While the general Romanian trend was toward more decentralized trafficking cells, certain large-scale networks persevered. Ion Clamparu, though he topped Romania's most-wanted list, continued to enslave young women. He drew from the waves of Romanians who were still heavily trafficked to Spain—60,000 in the first four months of 2006 alone, hidden among the 30 million foreigners in Western Europe.

Costache himself was to be paroled shortly after accession. I asked him about his plans.

"I'm going back to business," he said.

I asked him where he would sell women next.

"Far. Spain. Japan. In Romania, it's too hard right now." He explained that he still had two women working for him in Japan.

"But they can't send you money in jail," I said.

Costache just smiled. The guard sitting with us responded for him. "Yeah, he gets all the money here. No cash, he has an account. They have a store here—they have to be able to go shopping," the guard explained, as if shopping were a human right.

Costache's wife, a former prostitute, was now in charge of his business. She had several girls working below her and made sure he got all of the money they earned. Romani tradition absolutely forbade betraying prisoners, Isabel Fonseca writes in her magnificent book *Bury Me Standing*, and Romani folk songs celebrate wives' loyalty to incarcerated husbands. Costache planned to join his wife in Japan.

"Send me a postcard," I said.

While Costache looked overseas, the growing Romanian middle class looked on EU accession as a reason to stay home at last. Unfortunately, as happened in Hungary, the Czech Republic, and Poland, accession meant little for women from impoverished villages in eastern and northern Romania, except that they were more likely to wind up enslaved in Bucharest than in London. The most visible prostitutes, the girls working the lobby of the Intercontinental, for example, were the most likely to trigger moral outcry from an international audience. They were also the least likely to be held in abject slavery.

The girls in the Basarab brothel, however, enjoyed no public spot-light. They benefited from no American-led initiatives. Their freedom carried no public relations value. It is possible that "Britney Spears" succeeded in freeing herself the only way she knew how, and ended her life.

If not, she is still in hell.

6

The New Middle Passage

At three in the morning, a loud bang sounded on our compartment door.

"*Poliția!*" a border guard yelled.

I had convinced Petrică Răchită to join me as I traced the new Middle Passage: a slave trail that began across Romania's northeast border in Moldova, a country that used to be the Soviet Union's smallest republic. Now the nation was Europe's largest source of sex slaves.

From there, we would carry on through the breakaway region of Transnistria to Ukraine, then finally across the Black Sea to Turkey. Once in Istanbul, we would pose as entrepreneurs, looking to purchase a group of women at wholesale. The plan was to explore the slave catchment areas, then to spread out to the developed countries where dealers sold women to wealthy buyers.

For veteran slave dealers with phone books full of corrupt officials, the route from Third World to First World was a Sunday drive. For us, it would not be so easy. We had bidden farewell to Tatiana in Bucharest, and boarded a Soviet-era train bound for the Moldovan capital of Chişinău. The train was charming, with varnished wood paneling, white curtains, worn Oriental carpets. Petrică, unimpressed, spat when he saw the signs in Cyrillic.

"Communist train," he said. For young Romanians with a healthy disdain for the past, "Communist" was an epithet synonymous with "backward." Moldova, the poorest country in Europe, epitomized the term.

After eight hours of travel, Romanian police threw us off the train at Iaşi, several miles short of the border. It was my fault, as I did not have the visa. I had planned on driving, as most traffickers would do. But a village police officer had taken my license a week earlier when he caught me hurtling at 120 mph to make it to an interview, ironically, with a local detective. I apologized to Petrică, but he smiled, lit a cigarette, and again cursed the past.

"Fucking Communist train."

We hauled our bags to the only cab, and rode to the first border post, bathed in pale green fluorescent light like a gas station. Wary of Moldova, our driver refused to drive us across. "Watch out for those girls," he said. "And don't take a car when you get to the other side. Russian mafia."

Sixty-five years ago, this was not a border at all. Moldovans and Romanians shared language, culture, ethnicity, and, until the Hitler-Stalin nonaggression pact of 1939–41, they had shared a government. After 1989, many on both sides pressed for one country again, including the Romanian president, who had recently invited Moldova to reunite before Romania's EU accession. The day after we arrived, the Moldovan president called the overture "out of the question."

With that rejection, this would soon be more than a national border; it would be the new European political frontier. Already, above the first guardpost, the EU flag flew alongside the Romanian tricolor and the NATO emblem. In the late 1990s, this was a marketplace for traffickers selling Moldovan women to brutal Albanian gangs, to the Cămătarii, or to smaller-scale networks. Now European and American pressure had led

Romania to tighten this and other border points to stanch the flow of sex slaves.

Standing here in the dark at 3:30 a.m., Petrică and I would have appreciated slightly less border reform. The young guard would not let us travel the remaining 600 feet to Moldova on foot. So we waited to hitch a ride. One truck came, but rejected us. For two hours, that was the only vehicle to head our way.

The guard asked me how much cigarettes cost in the United States. I told him I didn't smoke. He asked for some chocolate instead. Two stray dogs came over to investigate, and Petrică, who loved animals, gave them the last of our food. At five thirty, a red-faced old man wearing a floppy hat staggered up to me, his breath reeking of hunting vodka. "You're a white knight, my son," he said, before stumbling on.

Eventually, as the orange sun burned through the clouds, a young man returning home in a beat-up station wagon pulled up and carried us to Moldova. We were met by a large, imperious border guard with heavy lipstick awkwardly skewed to cover a cold sore. She looked at my passport.

"American?" she barked. "Why are your jeans so dirty?"

She demanded to know how much money I had, and directed us to a blue-and-white customs building, where we waited for a visa. For two hours, we slept on the concrete floor of the lobby, getting mauled by mosquitoes in the process.

At 8 a.m., a consular officer showed up, and an hour later, we were doubled over, flush against the door of a dented commercial minibus at twice its capacity, slouching toward Chişinău. Just past the border, two women with stacks of Moldovan lei exchanged money with passengers in a frenzied, hand-over-hand scene. Most changed no more than the equivalent of $5.

A drive through the countryside left little doubt that Moldova was not prospering. Parts looked like rural Haiti, which made sense, since Moldova's GDP per capita was on par with Haiti and Sudan. When we slowed through villages, I noticed something different. Horse-drawn

carts outnumbered cars, but both were scarce. There were very few people on the streets and no young women at all. Certain villages were just
a few gaping houses, their paint peeling, their roofs rusted. Across the
country, a million Moldovans, or a quarter of the population, was gone.
It had become a country of ghost towns.

Outside Chişinău, we passed a billboard funded by John Miller's
office. An antitrafficking hot line ran over a stark image of a man paying $500 for a woman, clutched in the fist of another. YOU ARE NOT A
COMMODITY! the sign read.

For many, the sign came too late. Up to 400,000 women had been
sold into bondage since independence. In effect, it was a silent, disorganized genocide. Even Miller, publicly bubbling with optimism despite
his grim subject, was deflated privately. "Oh, Moldova is such a sad
case," he said. "Now they're just trying to focus on healing the wounds
and arresting some of the traffickers. That's a sad case."

As we entered downtown Chişinău, we passed a dozen Western
Unions. Remittances were Moldova's number one source of hard currency. Officially, in 2005, they constituted nearly a fifth of the $2.4 bil-
lion GDP. Unofficially, remittances reached as high as $5 billion.

A young woman finally appeared, walking with a switch in her hips
and a flip in her ponytail. Then there were two, three, then dozens. They
wore high-heeled Roman sandals, Daisy Dukes or short skirts, midriff-
baring tank tops or transparent blouses. Many preadolescent girls wore
a disturbing amount of makeup.

The provocative style of the women contrasted starkly with the overall drabness of the capital. Chişinău is much less architecturally blessed
than Bucharest, and much less repentant of its Communist roots. Sculp-
tural odes to Lenin still stand, and even manhole covers bear the hammer and sickle. At night, few lights illuminate the rutted streets. Public
transportation has decayed steadily since independence. The government tried to spruce up the place with flowery billboards celebrating
MOLDOVA: PATRIA MEA, and a few private businesses helped out with
bold, sexy advertising scattered throughout the city. But overall, it was
a grim scene.

Petrică and I arrived at our destination, a dumpy hotel called Turist. A jut-jawed Russian with a nametag that read RESPECT slouched by the reception, but offered no help with our bags. He did offer Petrică one of the house prostitutes, and later chastened us when we brought two female colleagues back to the room, asking to see their passports and warning us that a foreigner had lost $3,000 to "an unauthorized girl" the previous week.

Our room had shattered floorboards, periodic hot water, and plastic tubing connecting the faucet of the sink to that of the tub. Petrică checked the light fixtures and pulled off the mirrors to look for listening devices and cameras.

"Communist hotel," he said.

In 1907, Pablo Picasso gave Paris a masterpiece of discomfort: *Les Demoiselles d'Avignon* portrayed five nude prostitutes, all staring down the viewer. Picasso painted each with a different style, including his first foray into Cubism, and imbued each with a different personality. Two stood, arms raised, confident and inviting. Two inhabited the shadows, their eyes darkened, their silhouettes uncomfortable as they pulled back the curtains. One prostitute sat with her back to the viewer, her head turned 180 degrees. Her face, the most striking feature of the painting, was an oblique African mask, foreign and tortured.

As I traced the traffickers' arc from the Budjak steppe to the Arabian Desert, from the Bosphorus to the Danube to the Amstel rivers, I found that the sex trade, like Picasso's painting, had many faces. Many of the trafficked women I spoke with were plainly slaves, having landed in prostitution through fraud reinforced with violence. But prostitution was not always slavery. Or was it? I put the question to Michael Gerson, one of President Bush's most trusted aides, during an interview in the West Wing.

"Whoa. That's a tough one." He laughed, pausing for the first time.

"A fascinating question. Women are driven by desperate need, of course. By your definition, if they kept the results of their own labor, it may not be. I don't know about the slavery question. But it's the sign of a society that hasn't served women well. That hasn't given them opportunities and education outside of this, which I think is not something you choose."

Bush administration policy reflected none of Gerson's contemplative ambiguity: voluntary prostitution simply did not exist. Still, the debate raged in Washington during the Bush years, dominated by the strident Michael Horowitz, who rhetorically and politically crushed anyone who suggested that poverty, not prostitution, was the real culprit.

Although the role that legalized prostitution and poverty played in sex slavery was a lovely little tiff for others to carry on inside the Beltway, those seized with repairing the lives of former slaves had more immediate concerns.

Five thousand miles away from Washington, a single floor of an ugly Soviet-era Chişinău tenement served as Moldova's only functional shelter for former sex slaves. It was always full. In its first five years of operation, nearly 2,000 victims, many with severe physical injuries from their enslavement, attempted to heal here. The massive assaults on their humanity were more indelible.

I spent several hours with Natasha, a graceful blonde whose porcelain skin was marred by telltale razor scars, and whose twenty-one years of life were a blur of slavery and abuse. Born in Chişinău, she had never known her parents. Her mother, a prostitute herself, had left her, like 40,000 other Moldovan children, in an orphanage.

In 1991, a Russian woman plucked the six-year-old from the orphanage, only to turn the girl into an unpaid domestic and agricultural laborer. Like most women who wound up as prostitutes, Natasha was sexually abused: her adoptive father molested her for seven years. To punish the child for tempting her husband, Natasha's mistress often beat her so severely that her delicate face bore the scars years later. When Natasha was sixteen, the woman threw her out. Desperate, unemployable, and penniless, she yielded to traffickers and entered prostitution in Istanbul.

She escaped after seven months of forced, unpaid servitude, only to wind up with another man, who forced her to sell sex to pay his rent. The cycle went on and on—escape, retrafficking, enslavement, escape, retrafficking, arrest, deportation, abuse, torture, rape. She found herself starved in a Turkish jail and forcibly drugged in a desert prison in Dubai. Pimps forbade condoms, and twice they made her have back-alley abortions. After a childhood in bondage, she was bought and resold repeatedly for as little as $100, as much as $8,000. Over the span of five years, a dozen slave dealers and pimps forced Natasha to prostitute herself, and took every penny she earned. Finally, she reached temporary safety in this shelter. Her plans?

"I want to go back to Dubai," she said. "Because here there is nothing."

Dr. Lidia Gorceag, the psychologist who operated the shelter, had heard that many times before. "Most girls just resign and give up hope," said Gorceag.

But was Natasha a slave? For nearly her entire life, she certainly was. And yet now, given the chance for a fresh start, she again opted for bondage. In brothels in India, the Netherlands, and the United Arab Emirates, I found women in similar situations. Some had been freed in police raids, or escaped after having been trafficked initially. Many reentered prostitution. A few reentered slavery. So, can a slave be a free agent? Abraham Lincoln would call that a paradox. Jotting a note in 1859 to clarify his own thinking, he wrote: "Free labor has the inspiration of hope; pure slavery has no hope."

Slavery is a situation that inspires its sufferers to justify it in order to explain their own existence. This is particularly acute with the deep shame of sex slavery. Any woman who has been raped once knows the tremendous "internal resources," to use Gorceag's term, necessary to repair a shattered psyche. For those who are raped regularly and repeatedly, psychic will mutates into something unrecognizable. Natasha had no life skills beyond mere survival; she knew no male affection short of rank exploitation.

Survivors in Dr. Gorceag's shelter often exhibited the same characteristics of Afghan war veterans that she had encountered early in her career. They were numb when they should be compassionate, enraged when they should be reflective. A woman slept soundly while her crying twin babies woke up those around her. A sudden move in a tense moment—my hand slapping the table, for example—would spark a massive fight-or-flight response. One woman stabbed a stranger simply because he raised his voice at her friend. Another ate napkins compulsively.

The women endured insomnia, nightmares, hallucinations. One girl whose owner broke her leg always had the impression that someone was chasing her. Many experienced blackouts and memory loss, complicating depositions against their traffickers. Most suffered depression; some tried to kill themselves.

Researchers found that prostitution—regardless of whether it was coupled with slavery or not—produced women who were, in effect, torture victims. A majority of the prostitutes in a 2003 study had severe post-traumatic stress disorder. Most were clinically depressed. As John Miller often pointed out, 90 percent wanted to leave prostitution. And among trafficking victims, 95 percent of whom were physically or sexually abused, the situation was even graver.

Such odds did not inhibit Dr. Gorceag, a lovely woman with soft brown hair, a warm, ready smile, and an unalloyed sense of healing about her. She was one of a handful of people I met in several countries who took in throwaway sex slaves and took on traffickers. A Romanian shelter operator regularly faced death threats. Embarrassed public officials trumped up charges against another shelter operator in Dubai and another in Varanasi, India.

Dr. Gorceag was fortunate enough to have American backing through the International Organization for Migration (IOM). But her passion drove her work. She spent hours on end with victims, even reaching out to their families to show them that the women were not whores. She was also pragmatic, and addressed the second element of Natasha's despair: "Here there is nothing." Gorceag and IOM helped women reintegrate by offering them assistance to start small businesses. One woman sold sunflower oil; others worked in hair salons.

The doctor was a living response to Horowitz's line of attack: with her, there was no compromise between fighting trafficking and fighting poverty. And because of her, for some women, sometimes, hope survived slavery.

During my month in Romania, I had been accompanied by a living reminder of the human cost of bondage. But Tatiana was also someone who proved that while traffickers can seize flesh, some souls remain unconquerable.

In the summer of 2002, Tatiana had her freedom seized by sex traffickers on arrival in Amsterdam. Any day, at any moment, she knew she might also lose her life. She desperately hoped to escape, but the thought of the traffickers' response against her family chilled her. Still, she plotted. Wanting her to better handle the requests of clients, Anton gave Tatiana English-language books. Always a top-flight student in school, she studied hard and learned fast. But she had her own reason for doing so. "I will find a way to escape this situation," she told herself. "But I need to know how to communicate with people."

She befriended a Moldovan named Maria, another of Anton's captives. When Maria was sixteen, the mother of a friend sold her to a Turkish trafficker, who enslaved her in a basement brothel near Ankara. There, a steady stream of men raped her without a condom. Still a slave in Amsterdam, Maria saw a way out: she confided in Tatiana that a client of hers might buy her freedom.

Tatiana wanted someone to do the same for her. But the "price of freedom"—the amount Anton wanted in order to release her—was $20,000. It was a lot for a stranger to pay, and she worried that once a client bought her, he might act as if he owned her. Tatiana kept her escape thoughts secret: she knew she could not trust the other girl, Olga, whom Anton had held for even longer than her and Maria. "Most girls just tried to survive," she explained. "They told on other girls so that the pimps would like them more."

Once, a client gave Tatiana $20 directly. It wasn't much, but she saw it as a foothold toward freedom. She stuffed the money in her purse, then passed it to a cab driver, asking him to buy a scratch card for her cell phone. By keeping her balance empty, Anton had restricted her phone to incoming calls. But if she added minutes, she might be able to call her parents and tell them of her plight. Olga overheard the conversation with the driver, and told Anton.

"If you do that one more time," Anton told her, "you will have an extra debt of two thousand Euros."

Tatiana could never smile at Anton. For one thing, he constantly menaced her. He was armed, violent—and huge. For another, she loathed him, and Tatiana was not one for hiding her emotions. Any time she needed something—cigarettes, food—Anton charged it against her debt. Even rent for a place she wanted to escape and transport to a job she was forced to do—all were charged against her. "There was always something extra to pay," she said. "I could never get out of debt." That summer, she made $15,000 for Anton. She didn't keep one dollar.

In mid-July, Luben, the man who sold her originally, showed up to deliver another girl. Tatiana wanted to kill him. "How could you do this to me?" she screamed.

"Shut up. One more word, and you will suffer. Save your words for something else," he said. "I think it's pretty clear what the situation is."

After a week in Chişinău, Petrică and I drove to a point of origin for the new Middle Passage: one of the hundreds of Moldovan villages that slave traders had drained of its women.

Chişinău has scant suburbs. As Petrică careered southeast, there was a sharp transition between the gray cinder block of tenement buildings and black-soil fields of corn, sunflower, wheat, grapes, and tobacco. After two hours, we were lost. For miles, the only humans were a smattering of solitary shepherds at some distance from the road. Finally, we came upon an old couple shuffling along the side of the road. Bewildered, they gave us directions.

"Don't go left," said the babushka, sporting a colorful head scarf. "But, instead, I would suggest that you go right."

We entered Carpeşti, a village of some 2,300 residents, and shrinking fast. Three old men spread piles of dried beans across the main road, and encouraged us to drive across them in order to crack the hard shells. There were few other signs of life. Stretches reminded me of Chernobyl. Weeds grew tall through upturned concrete; the only thoroughfare was buckled and broken; side roads were unpaved but still navigable by the town's main form of transportation, horse and cart. The only persisting signs of the village's former glory flanked a crumbling, Stalin-era cultural center: a statue of the iconic Moldavian prince Ştefan cel Mare and a faded memorial to the Great Patriotic War.

Carpeşti is a tough old town. Founded in 1469, it has survived the Black Plague and dozens of wars. It has passed from Russian to Romanian to Soviet to Moldovan hands. But the worried face of Ion Bîzu, the thirty-four-year-old mayor, betrayed his town's death throes. "This is a very difficult moment," he said.

Bîzu's office was the second floor of a simple, two-story farmhouse. On his desk was a rotary phone and an early-model computer. Behind him the Moldovan flag was draped around a bikini calendar. In the Soviet era, his parents, like most people in the village, worked on a collective cattle farm. The older generations were nostalgic for that time. "We didn't know we were poor," said Bîzu. "We were happy."

In 1993, large-scale farming dissolved along with state ownership of the fields. Markets for local products soon evaporated as well. While two families bought up nearly all of the land at $250 per hectare, most were reduced to subsistence farming. Real income fell by over 70 percent. The average man earned $20 per month and was dead by age sixty. "Ten percent of the people can survive here," the mayor estimated.

Illiteracy grew as schools closed and teachers emigrated. Most who remained had no job, as all but six small businesses went bankrupt. No one read newspapers; no one had indoor plumbing.

There was one piece of technology that nearly everyone did have.

In the 1990s, at a time when national polls showed nine out of ten young people wanted to emigrate, television stations replaced Communist propaganda with alluring images of life beyond Moldovan borders. TV became to the young women of Carpeşti what the AK-47 was to the young men of southern Sudan: a diplomat from the modern world, offering the hope of a better life—at a price.

Around 2000, the traffickers appeared. They were mostly women, and mostly well-heeled citizens of neighboring villages. They took girls, sometimes three or four at a time, to Portugal, Turkey, Italy, Spain, and Moscow. Once there, the girls had to work off a debt, usually about $6,000. Despite 20–25 percent interest rates, some women managed to emerge from debt bondage after a couple of years, and send some money home. Many wound up enslaved.

Bîzu held out a handwritten ledger of the women who had disappeared. The pages were filled. Eighty-five percent of the town's women between the ages of eighteen and twenty-five had emigrated. The average age of the remaining women was thirteen; soon they too would disappear. Divorce and child sexual abuse became epidemic.

There was a real sadness about the mayor as he described his town. Still, he put on a brave face. "It's not a problem economically, because the women send back money that sustains the village," he said. "But it's a big problem psychologically." His friend recently shot himself in the head, leaving behind six children, after his wife left him while abroad.

In 2002, Bîzu's own wife of thirteen years left for Italy. She was not a fast earner, unfortunately, and now the original debt stood, hopelessly, at $22,000. According to a Council of Europe study, over the last ten years, 1 percent of Moldova's population of women ages eighteen to forty left to become prostitutes in Italy. Still, Bîzu echoed a common refrain, denying that his wife had entered the sex trade. I asked why mostly young women, and not young men, had left. "It's easier for them to find a job," he said. "In the service sectors, in Italy taking care of old people, whatever."

His wife came home once, briefly. "Her style had changed," he said, his voice trailing off. "Her attitude was different."

As we left Carpeşti, a young woman, one of only two we saw in the village, walked into a dirt-floored shack. I asked if she would talk to me. She wasn't eager, but consented. She was twenty-seven, and had recently returned from Romania and Turkey where slave traders had forced her into unpaid agricultural work, then "restaurant work." A neighbor later explained that she had been a prostitute in Istanbul. She had gone willingly at first, she said, to escape an alcoholic and abusive husband, and to pay medical expenses for a sick child. I asked if she was angry at the traffickers.

"They cheated me," she said.

We turned around and shot across the steppe to Transnistria, a slip of land skirting Ukraine, and the main transshipment point for Moldovan women sold into Istanbul brothels via Odessa. On the way, we stopped briefly to pick up Petrică's young wife in Chişinău, where she had arrived the night before. She would be our stand-in trafficking victim as we tested the borders.

Transnistria, a no-go zone for American officials and most international NGOs, seceded from Moldova in a bloody Russia-backed revolt in 1990. Since then, an economic mainstay of this unrecognized nation has been smuggling. It was an open secret in Transnistria that police officers moonlighted as slave dealers. A shelter operator in Tiraspol, the Transnistrian capital, said that when parents lost contact with their children, they called her first, and didn't tell the authorities.

The same principle held throughout Moldova. A trafficked woman in the Netherlands explained what would have happened to her if she had asked her native police to help her escape slavery. "In Moldova, if you go to the police for help in such a situation," she said, "the police would sell you to the Albanians."

Recently, Moldova had taken some baby steps toward abolition. In 2005, under pressure from John Miller, the police finally arrested one of their own who had sold women to a Turkish slave trader. He received ten years; another policeman, who had trafficked women to Dubai, was free on bail at the time of my visit. But in general, Moldova had a shamefully high hand-wringing-report-to-conviction ratio. In 2004, there were twenty-three antitrafficking raids, resulting in eighty-six reports, fifteen arrests, and thirteen convictions.

By comparison, Transnistria made Moldova look conscientious. At the time of our visit, a police officer, wanted for selling women to the Cămătaru clan, fled to his hometown of Tiraspol to escape justice. When five Moldovan police officers pursued him, their Transnistrian counterparts arrested them on espionage charges.

Petrică clenched his jaw as three soldiers with Kalashnikovs waved us to a stop. "Put your camera away," he told me.

The border guards wore big, Soviet-style radar-dish hats, striped Russian navy undershirts, and camouflage uniforms. They ordered us out of the car, searched the trunk and our bags, patted us down. In theory, they were looking for weapons as a week earlier someone—the Transnistrians said a Moldovan agent—had bombed a bus in Tiraspol. In reality, as Petrică knew well, they were looking for a tip.

They took our passports, and motioned for Petrică to follow them into the command post. As Petrică negotiated, two young women in Lycra skirts and high heels sauntered unmolested into Moldova. The Moldovan government did not recognize the border, and therefore didn't patrol it. Petrică reemerged and got into the car.

"Ecological fee," he said with a smirk.

Movement, like everything else in Transnistria, has a price tag. *Foreign Policy* editor Moisés Naím labeled Transnistria "the epitome of illicit" partly because of the activities at its largest shipping company, Sheriff. Between October 2005 and April 2006, Sheriff, run by the president's son, imported 150 pounds of frozen chicken for every man, woman, and child in Transnistria. Of course, the meat wasn't for Transnistrians, whose average salary was half that of their dirt-poor Moldovan neighbors; it was for sale on the black market. Naím cited Moldovan claims that Transnistria also sold massive amounts of Soviet-era small arms— and radiologically tipped Alazan missiles—to the highest bidder.

In terms of gross profits, women outflanked even dirty bombs as the region's most valuable commodity. A Transnistria-based network might buy a woman for $700 from a local trafficker in a village like Carpeşti. From there, the Transnistrians would take the woman to Tiraspol, where they would sell her to an Odessa-based crew at a 100 percent markup. The Ukrainians would take her across the border with a false passport, then drive a short distance to Odessa. At this point the traffickers would feed and give new clothes to the woman, who might not recognize she had been sold. Then they would lead her down the gigantic Potemkin Steps—the *"escalier monstre,"* as one nineteenth-century visitor called them—to one of the bi-weekly ferries to Istanbul. There a Turkish intermediary would direct her to a restaurant or a bar where she would meet her new employer, who had bought her for as much as $4,000 from the Odessa cell.

In less than a day, she would have voyaged from the Third World to the First World to the underworld.

Transnistrians sold their own women as well: the region had the second-highest trafficking rate in Moldova. In fact, about the only things not for sale on the black market were the elections. In 2001, President Igor Smirnov, a former metalworker who enjoyed Saddam-like popularity, claimed 103.6 percent of the vote in one region. I imagined the adulation derived from his still ubiquitous campaign posters, which portrayed him in lithograph as a dead ringer for Lenin.

As we entered the first town, Tighina, I thought that if it ever wanted to replace smuggling, Transnistria could turn itself into a Soviet theme park. An enormous monument to socialism was emblazoned with white-on-red Cyrillic reading STRENGTH IN UNITY. Soldiers in Red Army–like uniforms patrolled the streets and, despite the fact that this was nominally the demilitarized zone, some 1,500 Russian troops joined them. We soon passed a reverently displayed T-34 tank. Everywhere flapped the Transnistrian flag, featuring wheat, grapes, hammer and sickle.

As we approached the Dniester River, Petrică, who had been driving with uncharacteristic restraint, was again pulled over. The policeman barked at him in Russian—which Petrică did not speak—that he had failed to use his indicator when switching lanes. Petrică struggled to respond, but the cop yanked him out of the car, leading him into a guardpost. There he told Petrică, in perfect Romanian, that he would take away his license for three months. Three minutes later, Petrică returned to the car with his license intact.

"Fifteen Euros," he explained.

As we pulled out past the umpteenth stern-looking bas-relief of Lenin, I found myself humming Prokofiev's rousing Soviet national anthem, and belting out the only lyrics I remembered.

Be true to the people, thus Stalin has reared us,
Inspire us to labor and valorous deed!

Petrică, clearly not happy here, finally cracked a smile. "Fucking Communists," he said.

We drove through Tiraspol to the Ukrainian frontier. As Petrică negotiated with the Transnistrian customs authority, I gave a cookie to a small dog finding shade beneath a new BMW M5. Then the owner of the car, a low-level border guard, got in and drove away. The average salary in Transnistria was $10 per month.

Again, Petrică paid a bribe. This time, the $25 was well spent, as it enabled us to pass without an exit visa but with his wife, our mock trafficking victim.

On the other side, the better-compensated Ukrainians declined Petrică's bribe overture. Natasha, the blonde in the Chişinău shelter, had once been forced to have sex with a Ukrainian border guard—or else face five years in prison for traveling on a false passport. Unenthused about yielding Petrică's wife to the sweaty, gelatinous sentry before us, we turned back into no-man's-land.

In this situation, a trafficker would make one of two moves. He might take advantage of the wide-open topography along the 310-mile border by crossing with his women at an unchecked point. Alternatively, he would fabricate documents and fly the women to Turkey, charging all transport to them upon arrival, ensuring long-term, forced, unpaid service.

I chose to fly, and Petrică turned around to drive me to the airport. On the way out, we were stopped again at the same border post where we had entered.

In the course of those few hours in Transnistria, I became conversant in the unspoken language of the shakedown. The officer's stern look at our papers. The furrowed brow which said: "We're going to have a problem. Unless . . ." In this case, the furrowed brow presaged a false claim that Petrică was trying to exit from a different point than he had entered. Petrică offered $8. "I can't even pay one bill with that," the officer sniffed. "For you? Fifty Euros."

The problems at the Ukrainian border meant that I would have just eight hours in Istanbul. The ongoing Israeli bombardment of Lebanon meant tighter preboarding for flights bound to the Middle East, my next destination. So my window was actually six hours. I planned to see if the Russian mob would sell me three teenage girls in that time.

Human trafficking is illegal in Turkey, and I had no yen to see the inside of a Turkish prison. Several women I had interviewed provided sufficient description. In winter 2004, Natasha was retrafficked from Chişinău to Istanbul. She arrived at a time when Turkey, facing possible sanctions thanks to a Tier Three TIP ranking, finally responded to John Miller's pressure to crack down. Natasha was arrested in a large-scale sweep of the city's foreign prostitutes. Before she was deported, she spent a week in a dingy Turkish prison where other prisoners abused her, and guards fed her nothing but bread and olives.

Realistically, I knew that I had little to fear from Turkish authorities, who routinely winked at the thousands of sex tourists who arrive here at Atatürk Airport every year. So I decided to be brazen in the search for one of the hidden, illegal brothels that dominate the Turkish sex market and make it the top destination for Moldovan slaves. Sometimes, pimps held the women, literally in underground cells, tiny and windowless. Thousands of women, mainly Ukrainian and Moldovan, worked for no pay while collectively earning over $4 billion for their owners.

After buying a visa, I randomly chose a small tourist agency inside the Atatürk arrivals hall. A Turkish woman stood at the desk negotiating her family of six into a three-bed hotel room. An elderly English couple quietly accepted an overpriced shuttle to their cruise ship.

Kerem introduced himself to me.* He was rail-thin, with pointed nose, receding gray hairline, and bushy mustache. His shirt and tie hung off his frame like sails on a ship. I told him that I would like to find a woman. He turned over his badge to conceal his identity, ushered me into the office, and gave me a cup of coffee.

According to online sex tourist forums, most Turkish travel agencies have a Kerem on hand. Kerem was the guy for the guys. He helped his clients engage in what John Miller sarcastically called "just some harmless recreational activities." Recently, when two women hereabouts refused to provide that recreation, their pimp had mangled their genitals with boiling oil.

I told Kerem that I wanted to pose as a slave trader looking to buy three women. In his twenty-five years as a tour guide, he had been privy to dozens of sales, mostly from Russians or Ukrainians to Turkish pimps. He knew just who to call. A pimp he sometimes worked with was trying to clear out some of his older girls and might be willing to sell them. The pimp, a Turk, was a buyer at the end of a Russian network, and ran a brothel deep in the city center, from where he would dispatch his girls to the hotels and apartments of his mostly Turkish, occasionally Middle Eastern clientele. While Kerem had little compunction about his own work, he occasionally flinched at the rank slavery of the young girls.

"These girls," he said in a naturally languorous tone, "they're seventeen, sixteen years old. The bosses—Russian, Turkish—they take their passports away. They don't pay them anything for three months. If they want to leave, they touch their families back in Moldova."

He dialed the pimp. "This is a guy I know for years," he said as the phone rang. "He's my countryman. But fuck him." No answer. Kerem

---

* At his request, I have changed his name.

suggested the pimp was still sleeping, as he and the girls were always up until eight in the morning. He slept during the days, but the girls stayed on call as escorts.

I told Kerem to take me to him. He wavered, concerned that I would do something rash, and put him in danger. An hour had already run off the clock, and I couldn't waste any more time. I convinced him with a hundred-dollar bill.

We drove out along the highway that traced the Sea of Marmara toward the mouth of the Bosphorus. Just as the strait divided Europe from Asia, so a hidden line divided the women who walked along the shoreline on this hot July day. Some wore black *abayas*, veils, sunglasses to hide even their eyes. Most dressed in modest Western styles. Kerem knew by name five or six who didn't wear much at all.

Past the Yenikapi Ferry Terminal and Topkapi Palace, at an intersection with children begging, we turned into the working-class Aksaray neighborhood in the heart of the city. The Soviet expat community had exploded here. Buildings bore Cyrillic script advertising cargo transport from Odessa, tourism services, or money transfers. An "Erotic Shop" stood next to a sign for Air Moldova flights to Chişinău, Kiev, and Odessa. Strapping West African pimps walked a step or two behind ample-figured Slavic women.

Three hours left. We drove into a dense cluster of steep, winding, bumpy streets, tied with corkscrew turns that revealed construction long before the automobile. Around one corner, a turn-of-the-century fortress sat directly on top of an ancient, withered wall with arched, bricked-up windows that survived despite the added weight. At the end of the block stood a faded green building. A blue-on-white sign identified it as the Turcan Hostel.

"This is the place," Kerem said.

We walked into a dusty foyer with frayed carpets. A portrait of secular reformer Kemal Atatürk in a white bow tie was the only adornment behind the front desk.

There sat a Turk wearing a tight-fitting T-shirt and jeans. Like Florian in Jilava Prison, he carried himself like a boxer, only he would have fought in the middleweight division, and he would have been less float, more sting. His hair was closely cropped to the length of his stubble. He had a scar on his forehead, a neck that was pure muscle, implausible deltoids, bulky forearms, and, by default, a glare.

I asked where his girls came from.

"Moldova and Russia," he said. "Two hundred Euros for the night."

"How old?" I asked.

"How old would you like?"

I responded, but before Kerem could translate, the pimp held up his finger. He took a calculator that sat on his desk and handed it to me.

I typed in the number 16.

He shook his head. He could do eighteen, he said.

"For sixteen," I said, picking up the calculator and typing in the number 300.

"Euros?"

"Euros."

I had his attention, and went a step further.

"Actually, I'm interested in a larger venture. I'd like to buy three girls for a business I'm setting up in Sharm el-Sheikh," I said. "I mean buy them outright."

He looked at Kerem, whom he recognized.

"Come upstairs," he said.

We walked up five flights of creaky steps, past the girls' rooms. As we ascended, he explained that he had recently bought the brothel from the pimp that Kerem knew. We reached the roof, overlooking the city. He lit a cigarette.

The pimp said that he wasn't really in a mood to make new friends, but if I was serious about business, then he would talk business. He said that he started dealing slaves in 1996, but spent the last four years in a Turkish prison, convicted of human trafficking. "This damn thing," he said, holding up his cell phone. "Interpol traced my phone calls."

"My friend," I told him, "you've got to do what I do. SIM and toss."

I dumped ten subscriber identity modules (SIMs) from my wallet onto the table. They read like a trafficker's phone book—Dubai,

Amsterdam, Moldova, Romania, Germany, Amman. I held up a Yemeni SIM. "This was when I was shooting Kalashnikovs," I explained.

He smiled for the first time, revealing teeth stained brown by tobacco. He pointed at the corner of the roof, where a marijuana plant sprouted from a cooler. "You know what that is?" he asked.

"That was my first business when I was eighteen," I said, spontaneously faking a criminal past.

He reached out and shook my hand. "Ours is a people business," he explained, "and trust is very important."

I asked if I could see the girls. He said they were all out, but would be back that evening.

"I don't want to waste my time if they're not quality," I said.

He brought out a color picture of a plump, blond girl. He proved that she was eighteen by showing me a photocopy of her Moldovan passport.

"Would this be the girl I'm buying?" I asked.

"I can bring girls direct from Moldova through Ukraine for you," he said. "It will cost less than taking girls who are already working here. Would you arrange their visas for Egypt? Would I have to come?"

I explained that I'd expect a price break if I had to secure their visas. He said he could arrange to make Moldovan passports for them. I pressed him to give me numbers. He demurred, but said he would need a deposit in case I decided not to give them back after six months. I asked how much.

"I have to make a call to Moscow," he said. The boss of his boss worked there. He said I could meet the underboss, also Russian, to complete the deal tomorrow.

I glanced at my watch. Two and half hours left. "What about tonight?" I asked. "What about now?"

Kerem began to lose his nerve, and refused to translate my request. Confident that the pimp spoke no English, he explained himself. "This isn't my job," he said, retaining a smile but expressing panic through his eyes. "I'm a tour guide. I have three kids. These Russians—they will touch you."

The conversation had become tense. Kerem, pouring with sweat, was on the verge of a meltdown. I thanked the pimp for his time, and asked him for his phone number.

"You know where to find me," he said.

Over the centuries, slave ship owners recorded that one out of every seven slaves died along the Middle Passage across the Atlantic. While masters at the other end were regularly bestial, they normally recognized that their slaves were investments, worth the equivalent of $40,000 today.

Today Ukrainian women generally cost more than Moldovan women; who cost more than Nigerian women; who cost more than Chinese women; who cost more than Cambodian women. But all were cheap and, in slavery scholar Kevin Bales's term, "disposable." And while some met the barbarity of their impending slavery as they left home, the journey itself would only hint at the test of survival they would face at the end of the new Middle Passage.

One evening in early March 2006, two Pakistani men in their early twenties went out for some harmless recreational activities in Dubai, the fastest-growing destination for sex traffickers. The men dropped by a hardware store in the neighboring emirate of Sharjah, then went to a studio apartment where they found an Uzbek prostitute from whom they had previously bought sex for 40 dirhams—about $10. This time, they wanted a price break, so one man raped her, followed by the other. She screamed for help, and the men used what they had bought in the hardware store to silence her.

Her cries became gargles as blood rushed into her windpipe when the men stabbed her seven times in the neck.

Meet the mongers. The sex tourists—or, as they call themselves, "mongers"—who rent the women at the end of the slave trail are a mysterious and varied lot. Most researchers have ignored them. Most governments absolve them. But as consumers of flesh, their impact on psyches is indisputable.

The Dubai murder sparked debate among senior members of the *International Sex Guide*, the Internet site that is the world's largest forum for mongers.

Normally, the uncomfortable topic of a woman's death would not bear comment in the forum. She would have been just another dead "whore," an unfortunate but inevitable by-product of their fun. In 2005 alone, Dubai police found over a dozen freshly slaughtered, often mutilated, corpses of prostitutes in the desert and various Dumpsters around the emirate. In the three months following the stabbing, mongers strangled another Uzbek, slashed a nineteen-year-old Ukrainian, threw a Bangladeshi maid from a third-floor balcony—all because they resisted sex slavery. Another Bangladeshi maid, who struggled against her captors but was forced into prostitution nonetheless, died of AIDS in the same period. The stories were a line or two, at most, in the local media, and were not mentioned at all in the *Sex Guide*.

But one aspect of the March story caught the eye of "Lomion," a husky, six-foot-tall American.

"Dh 40 huh . . . we are definitely being ripped off then :)," he wrote in the *Sex Guide*.

"You know . . . it's not so funny," responded a Los Angelean. "These ladies are people."

The next day, Lomion apologized for offending his fellow monger, and offered an explanation. "Spent the last 10 years bouncing from one 3rd world war zone / atrocity site to the next (Bosnia→Kosovo→Sierra Leone→Bosnia→Kosovo→Bosnia→Iraq→Afghan→Iraq) and was making a joke which I see now was in bad taste for the area," he wrote.

Then, in a moment of candor, he added: "Considering we all make use of a service which makes its margins on human slavery (lets get realistic, we are not getting with locals here) surprised to see such a backlash on this."

Like most who rented slaves for sex, Lomion was rarely so reflective. A contractor with the U.S. Department of Defense, he had deployed with every major American military engagement since Bosnia in 1995. "Where there are troops and contractors, there [are] whores," he wrote from Afghanistan. "Been that way since man invaded his first country thousands of years ago."

In Kabul, Lomion frequented brothels fronting as Chinese food restaurants. There, if he wanted, he could buy a girl outright for as little as 100 kilograms of wheat. In post-Baathist Baghdad, his fatigues and strawberry-blond hair were magnets for street pimps. But Lomion's dystopic Eden was post-conflict Sarajevo, where half of the sex slaves in local brothels were Moldovan. He viewed the women as an irresistible combination of Russian, Romanian, Jewish, Gypsy, and Ukrainian blood. They were exquisitely pleasing to the eye, fiery by nature, but tempered by poverty and domestic abuse.

At the time, the monger's fellow Pentagon contractors were being investigated for keeping Eastern European sex slaves in their residences in the Bosnian capital. Their comrades-in-arms, UN peacekeepers, had a particularly nasty reputation that was not limited to Sarajevo. Blue helmets pressed girls into slavery in the Congo, purchased sex slaves outright in Cambodia and Eritrea, and became-known "less for peace than for rape," as John Miller said. "The UN peacekeepers are the worst military in the world," Miller told me. "I demand you quote me on that."

On March 14, 2004, Lomion posted a review of Florida, a Sarajevo brothel, a few months after the proprietor was killed in a mafia hit. The place had recovered nicely, he reported, and now featured a Ukrainian girl, "1 Gypsie looking thing," and, best of all, three Moldovans. Unfortunately, "the blond Moldovan has a serious sag problem nor does she seem to enjoy her job. Just lays there till you are done." The other two Moldovans were young and perky, but there was usually a line as they "don't go for more than 10 minutes between tricks." Their captor did not allow the girls to speak, and insisted on collecting payment in advance.

When Lomion returned to Bosnia two years later, he found Moldovan sex slaves few and far between. The country had recovered somewhat from the hell of war, and regional initiatives like the U.S.-sponsored Operation Mirage had stanched the overland flow of slaves along the western corridor. UN Secretary-General Kofi Annan had issued a "zero tolerance" trafficking policy for peacekeepers, and President Bush, Secretary of Defense Donald Rumsfeld, and his deputy Paul Wolfowitz all did the same for U.S. contractors. While Miller testified that there was "zero compliance" with the UN policy, Lomion noted a supply-side effect.

"Think Bosnia is starting to go the way of Croatia and the mongering scene while still going strong is past its heyday. Its economy is improving, EUFOR and the UN are really really cracking down on the trafficking (and outright slavery)," Lomion lamented. "It is no longer a Dubai/Hong Kong/Bangkok free for all. Oh well, it was great while it lasted."

Lomion was not the only monger mourning economic resiliency. Some viewed the emerging market indicators from the back of *The Economist* as mongering tools like condoms or lubricant. In the fall of 2004, Moldova's economy received a slight bump from a German compensation package for wartime slavery. Mongers grieved, and looked to Belarussian women instead. In the spring of 2006, markets skidded after Russia boycotted Moldovan wine. The mongers then rejoiced: they knew a stifling of the country's number one export would mean a glut of the number two product.

"Now comes a really crazy idea," wrote a middle-aged Manitoban wholesaler. "Poverty is good. That's right. I said it. For guys like us, poverty is good because it keeps those women from getting arrogant, spoiled and demanding. Just think about all the countries that have a reputation for having the best women. What do they all have in common? That's right, poverty."

The members of the *Sex Guide* were only the most conspicuous consumers of the flesh. With 2 million women in forced prostitution at any one time, it couldn't have been only the 160,000 registered members using a dozen sex slaves each. Undeclared mongers were numerous, and few took the time to find out if the women they purchased had sold sex of their own free will.

Once, in her first month of enslavement in Amsterdam, Tatiana saw a glimmer of decency in the eyes of a Dutch client. She blurted out that she was being held captive, forced to be a prostitute against her will, humiliated and raped on a daily basis. She begged him to help her escape.

"He felt sorry for me, but he wanted to have sex, so that's what happened," she said. "That's what always happened."

To enter Dubai's most notorious brothel, the Cyclone, I paid $16 for a ticket that the bursar stamped with the official seal of the Department of Tourism & Commerce Marketing. Prostitution is illegal in Dubai, whose laws are rooted in Islam, with penalties ranging up to death. But the stamp was only the first of several contradictions in a place of slavery for women that one well-traveled British monger referred to as "Disneyland for men."

One sign read No Soliciting; another read No Camouflage in the Disco Area. In the club, no less than 500 prostitutes solicited a couple dozen prospective clients, some Western servicemen among them.

An Indian living in London owned the place, and had not updated the decor in a decade, as if taste would reduce the charm and thus deter tourists. I walked over to the bar, and two Korean girls, who looked no older than fifteen and claimed to be sisters, approached me.

"Do you want massage?" one asked.

While the strobe lights, the loud music, and the general whirlpool of anxious femininity lent an air of abject chaos, the place was carefully ordered by race. Stage left was a crush of Chinese, Taiwanese, and Korean women; center stage were sub-Saharan Africans; stage right were Eastern European and Central Asian women, who initially identified themselves as Russians, but later revealed specifically that they were Bulgarian, Ukrainian, Uzbek, and of course, Moldovan.

A young Chinese woman wore a childlike perfume. The club bathed her in black light, so that she appeared like a radioactive negative of herself. In broken English, she explained that she had arrived in Dubai twenty-eight days earlier, having been promised a job as a maid. Instead, human smugglers known as snakeheads sold her to a madam who forced her to pay off a debt by selling sex here. She trembled as she said that she just wanted to go home.

Her story was not unusual. A night earlier in another mega-bordello located in the three-star York International Hotel in the tony Bur Dubai neighborhood, a thirty-year-old Uzbek told me she had to pay off a $10,000 debt or "the mafia will kill my children."

In the Cyclone, every woman who spoke with me in depth explained that traffickers had taken their passports away as collateral until they paid off a debt. Both Lomion and a man who signed himself "Big Bob II" reported hiring prostitutes from here who were covered in bruises. But that did not stop them from having sex with them—or returning to the Cyclone for more.

Alina, a bleach-blonde from northern Romania, sat forlornly smoking and playing electronic solitaire along the back wall. She had a raspy voice, and a sallow complexion that made her appear much older than her twenty-three years. She came here in 2004, after divorcing the alcoholic father of her three-year-old son. A Romanian woman in Dubai had promised her work as a waitress in a local restaurant.

When the woman met Alina at the airport, she told her what her real work would be. Without her passport, without any money, without any local contacts, she had no choice but to go with the woman to the Cyclone. From then on, her life was a blur of clients—American, European, Indian, and mostly Arab. Some men purchased oral sex in the "VIP Room" above the bar, but they normally took Alina to a hotel or apartment. They were often violent.

"Many problem customers," she said, particularly among the Arabs.

Every morning at six she would return to the apartment of the madam, an abusive woman who took all the money. For Alina's efforts she was given one meal a day, coffee, and cigarettes.

Alina contemplated escape, but running to the desert would be a death sentence for her, and running to the police would be a death sentence for her son. Her health faded, her skin fell apart, and in the supply-saturated market of the Cyclone, she ceased getting customers, a fact that triggered the furor of her madam.

One night, the woman forced Alina to go with a Syrian man to the neighboring city of Al Ain. As soon as he picked her up, he started yelling at her in Arabic. She was terrified, and cried all the way to his apartment. There he tortured and raped her for two days. Shortly after the man released her, the madam announced that she was going back to Romania, and that she would manumit Alina.

For the first time in a year, Alina had a choice. Despite the horrendous abuse she had survived, and despite her illegal alien status, she went back to prostitution. She knew her reputation was shattered back home, and that she would never find legitimate work or a husband to provide for her son. So she stayed. But she insisted that "I am for myself."

In the Cyclone I found a range of nationalities, a wealth of sad stories; though most had been enslaved, some were now free. But for Alina, as for many others, there was no joy in freedom.

Before I left, I noted one sign that, unlike the rest, did not contradict the surroundings. On a coaster, embedded underneath the polyurethane finish of the bar top, was a quote by Martin Luther King Jr.

We may have all come on different ships,
but we're in the same boat now.

Dubai grew at breakneck speed during the 1990s, developing faster than any country on earth. In 1991, a handful of multistory buildings sat alongside a dusty, two-lane highway, with the occasional oasis, camel tracks, and plenty of sand.

Fifteen years later, Dubai was a sparkling metropolis of 1.5 million people. Mirrored glass was everywhere, and while the streets were well over 100 degrees Fahrenheit, the skycrapers were chilled to meat locker temperatures by massive air conditioners. Grandiose mosques and palaces gave variation to the skyline, and even the *adhan* was a sound effect–aided performance. Camel tracks still flanked the al-Makhtoum highway, but the first thing a visitor saw when entering Abu Dhabi, the largest of the seven emirates, was an ice rink. Since 1999, five of the world's tallest buildings were erected here.

The sheikhdom was still, at its heart, old-world Bedouin, but became well stocked with technocrats who laid the groundwork for a post-oil economy by building a playland for wealthy tourists, investing in infrastructure, and making Dubai a radiant draw for business conventions. Now the population is, at most, 20 percent Arab. Construction and service sector laborers from South Asia and the Philippines make up the bulk of the rest.

But with breakneck growth came whiplash. As the UAE steadily loosened barriers to investment and immigration, unscrupulous operators moved in. Drug-smuggling arrests increased 300 percent in the two years preceding my visit. Rogue nuclear scientist A.Q. Khan used Dubai as a transit point for illicitly traded weapons materials.

Dubai also became the Mecca of the new slave trade. Although slavery was abolished here in 1963, many still worked under threat of violence for no pay. On occasion, unpaid or underpaid laborers resisted. In March 2006, a small group of South Asian construction workers building the Burj Dubai tower—set to be the world's tallest building—rampaged through the emirate for several days to protest poor working conditions and low pay. Rami G. Khouri, the editor of Beirut's *Daily Star*, called it "our first modern slave revolt in the Arab region."

While the rioters were exploited, they were not enslaved. Tens of thousands of others were, but their plight was hidden. In addition to bonded construction workers, Filipina housemaids were regularly beaten, raped, and denied pay by their Arab masters. As many as 6,000 child camel jockeys—mainly from South Asia—languished in hidden slavery on *ozbah* farms, where their masters beat them and starved them to keep their weight down. In 2004, an HBO special on the jockeys personally embarrassed John Miller into dropping the United Arab Emirates to Tier Three in the *Trafficking in Persons Report*.

A year later, the day before Miller's office released its 2005 report, an embassy official hinted at the sheikhdom's impending demotion. I was in neighboring Abu Dhabi reporting for *Newsweek* on camel jockey repatriations. But the official explained that the downgrade partly would be due to the third category of underreported slaves: sex-trafficking victims.

At least 10,000 such slaves were in Dubai at the time. Though the emirates had moved to erase the stain of the camel jockeys by repatriating over a thousand of them, little had been done about the massive problem of slavery in places like the Cyclone. The day after the release of the TIP Report, the downgrade was of little outward concern to the man whose responsibility it was to free the slaves, Lieutenant Colonel Dr. Mohammed Abdullah al Mur, director of the Human Rights Section of the Dubai Police. "We don't need outside organizations telling us what to do," he concluded.

Al Mur saw trafficking as a moral problem, which the agents of the emirati leader, His Highness Sheikh Khalifa bin Zayed Al Nahyan, would eliminate by hewing to the laws of Islam, which forbade extramarital sex. On more than one occasion I heard the identical sound bite from emirati officials: "The Sheikh, God bless his soul, is always thinking of the people." Like Michael Horowitz, al Mur supported keeping prostitution a "per se" crime. For al Mur, the issue of whether or not a given woman was forced to sell sex was of no consequence, as long as the problem was eliminated from public view. And despite his disregard for the report, his officers cracked down hard during the 2006 TIP review period. That spring, they arrested and summarily deported a thousand foreign prostitutes.

Natasha—whom I interviewed in the Chişinău shelter—was the reluctant beneficiary of U.S.-driven antiprostitution efforts once again. At the time, she found herself enslaved anew by a Russian madam in the Cyclone. One evening, Dubai police rushed the doors, turned on all of the lights, ordered all of the men to leave, and demanded the girls' passports. Natasha's was held by her madam, so the police threw her into an overcrowded desert prison for a month without trial. The conditions were appalling. She claimed that prison authorities laced her food with Bron, a codeine-based drug that supposedly killed her sexual appetite. The drug left her in a stupor and made her an easy mark for other prisoners. A month later, she was back in Chişinău, penniless and hopeless once again.

Miller's office upgraded the UAE in the 2006 report, yet the deportations did little to diminish the slaughter and slavery of the prostitutes. The mongers were blasé. "Life goes on as usual," wrote one regular at the York. "Except that the rates are more flexible these days." Another reported being "gutted" when police arrested and then deported a favorite to her native Kyrgyzstan. But he added that she was stupid to have chosen the risky lifestyle in the first place.

"What choice?" asked "11Bravo," a Cyclone regular. "I have no real knowledge, but just something about it suggests that the debts incurred to originally get here are not forgiven due to extenuating circumstances, especially if borrowed from 'certain' people.

"Unfortunately, you're seeing the dark underbelly of the 'fun and frolic' nights," he continued. "When you see her disappearing in the taxi, best to go into 'out of sight, out of mind' mode.

"Her reality outside of the 'time with you,'" 11Bravo concluded, "not fun to think about."

Shortly before my second visit to the Netherlands, Michael Horowitz registered his opinion of the Dutch approach to sex slavery with the U.S. House International Relations Committee. "Now, that country, which shall remain nameless, whose name—whose major city is Amsterdam," he said in May 2006, "has been a kind of symbol for this evil."

The previous fall, I had asked John Miller which country had the most slaves. "It's hard to say which is the worst country," he said. "I think on a per capita basis the Netherlands is pretty bad." Miller's efforts to downgrade the Netherlands to Tier Two had been consistently rebuffed by his superiors at State. But his disdain for the Dutch model was undiminished. Miller likened Dutch legalizers to Wilberforce's regulationist opponents, who argued "for getting better mattresses in slave ships."

For the American neo-abolitionists, Amsterdam was a latter-day Sodom. In addition to prostitution, gay marriage was legal in the Netherlands, and on the day that I arrived in that country, the Charity, Freedom and Diversity Party announced its goal to legalize pedophilia, child pornography, and bestiality.

But Bush administration shock did not awe the Dutch. On the contrary, among the elite, it was political suicide to subscribe to American logic on questions of vice. "Here in the Netherlands, there *is* a taboo," said Amma Asante, a member of Amsterdam's city council. "That is the shame of being called a moralist."

Mainstream Dutch antitrafficking organizations scorned Miller's efforts, and labeled prohibition a draconian measure that would only increase "the marginalization and stigmatization of sex workers." Dutch government officials also scoffed at Bush administration pressure. The threat of sanctions would be purely symbolic, and despite bluster from Horowitz and Miller, the TIP office ranked the Netherlands in its top tier since the first report in 2001. "I spoke to Mr. Miller when he was in Amsterdam," said Harold van Gelder, an erudite detective who headed Amsterdam's antitrafficking vice squad. "He promised to send me a copy of his report. He never did. No problem. I'm not so interested."

At the same time, I found no one in the Dutch antitrafficking vanguard who felt that prostitution was a good thing; it was just that prosecuting it would not be pragmatic. Mainstream Dutch opinion holds that prostitution can be an integrated and open "economic activity," and in fact Amsterdam's Red Light District yields millions of dollars in annual tax revenue.

But there is a fine distinction between legality and legitimacy. I asked three vigorous Dutch defenders of "sex work" whether they would like to see their own daughters sell their bodies. Their responses were cool.

And the 1990s brought a new surge of slave traders who did not follow the Dutch honor system. Though women had been sold into sex slavery in Amsterdam for centuries, the fall of the Berlin Wall changed the game, if not the rules. At first it just seemed as if Eastern European women had taken advantage of their newfound freedom of movement to make a quick gilder. Then the bodies started turning up. One woman was killed after she told the story of her slavery to a foreign journalist. The bullet-riddled corpse of an enslaved Yugoslav woman was found in the street after she sought help from the main Dutch antitrafficking organization. Only a sliver of the sex slaves wound up murdered, yet they stood out in an otherwise placid city.

The Dutch scrambled to keep order. When the first wave of sex slaves came from Southeast Asia in the 1970s, officials began to tolerate prostitution formally. Now they moved a step further, legalizing brothels and opening the *tippelzones*. The idea was to bring the trade out of the gray, to regulate it, to repair the beds in the windows, to make sure the women received regular health checks, to tax the brothel owners, to hold those responsible for the flesh trade to financial, if not moral, account.

Unwittingly they also breathed life into pimping, hitherto moribund. The slave traders leaped at the easy money of destination-point sales in an open sex market that grew by 25 percent in the following decade. At first, it was the Turks and the Moroccans; then the Albanians, Antilleans, Moldovans, Romanians. In 1988, three mafia syndicates had infiltrated the Netherlands. Four years later, they numbered nearly one hundred.

Regardless of whether prostitution was legal, women like Tatiana were not. This meant they saw no benefits from the reforms of the 1990s. In 2003, Amsterdam finally acknowledged that the *tippelzones* were horrendous places of abuse, and closed them down. Moreover, in order to encourage victims to testify against their traffickers, the Dutch government gave freed slaves the option of staying with a temporary residence permit. Both were progressive ideas, and both still meant little for illegal immigrants. When the *tippelzones* closed, unregulated escort services exploded; when officials offered temporary residence, traffickers did not tell their slaves about the option. Their abuse in the hands of the lawless was not tempered by the good intention of the law.

"Five years after the lifting of the ban on brothels," said Job Cohen, the mayor of Amsterdam in 2005, "it has to be established that the goals of that law have not been met."

Over the course of a month, I visited over a dozen sex clubs, brothels, swinger lounges, and window prostitutes in Amsterdam. I posed as a client to talk to women—although I always revealed my identity when we started interviews at a safe distance from pimps and brothel owners. I posed as an arms dealer to talk to traffickers.

My work yielded pages of fascinating anthropological notes. Almost every woman that I spoke with despised the work—one comparing her status in the eyes of the clients to that of an ashtray. Albanian slave traders found Kalashnikovs a much harder commodity to acquire in the Netherlands than women. But no woman acknowledged that she was a slave at the time we were speaking. And several prostitutes claimed they made a fair amount of money for themselves.

A Brazilian who loathed the work claimed she had financed her child's education with the money she made. She rarely allowed men to penetrate her, forbade them to use their hands, and simulated coitus by holding their penises just off of her vagina. One twenty-nine-year-old Austro-Italian said that she was traveling around Europe and soliciting World Cup fans, often too drunk to perform sexually, but not too drunk to hand over 50 Euros after the failed attempt. "I know this may be hard for you to believe," she said, "but I started in this job for fun. I love sex!"

I heard darker stories as well. Six of the women I interviewed said that they had originally been sold into slavery, and told heartbreaking, complex stories of seduction, despair, inhumanity, and survival. Slave traders showed one woman pictures of her family in Albania with one clear message: run and they're dead. A woman from rural northern Nigeria told me how she had been enslaved, but feared freedom as her bondage had been ordained in a vodou ceremony.

On five separate occasions, young Eastern European women were too frightened to talk to me. Each had been in the country no more than a month. A Bulgarian said that her "protection" would be suspicious. All had pimps nearby. Knowing that others had been killed for speaking to the media, I was always quick to desist.

Authorities found around 400 trafficking victims within Dutch borders every year. A top police official told John Miller that 40 percent of the country's 30,000 prostitutes were slaves. But business in the well-regulated Red Light District shrank by half since 1999, and the police were unwilling and unable to probe deeply into the burgeoning escort services. Tatiana guessed there were 5,000 who, like her, were enslaved in the Netherlands. No one could say for sure.

"I am realistic to understand that what we are trying to control is just the tip of the iceberg," said Detective Van Gelder. "And I don't have even the faintest idea what's below the surface."

The end of August 2002 was a pregnant time in Amsterdam. Humidity was well above normal, but it just wouldn't rain. Hair clung to skin and wrapped around ears like ivy. The blue-and-white trams, though air-conditioned, offered little respite. Hundreds crowded the city's beaches and parks, many parading topless or nude, grateful at such a stifling time that they lived in a permissive, or pragmatic, land.

For Tatiana, the atmosphere suited a growing dread. She had been looking to escape for ten weeks, and she sensed that her time was running out. Her original trafficker, Luben, had delivered stern news to her captor, Anton, during his visit. Tatiana did not know why, but Anton and Luben moved her and the other girls from the apartment to a hotel an hour away in Rotterdam. Then, the next night, another hotel. And then another. For a week they ran from something—or someone—that had Anton fearing for his life.

Tatiana overheard a conversation Anton had on his cell phone: They were going to drive to Spain the next day. He took the women back to the apartment, and told them to go upstairs and pack the rest of their belongings.

Tatiana's mind raced and she immediately thought of a young Turkish client who told her that he would help her escape if the opportunity arose. This felt like such an opportunity. Tatiana bolted upstairs first to have more time to think about how to reach him. She opened the door and stepped into the apartment.

There she was met by two big men and the long muzzle of a silencer. One man grabbed her cell phone, and threw her on the couch next to her landlord, who was gagged and bound. The other peeled off three rounds in the direction of Anton, Luben, and the other three girls, who had bolted as soon as Tatiana disappeared into the apartment. The shooter took off after them, and returned with a hysterical Maria.

"Shut up," the man said. "Don't move."

Knowing that the gunplay, muzzled though it was, would soon attract police attention, the men left the bound landlord, pushed the girls into the street, and hailed a cab. One man quietly explained to Tatiana to stay right next to him. If the police caught up with them, she was to act like a lover or he would use the weapon, pressed into her rib cage, to blow her wide open.

"In that moment," she later recalled, "it hit me that I could be shot, I could be killed, and they didn't care. I thought that my first day in Holland was the worst day in my life. But this day was worse than any other."

The men, who spoke no English, told her to direct the driver to the edge of town. She was desperate. But with a gun in her side, she couldn't signal to the driver what was really happening. So they drove to a building on the edge of a forest outside of Amsterdam. They walked up to a second-floor apartment, where three other men were waiting, including a rival pimp whom Tatiana recognized from the street.

As the men spoke, she began to understand what was happening. This was an asset seizure, a move to take over a rival business, or a rival faction within the same network. Apparently, a 1999 deal had gone sour when these men tried to sell three girls to Anton. Now they wanted to find him and kill him and Luben.

"Start talking," they told the women, "or you won't get out alive from here."

"I don't know nothing," Tatiana cried. "Don't you think if I knew where they were I would tell you so I don't have to work for them anymore?"

The kidnappers tried a different tactic, bringing out two bottles of vodka and telling the women to calm down and drink. They began making jokes, and told them to stand up, dance, and perform as if they were lesbians in a strip club. Then the men discussed what to do with them.

"Maybe we should sell them to the Albanians," one said. "We could probably get twenty-five hundred Euros for each."

After an hour, the girls still hadn't talked, and the men became more aggressive. One grabbed Maria and dragged her into a bedroom. Another grabbed Tatiana. Her mind raced as he pulled her into a bedroom. This felt like the end game. "Okay, there's no longer five, there's one," she thought. Sounds of a muted struggle came from next door.

Outside the window was a balcony. She knew that if she could manage the twenty-foot drop without breaking her leg, she could run to a neighbor and pound on the door, hoping that someone was home and would give her shelter.

Breaking free from the man would be a challenge. As he threw her on the bed, she reached back for the side table. Her thought was to smash him with it, run, and jump. A huge crash sounded from the main room, and lights flashed through the window. She heard screaming, her captor rolled under the bed, and she ran to the balcony. Maria, naked after being raped in the next room, ran to the balcony as well. The bedroom door burst open.

"Police!" a Dutch officer yelled.

Tatiana was still in shock as another officer covered her with a blanket.

"We know what's happened," he said. "It's over."

Sometimes she would close her eyes and see the wheat fields of her homeland. In those moments, a dropped bottle did not frighten her, the stranger on the train did not appear to loom, and the dusk did not bring shudders.

In other moments, starting after she testified, the beast visited Tatiana. It visited her after the men who were minutes away from killing her received just two years in prison. It visited her after Luben and Anton, who had shattered her life in the first place, disappeared into the ether. It visited her while she was applying for permanent residence, an uncertain process even though repatriation could well be a death sentence. It visited her after she had moved into an apartment by herself—her first time alone in her life. It visited her after she went to sleep. It visited her every night.

The beast was a human form, a shadow of a man that came in through her door, illuminated by the moon. She was asleep, but she was conscious, and she saw her cat, she saw the window. She could not move but, as if frozen in Munch's tempera, she heard herself scream.

The beast that haunted Tatiana probably did not visit the men who enabled her enslavement, those clients who resided in their own insouciant paradise at the end of the new Middle Passage.

In 1999, Sweden became the first country in the world to decriminalize the role of the mere provider in prostitution. At the same time, the Swedish authorities outlawed pimping, trafficking, and the purchase of sex. While the law sounded contradictory, and while some claimed it would just drive the whole trade underground, Sweden thus offered women like Tatiana a helping hand while raising a mailed fist to men like Florian Costache and Lomion.

It was difficult to meet with as many sex slaves as John Miller had and argue that the solution to their bondage was to treat them like criminals. Publicly, Miller hewed to Michael Horowitz's hard line. Privately, he confided that his tenure as trafficking czar left his thinking more nuanced.

"Do you support keeping prostitution a 'per se' crime for the women?" I asked him in November 2006.

"The Justice Department argues that they need the leverage of prosecuting the women, but in my heart . . ." He paused. "In my heart: yes. I, in my heart, I'm with the Swedish model."

Miller, quietly, had applied pressure for more flexibility in U.S. policy. At the end of the president's first term, Miller argued face-to-face to Colin Powell that if a European country was considering adopting a Dutch model of legalized prostitution, the United States should press it to legalize the role of the women, but crack down on the role of the men. Quietly, Powell approved this subtle, but significant, change in the American stance.

In her waking life, Tatiana also had her views changed through contact. She used her newly won freedom to help others escape, but she did not judge those who entered prostitution willingly. Her concern was slavery. In her view, politicians expended too much air on the legalization debate. Meanwhile, across the globe, millions of women and children were struggling to breathe.

Tatiana and I made peace in Bucharest, and while she never yielded an inch in an argument, she laughed about her volcanic personality. "You took on your head a difficult person," she said. "And another thing, this person is a woman! And she was a victim. And she's aggressive and stubborn." I told her that her stubbornness was probably what kept her alive, and I told her about the young woman in the Romani brothel who, by contrast, had given up on life.

"She can be freed physically," said Tatiana. "But she will never be freed emotionally.

"That shame is a shadow you can't shake," she added. "Sometimes it's smaller, sometimes it's bigger. But it's always with you."

7

John Miller's War

You don't generally get involved in this issue unless you're driven by faith, or you see slavery, and feel it and taste it," said Congressman Frank Wolf. "It's hard to just fabricate the commitment and the interest and the desire."

When Wolf approved him to lead the human trafficking office, John Miller was driven partly by faith, but mainly by ambition. That changed on September 20, 2003, when Miller met his first survivor of slavery.

Katya was a teenager from the Czech Republic who, like Tatiana, had made some mistakes. First, she married the wrong man. Then, after he left her with a two-year-old daughter, she responded to an ad for a restaurant job in Amsterdam. But neither of those actions justified what happened next. She was taken into the country by a Czech man, who, upon arrival, sold her to a Dutch thug, who drove her to the Red Light District.

"I will not work here," Katya told the trafficker.

"Yes, you will!" he responded. "You owe us twenty thousand Euros."

Katya continued to resist. Finally, the man broke her will by presenting her with a choice: submit, or her daughter dies. Thus, he forced the teenager to have sex with over a dozen men each night, and kept the money she earned. After several months, as a "reward" for good behavior, the Czech trafficker brought her daughter to Amsterdam. Severely depressed, her mind warped by the daily rape, Katya considered killing her child. Finally, a sympathetic cab driver organized a posse to confront her captor. After a struggle with the pimp, who demanded a redemption price, the driver won her freedom.

In that two-hour meeting in Amsterdam, Miller learned more than he had in several thousand pages of Michael Horowitz's briefing books. He learned the deep trauma and self-blame that comes with being a victim of trafficking. He learned that, at a certain point, a victim is no longer a victim: he or she is a survivor. And he learned that survivor and victim alike are human before all else. Katya had married her rescuer, and found work in a hospital. Her life was shattered, but, slowly, she was reassembling the pieces.

Katya defied Miller's expectation that someone who had been through such humiliating trauma would never lead anything approximating a normal life. But she also confirmed his early belief, based on the assertions of Horowitz and others, that "there is no more demeaning form of slavery than sex slavery." Over the next few weeks, survivors of other forms of bondage shook even that belief.

Miller flew east, stopping in Sweden, Greece, Russia, and India. At each stop, he met dozens of survivors, and as he heard their stories, he came to see that the degradation of slavery was not limited to those kept in a brothel.

In Bangkok, the last stop on his trip, he met a girl called Lord in a government shelter. When Lord was fourteen, her parents sold her to a trafficker in Laos. The trafficker then sold her to an embroidery factory in Thailand, where she was forced to sew for fourteen hours a day. When she resisted against the unpaid labor, the owner's son held a gun to her face and pulled the trigger. For a moment, she thought she was dead, but when a BB ripped through her cheek, she realized she was just scarred. She continued to resist, and he deformed her face further with caustic chemicals.

What struck Miller most about Lord was not the horror of her experience, but the joy he saw in her now that she had been freed. A nongovernmental organization had sponsored reconstructive surgery. When Miller saw her, the scars were unmistakable, but she smiled like any other girl.

That night in his hotel, he avoided nightmares because he could not sleep. His whole body was aching, and for a fleeting moment, he feared he was having a heart attack. It was the first of many restless nights for Miller. A million trafficking victims every year had meant nothing to him until he met one. Now, he had met dozens, and their plight overwhelmed him. Sex slavery might represent the greatest proportion of cross-border trafficking, but the evil had many faces.

If the tens of millions of slaves were hopeless, disposable people, he would not feel the burden so deeply. But Lord was smiling. That smile said one thing to Miller: Get to work.

The biggest guns in Miller's arsenal were economic sanctions, and from his time battling China as a congressman, he had a reputation as one of the fastest draws in Washington. The Trafficking Victims Protection Act streamlined the process by requiring the president to initiate sanctions against a worst offender country if, three months after being ranked in Tier Three, it had not made "significant progress" toward abolition. The path to sanctions began with the initial assessment made by Miller's office. His staff—which grew from thirteen to twenty-four during his time in office—leaned hard on foreign governments and U.S. embassies for trafficking intel that they were often reluctant to serve up.

In 2001, the United States assessed twenty-three countries as grossly inadequate in combating modern-day slavery. Each year, that number dropped steadily until, by 2006, only twelve countries were placed in Tier Three.

Other foreign-policy interests dominated the process. After Miller submitted his recommendations to Paula Dobriansky, regional bureaus, dreading the complications that sanctioning friends would cause, would nearly always press for an upgrade of countries in their domain. Normally, the bureau chiefs would prevail, particularly when the final decision was made by Colin Powell, or later Condoleezza Rice. In total, over two dozen people had to clear each ranking.

The only states that regularly faced sanctions read like a rogue's gallery of reprobate American enemies: North Korea, Sudan, Cuba, and Myanmar (formerly Burma). If a friend of the United States wound up on Tier Three—as did the United Arab Emirates in 2005—it would invariably demonstrate "significant progress," and the Secretary of State would reassess it as a Tier Two watch list country before the sanctions provision kicked in.

"What does 'significant progress' mean?" I asked Miller.

"I think passing a law can be significant, and that should be recognized," he said. "But the next year if they haven't enforced the law, then you know, there's got to be appreciable progress. It wouldn't be enough to just pass a law two years in a row."

In the rare instance that the United States drew the sanction gun against an undeclared enemy, as it did with the tiny kleptocracy of Equatorial Guinea, it fired rubber bullets. Trade was unaffected, as were some types of aid. The United States might still consider a nation sanctioned under the TVPA a Most Favored trading partner. An unwaived Tier Three country would get a "no" vote from the United States on any application for loans from the World Bank—but that didn't mean other countries would not override the American veto.

On June 25, 2003, during a hearing of a subcommittee of the House International Relations Committee, Democratic congressman Brad Sherman challenged Miller.

"I see sanctions in which countries that might have gotten $50 million only get $25 million," Sherman said. "And I want to say if getting $25 million is being sanctioned, I'm ready to be sanctioned."

In public, Miller defended his superiors by saying that the point was not to sanction, but to embarrass governments into acting. In private, Miller chafed at the fact that broader sanctions were not available. He particularly disliked that his superiors would not sanction the kind of country that countenanced the enslavement and mutilation of children like Lord. But he was unsure that, even if the threat of sanctions were real, they would be effective.

"I got to admit you can't prove it," he said. "I mean, what are you going to do, go interview officials in a foreign country and have them say, 'Well, we did this because of the threat of sanctions'? Of course not."

Still, Miller was effective at leveraging his most potent weapon: shame. Nationalism was a tricky thing, particularly at a time of limp American prestige due to perceived recklessness in Iraq. But Miller knew his subject was transcendent. In 2004, the president of Guyana flew to Washington to meet him and beg his country up from its Tier Three ranking. The previous year the Kazakh foreign minister responded to his country's demotion by offering a half-hour televised speech against trafficking.

After Miller met Lord and Katya, he began insisting that foreign officials visit trafficking shelters and talk with those who had endured slavery. Few did, and many offered bald denials that slavery even existed. One year, seventeen enslaved maids jumped out of skyscrapers in Singapore. Miller confronted national officials with the fact.

"Their explanation to me was that they had trouble hanging out the wash," he said. "That was their explanation."

Miller really didn't need to be confirmed. His initial appointment in 2002 was a low-rent affair, which was fine by him. He hated receptions and ceremonies, particularly when they honored him. But in the summer of 2004, Congressmen Frank Wolf and Chris Smith tailor-made an ambassadorship for him. Shortly after Bush signed the legislation which elevated his rank, the Senate confirmed Miller without a hearing.

As an ambassador, Miller gained leverage both inside the government and in bilateral negotiations. With the presidential coin spent on an ignored UN General Assembly speech, and the sanctions weapon a dud, Miller was left with two tools to combat slavery: diplomatic pressure and grants to abolitionist groups. Both would require a lot of behind-the-scenes effort, and every bit of clout helped.

Even as he took the oath of office on September 7 under the exquisite chandeliers of the State Department's Benjamin Franklin Room, Miller used that added clout to make clear his belief that the issue of slavery was worth occasionally soiling the pristine, dispassionate diplomacy of his colleagues at the State Department. He cited Wilberforce as an example of an abolitionist who was labeled a moralist who sought to "impose British values on the world," but who ultimately changed that world for the better. He praised, but also gently chastened, those in attendance, including Colin Powell, to "get our language straight" and call a slave a slave.

Staffers described an obsession that overtook John Miller after he met Katya and Lord. Some worried for his health, and for their own, when he began pulling eighteen-hour days, often through the weekends. He became frustrated trying to count slaves, and poured his energy into freeing them instead. At times, the obsession bordered on mania. Though he always apologized for doing so, he would call and visit staffers at their homes late at night. Often, he called to invite criticism of an idea that had hatched in his fertile mind.

"Here's an idea," Miller would say. "Now tell me the reasons I'm wrong. Talk me out of it!"

In direct overseas negotiations, Miller was more forceful, and less open to dissent. If an American Embassy staff resisted his efforts to visit with survivors, he would ignore their objections and visit shelters on his own. At those shelters, he would gather stories with which to confront foreign officials. Occasionally, the confrontations got ugly.

In 2005, Miller won a symbolic victory when he convinced Condoleezza Rice to drop Saudi Arabia to Tier Three. The Saudis abolished legal slavery in 1962. But international organizations reported that the malfeasant rulers and other elites countenanced domestic slavery, and often held slaves themselves. Surprising no one, President Bush waived sanctions against the kingdom. With Iraq disintegrating, the United

States was increasingly reliant on its authoritarian partners in the region. None was bigger than Saudi Arabia, against whom Miller later acknowledged that the sanctions threat was always "purely theoretical."

Four months after the president's waiver, Miller met a twenty-five-year-old woman named Nour Miyati at a Starbucks in Riyadh. Modestly attired in a black *hijab*, Miyati quietly recited her story of slavery and survival. Miller had heard several such firsthand accounts in Saudi Arabia, but Nour's stood out. Immediately, his attention fell from her sad eyes to her hands. They were mangled, stunted and twisted, a result of months of horrendous torture.

She had worked as a maid for four years in order to earn enough money to support her nine-year-old daughter in Indonesia. Then, when she switched employers, her new bosses forced her to work up to eighteen hours a day for no pay. They beat her regularly, and confined her to a bathroom for one month, where they tied her hands and feet until gangrene set in. In an attempt to "repair" their "commodity," her masters wheeled her into Riyadh Medical Complex, where doctors removed several of her fingers and toes. The doctors filed a report on her behalf, and a Saudi court responded by sentencing Nour to seventy-nine lashes for "false accusations."

Miller decided to use Nour's case to bring shame on the House of Saud. On January 22, 2006, the last day of his visit, he described Nour's hands to Crown Prince Sultan.

"This is unacceptable," Miller said.

The Saudi heir apparent, who had walked hand-in-hand with Bush and Cheney, was vexed. He claimed to know nothing about the matter, but said he would look into it. Miller explained that President Bush cared deeply about the subject, and that the Saudis were under review. In short order, Nour's sentence was overturned.

Ultimately, Miller's bullheaded approach resulted in more than a hundred new antitrafficking laws and over 10,000 trafficking convictions worldwide. But Miller knew the reports, speeches, diplomatic pressure—even the laws and convictions—were only means to an end.

"All of these other things are tools," he said. "You've got to want to do this because you've got to free the slaves."

The most direct agents of that freedom were sometimes the police, but more often they were completely separate from government. In the nineteenth century, the British used the Royal Navy to combat the slave trade. Miller's troops were decidedly less imposing. They were the non-governmental organizations, often low profile, frequently locally based, that worked to free and rehabilitate slaves in over a hundred countries.

Most of the $375 million that the United States allocated for antitrafficking went via grants to such organizations. Miller viewed them as the true heroes, and did battle with the State Department to get them money faster, as, for a slave, delay was deadly. "The delays in getting the grants out of the door are just atrocious," he said. "We've got so many checks and balances that have become meaningless. People signing things that don't do anything."

Miller had great respect for people of faith (he considered himself one, up to a point), and under his watch the proportion of those groups receiving G-TIP funding that were faith-based increased from less than one in ten in 2002 to around one in three by 2006. He felt that, prior to his arrival, faith-based groups had been unfairly discriminated against. Thus he rewarded evangelical groups that did solid work, like the International Justice Mission. IJM, which freed girls from sex slavery in Cambodia, received millions.

Yet the man did not suffer fools: faith was fine, but for a group to wield influence with Miller, it needed to demonstrate reason as well. Though they regularly lobbied him, he did not buy the bill of goods that John Eibner and Christian Solidarity International tried to sell him on Sudan. He learned quickly the difference between a speculative talking point provided by the Horowitz coalition and a fact that his diligent staff could demonstrate.

"He's pretty good at telling the difference between bullshit and data," said Kevin Bales, a pioneer in contemporary slavery research whose umbrella organization, Free the Slaves, distributes G-TIP funds to some of the most effective and least heralded grassroots groups. Miller respected Bales greatly but openly challenged his assertions about the total numbers of slaves, not because he disbelieved them, but because he wanted proof.

The organizations that Miller funded through Bales not only freed slaves but also rehabilitated them through retraining and income generation programs. It was a commonsense approach that Miller grew to appreciate over the course of his tenure. Miller had pressed the first President Bush to tackle global poverty, and began work for the second President Bush believing that tackling poverty was essential to abolishing slavery. But many in the Horowitz coalition resisted any focus outside law enforcement.

"You know, if we had an easy, consensus solution as to how to get a job for women in poverty—hey, sure, go for it," said Michael Horowitz. "You know, maybe, it's Jesus' second coming. Maybe it's Paul Krugman redistributing my income to Sri Lanka. But nothing I've seen really works."

Miller himself often cited instances where trafficking victims were not the poorest of the poor and argued that his office "can't just be a general poverty fund." But he came to view organizations that focused on prevention and rehabilitation, as well as emancipation, as the vanguard. Several international studies showed that increasing prosecutions did little to affect the aggregate levels of trafficking, while poverty alleviation tended to keep the vulnerable from becoming victims. Miller began pursuing a much more integrated strategy with the U.S. Agency for International Development and the World Bank.

He was regularly frustrated by the State Department or by foreign governments, but he was also excited at the progress he saw in second and third trips to countries. Embassy staffers knew what "trafficking" meant. An increasing number of foreign ambassadors felt the heat, and did preventive diplomacy, if not preventive law enforcement. Critically, Miller met more slaves like Lord and Katya who had found freedom and were rebuilding their lives.

Still, he knew that for every free slave, there were ten, twenty, a hundred who suffered in the shadows. It was knowledge that came to dominate his life.

Among those at his 2004 swearing-in was his son Rip, who had become a standout high school football player in Seattle. At five foot nine and 162 pounds, Miller's son was small for a defensive back, but his coach reported that he "hit like a ton of bricks." Miller adored the boy. After the ceremony, Rip asked if he could travel with his father. The request reminded Miller that his obsession with the slaves had caused a blackout in his family life.

June, his wife, needed no such reminder. Then formally separated from her husband, she did not attend the ceremony.

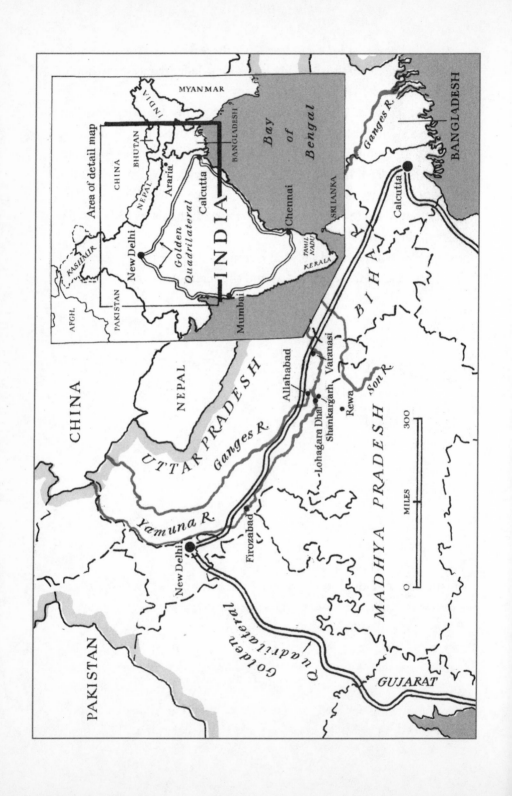

8

Children of Vishnu

At first glance, Gonoo looked like Frederick Douglass, in a particular 1866 photograph.

That portrait of Douglass was not his most distinguished, but it hangs on my office wall in Manhattan. It contrasted with the earliest Daguerreotype of the great abolitionist, taken some twenty years earlier, that showed a wan and angry young man. At the time of that first sitting, Douglass had escaped twenty-one years of brutal bondage. But in the eyes of the law, he was still the property of his master. After that first picture was taken, British abolitionists paid $710.96 to secure his emancipation. Douglass appreciated the act, but thought it unnecessary: he seized his freedom the moment he decided not to be a slave.

The 1866 photograph captured a fifty-year-old Douglass, and a ninety-year-old America, in a moment of transition. It was his first photograph after the Civil War, at the outset of Reconstruction. Douglass was in a time of professional triumph and personal loss. In 1860, his adored daughter died just shy of her eleventh birthday, and Douglass blamed himself for not being there to keep her alive. His hair was still long, but now streaked with gray. His face was no less resolute, but somehow the features were softer. He had the same stern brow, but he was fuller-bodied. Though well short of the bushy white beard of his more famous portraits, he was experimenting with a goatee.

I liked the picture because it showed that this icon was a man, flawed and, at times, unsure of himself. Once, in its first century, a high-minded nation was also insecure as it struggled to correct its greatest birth defect and fulfill its greatest promise—a vow of freedom for all. One hundred and forty years later, India, like Reconstruction-era America, was poised for greatness but cursed by pervasive, if illegal, slavery.

I stumbled on Gonoo Lal Kol one cold evening in early December 2005, in Lohagara Dhal, an unmapped hamlet in a forgotten, silt-covered corner of Uttar Pradesh, a North Indian state that contains 8 percent of the world's poor.* The forty-six-year-old was at once alien and, thanks to that resemblance to Douglass, familiar. He was a member of the Kol, a tribe that one administrator in the British Raj described as "the oldest and most characteristic race of the land." He had dark skin, a full goatee, a stern brow, and long, wild gray hair.

Gonoo lumbered along with two dozen other weary laborers, their clothes tattered and filthy. Behind them lay a stark gash in the earth, a white wound in otherwise flat and dark ground. In that pit, Gonoo's master forced him to work with his family for fourteen hours per day. During the summer the heat was unbearable. "If a man sits on a stone," Gonoo said, "it's as if he's sitting on a fire."

His family harvested the local cash crops, gravel and sand, by smashing rock and hauling the backbreaking loads to a truck. In that hole, like the quarry slave of William Cullen Bryant's *Thanatopsis*, Gonoo was "scourged to his dungeon."

Periodically, slaves packed a primitive blasting agent into the rock face, lit a fuse, and ran. Often, children set the explosives, as they could crawl into tighter spaces. Gonoo saw dozens of accidents when falling

---

*At their request, I have changed the first names of Gonoo and his eldest son. Most of the people in his village share his last name, so it remains unaltered here.

rocks crushed slaves. Some died instantly; others were mangled for life. In 2003, a young boy blew off his arm. The slavemaster, a tall, stout, surly contractor named Ramesh Garg, forced the child to return to work before his wounds fully healed.

Gonoo's tools were simple. They were a rough-hewn hammer and an iron pike. His hands felt like plastic and were covered in callus upon callus. Riddled with arthritis, they had lost their function beyond quarry use. "I can't catch chapattis anymore," he said. "I can't tell when bread is hot in my hands." His right purlicue was torn; his left thumb was smashed. His fingertips were worn away. The man had no fingerprints.

Garg's tools were not so simple. They were the men, women, and children who worked for him. Their only use was to turn rock into silica sand, for colored glass, or gravel, for roads or ballast. Any human concerns beyond that were a bother. Garg was one of the wealthiest men in Shankargarh, the nearest mid-sized town, founded under the Raj but now run by nearly 600 quarry contractors. He made his money by administering terror and savagery to entire families whom he forced to work for no pay beyond alcohol, grain, and bare subsistence expenses. When necessary, he bought the slaves essential medicine; sometimes he would pay for a modest wedding or a funeral.

In other words, Garg funded the upkeep, stupefaction, and the odd ceremonial expense of his human jackhammers, and nothing more. Kevin Bales has estimated that a slave in the American South had to work twenty years to recoup his or her purchase price. Gonoo and the other slaves yielded net gains for Garg in less than two years. Only through slave labor could one turn a profit on handmade sand, Bales observed after he visited Shankargarh in 1999.

Every single man, woman, and child in Lohagara Dhal was a slave. But in theory, Garg neither bought nor owned them. In theory, the slaves were working off debts to Garg. For many, the debts had started under $10. But interest accrued at over 100 percent annually here. One hundred of the 150 families in the village had debts that spanned at least two generations. The debts had no legal standing. They were a fiction that Garg carefully constructed and maintained.

The seed of Gonoo's slavery was a loan of 62 cents. In 1958, his grandfather had borrowed that amount from the owner of a farm where he worked, to pay the meager bride-price of Gonoo's mother. Three generations and three slavemasters later, Gonoo's family was still in bondage.

Gonoo now estimated that he owed Garg around $500. But, like all except twenty-five villagers, he was illiterate and innumerate, and Garg kept the books. Once, when he challenged his fictional debt, Garg's men beat him until his eyelids swelled shut. According to the slaves, the contractor had killed over a dozen others after they resisted their role as cheap and expendable instruments.

Gonoo's life now was contained within a 300-yard radius of the quarry. The stagnant brown pool in the excavation was Gonoo's primary water source, and that of the other slaves. Gonoo's home was a twelve-by-five-foot *jhopari* hut that encapsulated his epigeal existence: its grass thatch was four feet high, though Gonoo himself stood about six feet. Even his children crouched to enter. A cooking fire had singed the mortarless, outer wall; inside, on the dirt floor, all seven members of the family slept on hay and tattered blankets. When Gonoo told me that he never slept with his head toward the quarry, I imagined it was because of the dust. In fact, it was because the quarry lay to the north— the direction the Kol position their dead.

That *jhopari* contained all of his possessions. In one corner were the quarrying implements—long simple crowbars, and a couple of wood-handle pickaxes, all fashioned by hand. Immediately next to these was a small, ashy firepit with a blackened kettle on top. There were six dented pans, two long metal spoons, a makeshift lamp made out of a candle and a bottle of kerosene, a white plastic bucket, five or six saris hanging from the ceiling, a small pile of threadbare raiment in one corner, and a comb. That was it. No chairs, no furniture except a handmade *khatiya* cot out front.

An observer once described Frederick Douglass's voice as "highly melodious and rich, and his enunciation quite elegant." Gonoo's high-pitched voice, strained by asthma, was at the mercy of a chronic cough because the omnipresent silica dust inflamed his airways. Tobacco, which he mixed with a white limestone powder, garbled his words. His smile appeared to be a grimace, as over the decades betel nut had turned his few remaining teeth dark brown.

Upon first meeting me, he did not attempt to touch my feet. Many other *dalit*, or "crushed" caste members had done so, and I was always left standing dumbly. That convention aside, Gonoo was wholly deferential, and it took weeks before he truly opened up.

"What is a slave?" I asked him.

"A *ghulam* is me," he said, using the Hindi word. "When you take a debt, you become a slave."

In the eyes of the law, he was free long ago. In his own eyes, he would be a slave forever. I pressed him to think what he would do if he ever escaped. He thought for a while. "I would try to survive," he said. "I would try to eat and feed my family."

He had once thought about going to Allahabad, the nearest big city, to pull a rickshaw. "But I could not do any other work than quarry work. Ramesh would not allow it," he said. "I have no hope of paying the debt off in my life. It will be the same for my children."

Over my two months with him, something remarkable happened: Gonoo stumbled into freedom. But freedom, to this slave who had accepted his fate, would pose an even greater burden than bondage itself.

Gonoo's India, like Frederick Douglass's America, is in a state of suspended emancipation. While government estimates differ wildly—from zero to millions—most observers put the number of Indian slaves at between 10 and 20 million. Take the smallest estimate of slaves in South Asia—principally in Nepal, India, Pakistan, and Bangladesh—and it blows away estimates for the rest of the world combined. There are so many slaves, and so few who give a damn about them.

India has become an avatar of the free market, a development success story that blinds the world, and many Indians, to the bondage that lives close beneath the surface. In 1991, the government of India opened up its country for business by lowering tariffs, privatizing state-run industries, slashing subsidies, and promoting competition. For a country whose most successful states were headed by Marxist leaders, it was a bold move, but a sensible one given the collapse of its longtime ally, the Soviet Union. The gamble paid off. India is second only to China as the world's fastest-growing major economy.

Indian expats are justly proud of their country. My *desi* friends were not thrilled when I reported the mass bondage in their homeland. Many had heard about Indians trafficked to the Middle East for forced domestic service or indentured construction work. But few knew of the remaining 90 percent of Indian slaves who never cross the country's borders.

The scale of bondage in India overwhelmed me. I spoke with children who had been slaves in tea stalls and sari factories around Delhi, the nation's capital, where at least half a million children were in bondage. Hundreds of thousands are forced to weave carpets around Varanasi, harvest fish in the Bay of Bengal, or roll *bidi* cigarettes in Gujarat.

I visited Firozabad, the soot-choked glass capital of India. There, until 1993, *dalit* kids from nearby *jhuggi* slums were bought and sold in an outdoor "children's bazaar." The factories where the buyers put the children to work looked like something from the dawn of the Industrial Revolution. The 3,000-degree heat of the coal-fueled furnaces crimpled the cold winter air as boys spun long thin metal polls tipped with molten orange glass. Others pounded the glass into bangles for sale in stores like the chic emporium next to my Brooklyn apartment. Nearby, arsenic trioxide powder—a substance banned in Europe but handled by children here—spilled out of an unsecured warehouse. Were the boys enslaved? I could not tell in guarded interviews abbreviated by the watchful eyes of the factory owners; earlier, Anti-Slavery International had well documented their bondage.

Most slaves do not make products for export. Thousands of children work for no pay under threat of violence in begging stables around Mumbai or Diwali fireworks factories in Tamil Nadu. Across the country, perhaps 8 million toil in the oldest form of bondage, agricultural slavery. Some farmers enslave girls in cotton fields because, lore had it, the crops would not replenish if men reaped the harvest. In 2001, investigators found farm slaves literally in chains.

In the holy city of Varanasi, I found brothels where pimps paid prostitutes only with food, confined them to four-by-six-foot cells, and forced them into unprotected sex with hundreds of men. In southern India, tens of thousands of girls are *devadasi*—ritual sex slaves.

Denial of bondage has long been the hallmark of India's unenlightened rulers. In 1833, the British banned slavery throughout their empire, but left it alone in India. A decade later, the British did declare that Indian slaves had no legal standing as such, and were free to leave their masters if they wished. The masters had other ideas. Soon, officers of the Raj began referring to "voluntary" or "benign" slavery. In 1926, the British formally declared that slavery no longer existed in India. Today, there are no slaves, only "bonded laborers," "exploited workers," or simply "backward poor people." And no one denies that there are a lot of poor people. Six hundred million live on less than two dollars per day; 260 million survive on less than a dollar.

Many national officials correctly argue that, while India has more children working—100 million—than any other country, the great majority of those children earn money. Often the alternative to work is starvation. But those same officials conveniently overlook that while not every child laborer is a slave, millions of slaves are child laborers. Denial of slavery is standard operating procedure here. Despite the efforts of a small team of lawyers who were petitioning on my behalf, officials from the Labor Ministry in Delhi refused to speak with me when they learned of my subject.

One day, I went undercover to interview four slaveholding loom owners near Varanasi. Under the guise of carpet buyer, I toured a windowless underground factory with row upon row of unpaid Bihari children. They worked up to fifteen hours a day at the looms, seven days a week. Many had faded eyesight and respiratory illnesses. Two weeks later, I interviewed three human traffickers in Bihar, and met two dozen freed slaves, as well as families whose children were still in bondage somewhere in India's carpet belt. In some cases, the cramped workspaces had deformed their young bones. One now walked only with the aid of a stick.

After those investigations, I met Jay Kumar, the Social Secretary of Araria, one of the poorest districts in Bihar, the poorest state in India. A portly man, with four rings, a thick black mustache, slicked-back hair, and a tinselly, turquoise, crocheted sweater vest, Kumar spoke to me from his one-room office building. He was responsible for responding to charges of child labor here. And his response was adamant: I had not seen what I had seen.

"For God's sake, don't go talking about brutal slavery here," Kumar said. "We have no steel pens: everyone is free. While it is not the highest virtues that govern the universe, it is not possible that slavery exists in this district."

It was the starkest denial of slavery that I had heard since I spoke with Mauritanian officials three years earlier about the persistence of chattel slavery within their borders. Sensing my confusion, Kumar explained the situation. "You see, poor people are not rational," he said. "So I compare them to monkeys."

He proceeded to tell a story. On a hot day, a mother monkey dropped her baby to the scalding earth in order to climb a tree and keep from burning her own feet. This, he said, is why parents sold their children.

Gonoo has taken three trains in his lifetime. The first brought him to the quarry as a toddler, and the second brought him back to his birthplace as a young man. Each of those trains was supposed to carry him to freedom. The third train brought him back to bondage.

He was born in the neighboring state of Madhya Pradesh in 1959, a year after his grandfather, after borrowing 62 cents, became a slave to a Brahmin farmer. The minuscule debt that bonded his family was not unusual. Two decades later, a survey of Madhya Pradesh found that 80 percent of the state's half million enslaved farm workers had sold their freedom for less than $11. Ninety percent of them were *dalit*, or what used to be called "untouchable." In theory, Gonoo and his tribe, the Kol, lived outside the caste system. The Kol are one of many tribal groups among the 67 million indigenous Indians, the *adivasis*, whose African ancestors probably emigrated 70,000 years ago. Millennia later, their Aryan-origin countrymen came from Central Asia, introduced Hinduism, and, with it, the caste system.

In their folklore, the Kol were not always oppressed. One day, a Kol on horseback came upon a Brahmin pushing a plow in a field. Having never seen the process before, the Kol horseman, fascinated, asked if he could have a go. He did, the Brahmin jumped on his horse and rode off—and the Kol have plowed the fields of the Brahmins ever since. Today, Indians lump the Kol with the 250 million *dalit*. Their lot is that of the shit shoveler. Their slavery is karmic destiny. Sadly, India remains firmly in the grip of what Frederick Douglass called "the matchless meanness of caste."

In 1962, at age three, Gonoo rode his first train. At the time, he did not know why his family was oppressed. He just knew that, after the farmer nearly beat him to death, his father took his family on a ticketless ride several miles on top of a train to Shankargarh. There, he had heard he could earn enough to feed his wife and child by working in a quarry. For that fleeting moment, Gonoo's family was free.

When Gonoo was six, he started working alongside both of his parents in the quarry of Devnarayan Garg. They had no debt at that point: poverty rather than violence compelled them to work. At least that was Gonoo's version of events. Village elders contradicted him. They told me that Garg held Gonoo's family as slaves from the moment they first arrived in the quarry. The elders' version is more likely. The Kol from Gonoo's area had previously survived by beekeeping and subsistence agriculture. Around the time India won its independence in 1947, upper castes grabbed land amidst the chaotic mass migration of the partition with Pakistan. The Kol, who never had titles to the land, fell into debt bondage. In some cases, the slavery was even older, spanning two centuries across eight generations of a single family.

In Gonoo's version, his family fell back into bondage in 1969. That year, his mother became ill. He sensed that the quarry work had led to her strange and sudden ailment, which involved spasmodic, bloody coughing spells. The other laborers, most of whom had some form of the disease, called it "*Shankargarh-wali* TB," the tuberculosis of Shankargarh. Researchers would later identify it as pneumonoultramicroscopicsilicovolcanokoniosis, better known by its more manageable abbreviation: silicosis. The disease turned workers already withered by poverty and malnutrition into walking skeletons. The sand that made Garg rich slowly tore apart his slaves' lungs and swelled their blood vessels. Often, silicosis led to tuberculosis or cancer. The disease was incurable. It is a miserable way to die.

Gonoo's father faced a choice: He could watch his wife slowly expire. Or he could sell his family's freedom to Garg in order to receive a loan for the treatments that might save her. He chose the latter. That summer of 1969 was brutally hot; concerned for his mother, ten-year-old Gonoo chafed under Garg's yoke. Although she went undiagnosed, his mother probably developed full-blown tuberculosis. Her treatment, which may have amounted to nothing more than cough suppressant, did not save her. Gonoo guessed his mother was around forty when she died. Devastated by her death, and terrified of a future of slavery, he decided to run away.

In 1972, at age twelve, Gonoo caught his second train. He slipped away one morning, leaving his father and younger sisters behind, and ran to the neighboring village of Line Par. There he jumped on top of a freight car headed back to Madhya Pradesh, where he still had relatives. He found work as a day laborer carrying loads for the ACC Cement Company.

It was hard work, and paid precious little—but he was free, and he felt free. He remembered stripping down after work and swimming with another boy from the factory in the Son River, the largest of the Ganges tributaries. In 1973, he saw a movie for the first and last time—a Sujit Kumar Bollywood film.

"That was the best moment in my life," Gonoo said.

To drive to Gonoo's quarry from India's capital is to see the nation's rising glory. But slavery is never far below the surface.

Delhi, a grimy megacity, manages to broadcast crisp optimism reminiscent of Eisenhower-era America. A billboard advertising mortgages features a smiling couple and reads DELIGHT HER WITH A NEW HOME! A sign on the mudflaps of a truck reads MY INDIA IS GREAT! Political posters for the Hindu nationalist Bharatiya Janata Party (BJP) hail INDIA SHINING!

Much is endearingly idiosyncratic. Animals still hold sway. The job of corralling the 40,000 stray cows falls to police, but devout Hindus often impede their efforts. In some Indian states, cattle slaughter is still a crime. An overturned bullock cart or an impromptu herd of humpback oxen will snarl a mechanized stampede of rattling, three-wheeled, four-stroke *tempo* auto-rickshaws at incongruous angles.

Five thousand members of another holy species, monkeys, bound wild through the streets of Delhi. The metro recently trained a langur to stop other monkeys from menacing passengers. Car exhaust competes with wafting chapatti oil and incense from tea stands and temples. On one street, a small trash fire keeps men warm. Next door, a halal meat store sells goat meat across from a shop selling figurines of the Virgin Mary next to a stand selling statuettes of the Hindu god Ram.

Much is overwhelming—particularly India's swelling sea of humanity. Whereas Americans often throw around "hundreds" or "thousands" to describe populations; Indians, who reproduce at a rate of thirty per minute, estimate using *lakh* (100,000) or *crore* (10 million). A population clock in the center of Delhi counts determinedly to a point in the next decade when India, already more than 1 billion strong, will surpass China as the world's most populous nation.

Much is painful. Barely staying afloat in the sea of humanity, a polio-afflicted boy rolls along in a hand-peddled wheelchair. A swaddled beggar, her hands blackened and ravaged by leprosy, taps on car windows with a solitary fingernail. The contrasts become even starker along the northern section of India's new multibillion-dollar superhighway. The largest infrastructure undertaking in some five centuries, it runs from Delhi in the north to Calcutta in the east, Chennai in the south, and Mumbai in the west. Organizers dubbed the fifteen-year project the "Golden Quadrilateral." The moniker, like the local Ambassador cars, is clunky and bombastic. Driving east along the newly blacktopped four-lane highway, the eucalyptus-enclosed surroundings are a pleasant blur. Stretches could be midwestern America, save for the saffron-robed holy men sitting on a median, begging for alms.

Few Indians drive. In America, over 75 percent of households below the poverty line have a car. In India, less than 1 percent of the entire population owns one. But for the first time, more people travel by automobile than train, often quadrupling a vehicle's listed capacity.

The Golden Quadrilateral, viewed alone, is a stark metaphor for India's growth. And India's growth, viewed alone, is one of the great human achievements in modern history. Since the 1991 reforms, GDP per head has increased annually by more than 6 percent. During the same period, the number of heads grew by the equivalent of the entire U.S. population. Today, the country is still decades from becoming a middle-class society by Western standards. But, in parts, India is becoming fat and happy. Obesity rates are up. Porsche and Audi have set up shop in Delhi. Three hundred and fifty million people have risen above poverty and form, by Indian standards, a free and vibrant middle class. Average life expectancy was fifty-four in 1979; today, it is sixty-five. Even Rolls-Royce and Lamborghini sell cars in the capital. Eighty-three thousand Indians are millionaires, nearly 40 percent of whom joined the club since 2003. Fifteen are billionaires.

But a prosperous Indian is still an exceptional Indian. If desperation were recognizable at 70 miles per hour, the Quadrilateral would seem less golden as it stretches through the heart of Hinduism in Uttar Pradesh. After a while, the children pushing cattle along the road blend in with the pastoral surroundings. So do their cousins, who pull fish out of streams or haul hay. A few children squat in outdoor classrooms: most Indian schools have only one room or no building at all. India boasts the world's largest program to eliminate child labor. Yet the constitutional guarantee of a free education before age fourteen remains, like the abolition of caste, an unfulfilled agenda.

Like much of the developing world, India's cities are growing, but two thirds of the population still works the land. Most barely scrape by. Some sell their kidneys. Every year, thousands of farmers drink pesticide or shoot themselves rather than face a lifetime of bondage. A closer look at the placid scenery reveals ugly details. The brilliant yellow mustard fields are easy on the eyes; the possible slavery of the plowmen is harsh on the conscience. Deep green rice paddies stretching into the haze are a peaceable setting; but the lives of the harvesters are often bound by violence. The pyramidal smokestacks visible above a line of mango trees at first look like signs of industrial progress. Yet many belch the smoke of brick kilns that employ up to 100,000 slaves nationwide.

The bumpy two-lane highway to Gonoo's village peels off the Golden Quadrilateral in Allahabad, where the Ganges meets the Yamuna. Now parts of the countryside that were blurs appear in more distinct relief. Two thirds of all Indians still live in villages, and villagers along the road appear stunned by the speed of modern cars. A sign, meant to slow speeders, reads BEETHER LATE THRAN NEEVER in block letters. Men in their underwear look askance at passing travelers as they clean themselves with cupfuls of water from roadside pools.

After thirty miles, the air becomes particulate. Quarries and rusted silica washing plants flank the road. From space, the whole area shimmers from the silica flakes. A mile northeast of Shankargarh, a flashy, ultra-modern Reliance gas station seems radically out of place. Attendants—whose service is as snappy as their uniforms—pump gas in pristine bays designed by American consultants. A satellite dish and industrial floodlights sit atop the station. Next door, in front of a grass and mud hut, a barefoot woman in a sari pumps water using one of the area's few operating bore holes. Bulky, spiky-haired wild boars root nearby.

Finally, beyond a few, squirrelly acacia trees, the road reaches Lohagara Dhal. Blink and you'll miss it. On the left side of the road is Gonoo's quarry, and what the locals call "Ramesh *basdee*"—Ramesh barracks—a series of rock *jhoparis*. The huts are home to ten families, all slaves of Ramesh Garg. In front of one, a woman kneels and spreads glistening cow dung with her hands in order to purify the ground.

Across the road lies Gonoo's *jhopari*. Gonoo thought the highway that ran fifty feet from his front door was modern, but he had nothing to compare it to. He had never seen the Golden Quadrilateral. In a sense, though, a part of him was in that exquisite national road. The gravel produced through Gonoo's slave labor was the subgrade. Anywhere in India, slavery is never far below the surface.

A third and final train would soon take him from a life of his choosing to a world of brutality, but Gonoo enjoyed his two years of freedom in the early 1970s. While it was hardly a time of carefree pleasures for the fifteen-year-old, he had earned a little money and, for once, each day felt like his own. The work at the cement plant was backbreaking, but he had a day off every couple of weeks, and would use it to great effect, playing pickup cricket games with the other boys at the factory or just doing nothing.

Shortly after Gonoo returned to Madhya Pradesh, his grandfather and uncle arranged for him to marry a local girl. There were no flowers, nothing fancy, but several of his surviving relatives, and a few members of his wife's family, attended. The twelve-year-old girl who was to be his bride emerged, her head covered in a sari. Gonoo gulped. "This is my partner from here on," he said to himself.

At the end of the ceremony, he removed the sari from her head. She put it back. He removed it again, and they repeated the ritual seven times until, finally, she kept the sari on her head where, according to tradition, it would stay until her husband's death. In the flickering firelight, Gonoo never got a good look at her face. It was not until the sunrise the next morning that he could see his wife. "She is beautiful," he thought.

In the spring of 1975, ACC Cement Company was restructuring, and Gonoo lost his job. Adding to his hardship, a relative told him that his father had died, leaving Gonoo the sole caretaker for his three younger sisters and his cousin, all of whom still worked for Devnarayan Garg. Gonoo's father also bequeathed him his debt. With his sisters in bondage, Gonoo had no choice. He and his young bride climbed on top of the third and final train of his life to return to the quarry.

A year after Gonoo fell back into slavery, the government of India declared him free. But the declared abolition was pure politics. Prime Minister Indira Gandhi had campaigned under the slogan "*Garibi Hatoo*—Remove Poverty." At first, she took her election as a mandate to remove the poor themselves. Instead of creating wealth by initiating badly needed market reforms, she ordered slums demolished and forced mass sterilization of the *dalit*.

On June 26, 1975, an Allahabad High Court ruled that Gandhi's election was invalid. Massive street protests erupted, with organizers calling for her ouster. She declared a state of emergency, imprisoned political opponents, and suppressed the media and student movements. Her move sparked fears that the world's largest democracy was sliding toward totalitarianism. On October 25, 1976, to burnish her image, Gandhi's government passed the Bonded Labour Abolition Act.

The new law canceled Gonoo's debt, and provided for a three-year jail sentence for Devnarayan Garg and other slavemasters, as well as at least $400 in restitution to Gonoo—60 cents for every day of his enslavement. Not surprisingly, Garg did not volunteer to do penance, and with no provision for enforcement of the law at the local level, he continued to force his laborers to work for no pay.

Gonoo, who three decades later was only dimly aware of Gandhi's declared jubilee, slid deeper into debt. Garg ceased paying even a fraction of the 25 cents that, in theory, was Gonoo's daily wage. He provided basic foodstuffs, but not on a reliable schedule. "It happened sometimes that we would go for two days without food," Gonoo said. Garg's pay to the boy also included a bottle of the local hooch if he worked all night. During festivals, the master would render himself magnanimous by rendering his slaves drunk.

It was an old trick. Frederick Douglass's master also "paid" his slaves in alcohol. The reason, Douglass said, was to subdue them. "We were induced to drink, I among the rest, and when the holidays were over, we all staggered up from our filth and wallowing, took a long breath, and went away to our various fields of work; feeling, upon the whole, rather glad to go from that which our masters artfully deceived us into the belief was freedom, back again into the arms of slavery."

Alcohol was one more tool, along with violence and deception, that Garg used to prevent the slaves from organizing. "When a slave is drunk, the slaveholder has no fear that he will plan an insurrection; no fear that he will escape to the north," Douglass wrote. "It is the sober slave who is dangerous, and needs the vigilance of his master, to keep him a slave."

In his moments of lucidity, Gonoo realized that, at age eighteen, he would be a slave his whole life. He described a kind of peace that came over him. It was not a life of his choosing but, with the permission of his master and within the bounds of his servitude, he at least felt sheltered from starvation. The abdication of day-to-day decisions meant a simple existence. It was not pleasant, but it was, in a way, comforting.

The man charged with freeing Shankargarh's slaves was Allahabad's district magistrate, Amrit Abhijat, the area's highest civil administrator. One evening I set out to tell him about Gonoo.

I hired a bicycle rickshaw across the Yamuna River to the holy city. Traveling thus by night put me fairly close to the bottom of the mobile pecking order, but offered a close look at Allahabad, a heaving city of 2 million where the habits of rural India often ran roughshod over British Raj–era infrastructure. From a car, all looked like chaos, and driving was an act of faith. But from a rickshaw or a motorcycle, the constant negotiations between man, animal and machine had a strange, regular order. Smallness begat understanding. There were few streetlights, but the low-wattage headlamps of thundering trucks partly illuminated the road. The trucks always blasted their horns as they passed. Horns were as essential to automobiles here as brakes in America or bass tubes in Haiti.

A herd of water buffaloes rumbled on either side of the rickshaw, their bodies sweaty and enormous, their faces passive despite the exertion. A sign read TESTY BITE RESTAURANT: AN UNIQUE RESTAURANT. A few doors down, a gun store's wordless advertisement was less opaque: it featured a simple, handpainted, double-barrel shotgun, with a red arrow below pointing past a long, tin-roofed brick structure to a "gun house."

My driver skirted a slow-marching, roped-off wedding procession, led by a gaudy silver *diwana* machine, which blasted ear-splitting *bhangra* from twelve decorated megaphones. Orderly dancing, single-shot fireworks, strings of red lights and reverently hoisted candelabras did not diminish the sense that this was a somber affair, much more funerary than connubial.

Pilgrims had swollen the city's population to twice its normal size because of the annual *Magh Mela*, a *Hajj*-like event which takes place every winter at the confluence of the Ganges and the Yamuna. Many slept on cardboard, sprawled in front of the train station. Next to the entrance, a giant blue-and-white sign read URINAL in Sanskrit and English. Several men urinated below the sign itself, apparently unaware that it directed them to interior facilities.

Turning off the road into the District Collectorate felt like traveling back sixty years. The compound had the wood-paneled grandeur of Raj-era bureaucracy. The waiting hall in front of Abhijat's office featured a list of his predecessors that predated the Raj. Under the British, the administrators collected taxes that stripped the poor of what little land they had, and drove many into debt bondage. Under the Bonded Labour Act, the administrators now had to free these people.

I wandered over to a portrait of Mahatma Gandhi on an adjacent wall. In 1931, he had plotted the freedom struggle here in Allahabad, the birthplace of Jawaharlal Nehru, Gandhi's comrade and India's first prime minister.

"Gandhiji was a liar," said a voice from behind me.

Abhijat was a forthright fellow and, I would soon discover, he had a sharp wit. The thirty-eight-year-old also had a hard North Indian accent which transformed "lawyer" into "liar." "And so you see law is very important to our freedoms," he finished.

Abhijat's job, in part, was to create programs to meet national goals of poverty reduction. He had a zealous and, to put it mildly, unorthodox reputation in that regard. Abhijat often pointed out that his district, with over 6 million people packed into less than 3,000 square miles, was the most densely populated place in India. To fix that, he recently reinitiated Indira Gandhi's mass sterilization program among the poor, giving local schoolteachers until the end of March 2006 to meet "sterilization targets."

Less ghoulishly, Abhijat claimed to understand well his bonded labor mandate. Indira Gandhi's disastrous reign left 75 percent of agricultural households in debt, and in 1982, P. N. Bhagwati, an activist Supreme Court justice, ruled that the government needed to do more to end the resultant bondage. He defined bondage broadly, ruling that the state should consider anyone not paid minimum wage to be forced to work by "indebtedness and economic compulsions."

Effectively, Bhagwati had defined three quarters of all workers—half a billion people—as bonded laborers. Mere slaves, real slaves like Gonoo, were broad-brushed with a whole range of those who were struggling, exploited, but free.

The breadth of Bhagwati's definition rendered the law unenforceable. And his more specific orders to free brick and quarry slaves were wholly ignored. Over the next twenty years, a handful of homegrown abolitionists liberated several thousand bonded laborers, but the few police who bought into the program arrested only a handful of slavemasters. No one ever served serious jail time for slaveholding.

Abhijat read his mandate exclusively as an order to reduce disease and poverty, the elimination of which would end "exploitative practices." One plan, called *Sampoorna Grameen Rozgar Yojana* (Universal Rural Employment Program), provided manual wage labor, mainly to *dalits*, in rural areas. It was the rural Indian equivalent of Roosevelt's CWA and WPA programs. Without such alternative means of feeding themselves, few slaves would leave their masters even if they felt physically safe doing so.

But Abhijat underestimated the degree of force used to coerce workers like Gonoo. He compared the quarry slaves to Malaysian call center workers clocking long, rigid hours for paltry pay. "Human life wasn't meant to be that kind of straitjacket," he said. "That's also bondage."

"It's one thing if the punishment is to get fired," I said. "It's another if the punishment is to get killed or maimed, which is the case for people working for this Ramesh Garg."

When I met Gonoo's wife, she was a wisp. Invisible save for the few, covered ventures out of the *jhopari*, she was also silent save for the scroop of her sari, the occasional muffled cough. But once, I glimpsed a sign of a bolder time in her life.

"What's the tattoo on your wife's arm?" I asked Gonoo. He just smiled.

In 1974, to celebrate their wedding, Gonoo took his teenage bride to a country fair. There was a traveling open-air theater known in rural India as *nautanki*. And there was a tattoo artist. Kol women often got a tattoo around the time of marriage, and Gonoo's wife wanted a peacock. The artist embedded her name in the bird. It was a personal touch on an otherwise crude tattoo, but completely lost on Gonoo's wife, who never learned to read her own name.

Gonoo mostly remembered the fair for a show elephant. It terrified him, and from then on an elephant sometimes chased him in his dreams. In Kol lore, elephants in dreams normally portend good fortune, but not always. Gonoo believed that a death in the dreamworld meant a physical death. So he always woke up before the elephant crushed him. In the process, he often urinated on himself and his family in the *jhopari*.

After Gonoo returned to quarry slavery, his wife bore his first child. On the day of his daughter's birth, he was frightened by the responsibility, but he hoped that she might one day be free. Eight years later, reality set in when Garg forced her to work alongside her parents in the quarry.

In 1988, Gonoo's first son was born. Anuj was a frail infant, and the locals gave him a nickname which meant "skinny" in the local language. Still, despite the boy's poor health, Gonoo wanted to have a small celebration, a Kol tradition following the birth of a boy. Garg, who was by then quite old, refused to give him another loan.

Anuj developed fitfully, as his parents failed to provide enough food or care. Still, Gonoo wished that somehow the boy might be able to attend one of the schools in Shankargarh which, despite a 300-to-1 student-teacher ratio, were the only chance locally to rise up from bondage. "I hoped he wouldn't get caught in the same trap I did," Gonoo said. "But my dreams flew off."

Around this time, Devnarayan Garg's son, Ramesh, took over the quarry. In 1991, the old slavemaster, as a sign of his piety and magnanimity, ordered a temple built nearby. Other than the alcohol, it was his sole gesture of goodwill toward the slaves. Devnarayan was, Gonoo said, "very cruel." Gonoo soon found out that Ramesh was a monster.

Is a serial killer worse than a slavemaster? It's a moral judgment but an academic question. And, like much in academia, it doesn't much matter in the real world. For Gonoo, there was no distinction between the two. After Ramesh Garg took over the quarry, Gonoo and the rest of Lohagara Dhal became slaves to a serial killer.

There is a pleasant and unassuming gentility in this part of the world that belies the hard truth of rough men like Garg. "Any truism about India," the Indian scholar Shashi Tharoor has written, "can be immediately contradicted by another truism about India." While India's freedom struggle was a model of nonviolence, in rural India Gandhian *satyagraha* often yielded to another philosophy of Indian origin: the *thuggee* way.

Garg justified the villagers' slavery through fraud, but he ensured it with the gun. No one in Lohagara Dhal could say for sure when he killed his first slave, but they knew—and the Shankargarh police knew—that he killed his first Brahmin in 1989. Garg killed the man, a fellow contractor, to exact revenge for the murder of his eldest brother. The police, who often extorted money from truck drivers and provided protection for contractors like Garg, did nothing. With real justice frozen by bureaucracy and graft, murder was often the way to exact retribution here, and families passed vendettas from generation to generation.

The Shankargarh police had charged Garg with three subsequent homicides. Villagers counted at least a dozen other people that Garg had killed, but those victims were *dalits* and thus, to borrow Kevin Bales's term, "disposable people."

Gonoo recalled a hot summer day shortly after Ramesh Garg took over the quarry. A young, unmarried *dalit* girl had just begun working alongside her parents. In her innocence, she wandered from her work to play with a kitten that had strayed into the quarry to drink from the pool. Gonoo did not notice the girl until he heard the crack of Garg's Mauser rifle. The police never investigated the incident, and her parents never filed charges. That week, the girl's family cremated her small body. Garg paid for the death rites. He then added the cost to the family's debt.

Garg regularly thrashed the slaves if they missed work, or if they did not work hard enough, or if they asked for pay. Sometimes he beat them simply to assert his absolute power. Gonoo recalled one time in 1995 when Garg and his men tortured a ten-year-old boy named Gangu for seven hours.

Garg was particularly brutal towards female slaves, who were easier to control through physical violence. In 1990, when a man refused to work, Garg dragged the slave's wife by her hair to the quarry, yelling that she would stay there until she died or her husband showed up to work. In 2003, Garg's enforcers found an escaped slave woman in her father's *jhopari*. They dragged her back to the pit, where they raped her in front of her family.

Lohagara Dhal's other two slavemasters—including Ramesh's brother Bhola—also used sexual violence. Neighboring contractors had chosen Kol girls, starting at age twelve or thirteen, to be sex slaves. A master would first put a girl in a small *jhopari* by his house. But once she was too old, she would be cast back, broken by her master and resented by her tribesmen, into the quarry. One shamed young Kol immolated herself after a contractor raped her.

In total, the police had formally charged Garg with eleven serious crimes ranging from robbery to murder. They charged Bhola with five such offenses. But, despite two decades of blatant thuggery, the brothers never faced trial. The closest the Shankargarh police came to putting Ramesh Garg behind bars was in 1995, when, in a fit of anger, he shot the pig of a Brahmin. The Brahmin filed charges against Garg, claiming emotional duress, and the loss not only of the pig but of ten piglets the pig might have borne. The police apparently considered shooting a Brahmin's pig more serious than slaughtering *dalits*. Ultimately, Garg always avoided justice, even for pig murder.

I sometimes wondered what advice Mahatma Gandhi might give Gonoo. In speeches, the Mahatma often compared the status of the slave in bondage to that of India in the British Empire. Standing in Bombay in 1942 to urge the passage of the "Quit India" resolution by the All India Congress Committee (AICC), Gandhi said: "The bond of the slave is snapped the moment he considers himself to be a free being."

For Gandhi, slavery was a mental construct. For Gonoo, slavery was his world. In the first place, he did not renounce his bondage because he felt that to do so would lead to his destruction. He believed that Garg had a large network of criminals that would find him if he fled with his family. "Ramesh is a killer," he said, when I asked him why he didn't run away. "If I try to run away, he will catch me. I will never be able to leave this place without paying for my freedom."

Another reason Gonoo did not run away was because, although it would be intolerable to those of us who have been free our entire lives, Gonoo's bondage provided a measure of security. "You used to feed and clothe me, though I could have provided food and clothing for myself by my labour," Gandhi said to his hypothetical slavemaster. "I hitherto depended on you instead of on God, for food and raiment. God has now inspired me with an urge for freedom and I am today a free man and will no longer depend on you."

Gonoo had no such faith that God would share His bounty with his family. On occasion, he was able to supplement their diet by catching one of the low-grade, quick-breeding "*desi* fish" that swam in nearby ponds. Other than that, Garg was God, the giver of sustenance, the taker of life. And so Gonoo continued living as a slave.

"What was the happiest time in your life?" I asked him.

He thought for a minute, and then said: "I don't understand what you mean by 'happiest.'"

I tried to describe it in terms of joy, but quickly realized he had no frame of reference for that. I described it instead in terms of an absence of pain.

He recalled that when his daughter started work in the quarry, to stop her from crying, he tried to make a game out of the work. He would flick pebbles at her as she carried the basket of rocks that he had filled. At first she was annoyed. Then, sometimes, she would giggle. In those moments, he didn't feel like a failure.

But Gonoo described only one moment in his life as a triumph. In 1995, his wife gave birth to a son during the Festival of Diwali. "It was a great day for us," he said. "He had a big head! He was going to be very smart."

In a fit of optimism, Gonoo named the infant Vishnu, "the Sustainer," after the Hindu lord of the world. Others in Lohagara Dhal called him Pawan Kumar, "Pure Prince."

After burying Vishnu's umbilical cord, he was feeling flush with luck. He took the six dollars that his Madhya Pradesh relatives had given him as a birth present, and put it all on one hand of cards during the Diwali celebration. He won, and kept gambling. By the end of the day, Gonoo had nearly $500. It was not enough money to buy his family out of debt, but if he invested it wisely, he could build a new life starting at age thirty-five.

Instead, he spent some of the windfall on a celebratory dinner with others in Lohagara Dhal. He bought sweets, and even arranged for a *nautanki* performance in Vishnu's honor. Most of the winnings, however, went to moonshine. In a matter of weeks, the money was completely gone.

Still, he had Vishnu. And Vishnu gave Gonoo something he had not had since he hopped a train back to Madhya Pradesh at age twelve: hope. The child spoke early—his first word, *amma*, meant "mother." Before age one, he was standing with the *khatiya* cot as a railing, and soon he was toddling off on his own.

Because the whole family had to work, the only option for child-care was to bring Vishnu to the quarry on a daily basis. One cool evening, he fell asleep beneath an acacia. Gonoo figured he had wandered back to the *jhopari*. When he did not find him there, he panicked. He ran back to the quarry, yelling the boy's name frantically. Vishnu, groggy, wandered over, wondering what the fuss was about.

In 1999, Vishnu no longer had to spend his whole day at the quarry. A local organization named "Sankalp" had started a *bachpana kendra*, an informal education center, in a neighboring village. Every morning, before dawn, Anuj walked his little brother several miles to the center, where the boy studied hard to fulfill a promise to his mother to learn to read.

"He was smarter than the other kids at school," Gonoo said. Vishnu, Gonoo thought, would be free.

In 1997, Gonoo's wife bore a third son, whom he called Manuj. Unlike Vishnu, Manuj was born under a bad sign. Soon after he began to walk, he suffered a tremendous fever, which left one leg paralyzed. Two thirds of the world's polio cases are in Uttar Pradesh, and little Manuj accounted for one of them. Garg gave Gonoo an advance for the treatment, and after a month and a half Manuj began to walk again, albeit with a limp. Soon other events led Gonoo to doubt that Manuj would live free, if he lived at all.

Garg demanded that Gonoo's eldest son Anuj, who was then ten, but had not been in school, work in the quarry in order to repay the loan advanced for Manuj's treatment. Gonoo complained, saying that it should only be he who was responsible for paying his debt.

Garg dragged Anuj to his office, where he tied his hands together and whipped the boy ferociously as Gonoo stood by, powerless to defend his son. When Garg pulled out a straight-edge razor, Gonoo embraced his feet and begged him to have mercy on the boy. Instead of cutting the child's throat, Garg settled for humiliating the boy. "Ramesh removed his hair," Gonoo said. "I was very much angry at him."

It was only through that ordeal that Anuj learned of his father's debt. From then on, Anuj worked with the family in the quarry; he was paid solely in alcohol, and then only occasionally.

One evening at the outset of the dry season in 2001, Gonoo's wife began to cough up blood after returning from the quarry. Like his mother, she soon developed full-blown tuberculosis. Garg loaned Gonoo $200 for her treatment at Shankargarh's 200-bed community health center. The clinic nurses had plenty of experience with the disease. Lohagara Dhal was the pinpoint epicenter of tuberculosis worldwide. India had more cases than any other country, and accounted for a third of the world total. A 1999 study of Lohagara, the market town immediately after Lohagara Dhal, found that at least one member of every family had tuberculosis. In half of the families, every member suffered from the disease.

The treatment could not overcome a lifetime in the quarry, and Gonoo's wife gradually lost her voice. Soon she was unable to work in the quarries at all. With Gonoo's day-to-day existence a dreary purgatory, the miseries of life like his wife's debilitating illness faded into the surroundings. Alcohol helped.

The Kol believe that when a sleeper dreams, his soul breaks free and wanders across the land. Gonoo's dreams echoed his life, however. The sheer terror of an elephant attack was the only break in the monotony of the rest of his dreamworld. Mostly, he dreamed that he was breaking stones, and loading them in a truck, over and over. His wife told him that he would sometimes shout in his sleep, imitating the overseers: "Load in the right truck! Over there!"

In the rainy season of 2003, Gonoo felt something he did not remember feeling before. Real pain. Sharp pain.

One evening Gonoo noticed pustules on Vishnu's legs. Soon, the eruptions spread to his entire body. A fever followed. Gonoo borrowed again from Garg to buy medicine for the boy, but Vishnu vomited so violently that he could not keep the medicine down. His legs swelled to twice their normal size.

Over the next few weeks, Vishnu wailed in pain every night. And every night, his mother lifted him off of the floor and made him walk outside to try to calm him down. Gonoo was terrified. As the disease wore on, Vishnu became more peaceful, and Gonoo more frantic about his son's fate.

"Vishnu was a tough boy," Gonoo recalled. "He would not put up with any mischief from other kids when he was in school. He would fight!" The eight-year-old took that fighting spirit to his illness, and even as the mysterious disease raged, he tried to cheer up his family by mimicking fighting cats and neighborhood children.

Finally, three months after the symptoms first appeared, Gonoo feared Vishnu would not last much longer, and carried him to the clinic in Shankargarh. Two nights later, Gonoo asked Garg for yet another loan. This time, Garg refused, saying that it was already impossible that Gonoo would pay off even half of the loans in his lifetime. Gonoo briefly contemplated selling the grain that they lived on, but he realized it would not raise near the amount of money he would need for the medicine.

When the doctor gave Vishnu glucose for the last time, Vishnu removed the IV from his arm by himself. As Gonoo carried his son home, Vishnu looked up at him.

"I'm going to die soon," he said.

"I won't let you die," Gonoo said.

That night, Gonoo woke up when Vishnu's little hand shook him. Mucus was pouring out of his nose and mouth. He began to heave, choke. With his family surrounding him, he stopped breathing.

Gonoo was inconsolable, but he had to pull together enough money to give his precious son a proper funeral. Instead, he got a bottle of alcohol, and then got drunk before confronting Garg to tell him that he should pay for the expenses. Garg responded that if Gonoo would load trucks faster, he might give him the money. Gonoo's blood was up and, unwisely, he persisted in his demand, his tone rising to the point where he actually threatened Garg.

"We'll see who's the biggest *gunda!*" Gonoo yelled, using the Hindi word for hooligan.

Garg left no doubt about that. He and his men dragged Gonoo from the quarry to his office, where they stripped him, tied him up, and flogged him senseless. Gonoo's wife tearfully watched the whole event, and hauled her husband home after the whipping. He was thoroughly bloodied and broken.

It was not the first time, nor would it be the last time, that Garg beat Gonoo. But it would not be long before Garg's savagery would give Gonoo a chance at freedom.

"**This is an** act so unnatural," the American abolitionist William Lloyd Garrison wrote, "a crime so monstrous, a sin so God-defying, that it throws into the shade all other distinctions known among mankind."

Gonoo's hell is the forgotten heart of global slavery. Every credible study has estimated that worldwide, the number of slaves in debt bondage dwarfs the number that has been trafficked into all other forms of slavery. Yet, in trafficking conferences and press campaigns of the so-called New Abolitionists, Gonoo is the invisible man; sex slaves like Tatiana take center stage.

To one small band of brothers in a spartan, pink office in Shankargarh, the quarry slaves were not corpses to mourn but power to inspire. Sankalp, the group that had run Vishnu's informal school, was no ordinary NGO, and the least part of its work was teaching ABCs to children. They were in the revolution business. "Sankalp" meant "Determination," and here, where the state had disintegrated, they were determined to fulfill the promise of India's founding fathers.

Sankalp's organizer, Rampal, was a surly embodiment of the organization's ideals. He was contrarious, but not the loquacious, argumentative Indian that Amartya Sen describes in his book of the same title. When he talked, he barely moved his mouth, stained red by betel nut. Stout and stubborn, he moved at a glacial pace. If he were reincarnated as a water buffalo, it would be a short karmic hop.

But his eyes revealed both a wariness and kindness that came from a hard life and a passion for justice. Like Gonoo, he was born in 1959 into a farming family. Rampal's father owned a small amount of land in the hamlet of Majhiyari, near Allahabad. He made just enough money to support his family from a few head of cattle. Because there was no organized irrigation, his father's cattle grazed in the pasture of a local *jamidar* or landlord.

During the dry season of 1969, the *jamidar* showed up at the family *jhopari* and complained that the oxen had grazed excessively. Rampal's father said they had eaten no more grass than normal. Without warning, the landlord punched his father in the face, then kicked him on the ground as his wife cried and his son begged the man to stop. Rampal had seen the *jamidar* beat his slaves before, but he had never hit his father, a free man. It was a scene he would not forget.

When Rampal turned five, he began attending a free local primary school, and became the first member of his family to learn to read. Soon, he was reading history, and learning about why he, a *dalit*, was beneath the contempt of so many of his peers. He learned about Mahatma Gandhi's disgust with the caste system, about his attempts to undermine it by demanding that his wife and other upper-caste members clean up the feces of their *dalit* countrymen. Gandhi sought to transform his religion into one that enshrined equality instead of caste, going so far as to rebrand untouchables as *harijan*, or "children of Vishnu."

"If untouchability lives," Gandhi said, "Hinduism dies."

But Rampal could not shake a feeling that Hinduism itself underpinned his low status. He found his sentiment reflected in the writing of Gandhi's peer, Bhimrao Ramji Ambedkar. A *dalit*, Ambedkar became both India's Thomas Jefferson and its Frederick Douglass. He was the most well known advocate for his oppressed people, and today his bespectacled visage adorns *dalit* villages nationwide. He also headed the Drafting Committee of the new Indian Constitution.

"We are going to enter a life of contradictions," Ambedkar said on the eve of the signing in 1949. "In politics we will have equality and in social and economic life we will have inequality."

For Ambedkar, Gandhi's talk about caste was just that: talk, and paternalistic talk. Gandhi was sincere in his disgust with untouchability, but his appeals to religion rang hollow with Ambedkar, who renounced Hinduism in 1935. Talk was cheap; laws, if enforced, mattered. Ambedkar wrote into the Constitution a ban on forced labor, as well as provisions for affirmative action. He wanted to redress historic crimes against what he called "scheduled tribes," like Gonoo's Kol, and "scheduled castes," like Rampal's *dalit*.

Rampal's own most searing lessons about caste came outside the classroom. Once, when visiting an upper-caste friend, the friend told him that he could not sit on his parents' furniture. As a *dalit*, Rampal might contaminate his family. Rampal was appalled, and angered. At school, he was an average student, but upper-caste teachers treated him as if he were subhuman. He got in a lot of fights. He recalled that every August 15, there would be small celebrations for *Swatantrata Divas*, India's Independence Day. "We are supposed to be independent," he thought. "But people in my village are in bondage."

At first, Rampal felt that caste was the sole cause of that slavery. It was a logical assumption, as one study found that nearly 90 percent of the nation's 10 million bonded laborers were *dalit*. But, as he continued his education, he began to think of the problem in much more materialist terms. In 1978, he began his university studies as a scholarship student. There he joined the Jayaprakash (JP) Narayan Movement, started four years earlier when its socialist founder called for "Total Revolution" against Indira Gandhi's attempt to destroy Indian democracy in order to save it.

When Rampal joined the movement, he, like millions of other *dalit*, declared that he was no longer Hindu. He gave an even greater jolt to his devout parents when he also renounced his last name, a vestige of his caste status.

After he graduated in 1982, Rampal became a journalist in order, he said, "to expose the problems in my village." Five years later, while reporting for the Allahabad-based daily *Aaj* (Today), he came to Shankargarh. He wanted to interview workers for a story on silicosis, but several had completely lost their ability to speak due to irreversible lung damage. The more he heard from those who could speak, however, the more he realized that they were plagued not only by disease but by slavery. And the two worked in concert. Hearing the hacking coughs of children and seeing their backbreaking labor, he asked a man why he forced his son to work in such conditions.

"Because I myself am forced by debt," the man told him, explaining that earlier he had taken a loan of only a few rupees when he fell ill—but was unable to pay it off because of the high interest rate. "I'm in a trap."

Rampal felt his old anger refreshed.

At the time of Rampal's discovery, the quarry slaves of Shankargarh were invisible people. Culturally, racism led many to believe that the Kol were simply fulfilling their predestined role at the bottom of society. Officially, local and state governments flatly denied that slavery still existed in Uttar Pradesh. Personally, Rampal wanted to dig deeper.

He found that the tribesmen were not natural slaves. On December 20, 1831, the Kol in Bihar staged a bloody revolt against the local landlords who held them in debt bondage with the collusion of the British, whose interest was always stability over democracy. At a community meeting, as one Kol leader put it, "it was agreed upon that we should commence to cut, plunder, murder and eat." They killed hundreds and torched over 4,000 upper-caste homes and police outposts. Twenty-six years later, another revolt, again with Kol laborers among the rebel leaders, prompted the British to seize India and declare it part of Queen Victoria's Empire.

Given the chance, Rampal thought, the Kol would seize their freedom. In 1994, he formed a vanguard group of roughneck activists with the modest goal of, as he put it, "removing worker exploitation everywhere in India." First, however, he needed to raise enough money to buy a telephone. They scraped for funds but soon found "bourgeois sponsors."

The next obstacle, the most time-consuming, was tapping into what Rampal believed was the slaves' native desire for freedom. He slipped quietly into the villagers' *jhoparis* at night to explain the Indian Constitution. At first, the slaves feared he was an agent of contractors. Then they thought he was crazy. Then they started to listen.

Now that some knew they were legally free, perhaps, as Gandhi had recommended, they would "plainly tell the master: 'I was your bondslave till this moment, but I am a slave no longer. You may kill me if you like, but if you keep me alive, I wish to tell you that if you release me from the bondage of your own accord, I will ask for nothing more from you."

Rampal's vision, I thought, was a bit rougher. At one point, as I squatted to interview a worker in a nearby quarry, a goon of the local contractor saw Rampal's motorcycle and came over, yelling angrily. He was small, skinny, and wore a suit, tie, and glasses. Rampal stood up and stared him down. The man continued shouting, but Rampal never lost his cool. The man became increasingly unhinged. Finally, Rampal lifted his sweater to reveal a six-shot revolver tucked into his waistband. Argument over.

"We are not in the main of NGO activism," Rampal said with a stained-red grin.

"Are you a socialist?" I asked Rampal over lunch one day.

As soon as I asked the question, I felt awkward. To American ears, it sounded as if I had asked him if he enjoyed copulating with monkeys. As I waited for him to take offense, I buried myself in the *rasgulla* cheeseballs and deep-fried hot peppers that we shared from a common plate. Rampal did not hesitate once the translator relayed my question.

"Damn right!" he said.

In India, there is no shame in baring a red soul. The Communist Party is a major force in national politics, and a Marxist government runs Kerala, a state that boasts nearly universal literacy, a strong service sector, and the country's highest living standard.

But Rampal's response hinted at a much larger danger that lurks where slavery survives amid free market democracies. According to the eighteenth-century Scottish radical who first rationalized capitalism, slavery was fundamentally incompatible with the concept: "The experience of all ages and nations, I believe, demonstrates that the work done by slaves, though it appears to cost only their maintenance, is, in the end, the dearest of any." Adam Smith continued: "A person who can acquire no property can have no other interest but to eat as much and to labor as little as possible. Whatever work he does beyond what is sufficient to purchase his own maintenance, can be squeezed out of him by violence only, and not by any interest of his own."

Too often, when Indian slaves became aware of their slavery amid the world's largest capitalist democracy, they rejected the whole concept of the free market.

Enter the Naxalites, stage left. A forty-year-long armed insurgency with roots in the ideology of Mao Zedong, the Naxalites were corrosive to development, and capable of grotesque violence. Their banned political party pledged to abolish slavery when they gained power, and for many tribal people, they were an attractive alternative to bondage.

The rebels staged their war from India's forests, which included the ancestral homeland of the Kol and, officially, the quarry land around Shankargarh. Administrators in tribal areas estimated that half of the population approved of the rebellion. Already, their blood red brand of Maoism was the order in a fifth of the nation's forest land. Some 15,000 strong, the rebels recruited children as young as eight into their forces, and had acquired a formidable arsenal of machine guns and rocket launchers. They seized quarries, attacked construction projects along the Golden Quadrilateral, hijacked trains, broke comrades out of jail, and murdered thousands of upper-caste members, including landlords, police, and local politicians. They set up *jan adalats* ("people's courts"), where they denounced and summarily beheaded counterrevolutionary capitalist sympathizers.

The Naxalite vision was of one India under a totalitarian Maoist regime, and Delhi took notice. Indira Gandhi had used the group to justify the state of emergency, and her government succeeded in killing off the leadership in the early 1980s. After the 1991 reforms, rising inequality and falling prices for agricultural products led to tribal desperation, and a Naxalite resurgence. "It would not be an exaggeration to say that the problem of Naxalism," said Prime Minister Manmohan Singh in April 2006, "is the single biggest internal security challenge ever faced by our country." It is not, however, the only internal security challenge born of the government's failure to address slavery. And Maoists are not the only extremist group filling a developmental void left by the government of India.

During my visit to Bihar, the poorest and most corrupt state in India, I found that many families faced a terrible choice: watch their children starve, sell them to traffickers—or put them in the hands of radical Islamists.

One day I left the paved roads and pushed deep into off-the-map territory—which yearly floods wiped further off the map—against the border with Nepal. In one village, I visited the only school for miles: a *madrassa* where boys in skullcaps sat in a sparse, open courtyard and chanted surahs written by hand on wooden tablets. There they rocked back and forth, learning the Q'aran by rote.

Although Hindus retain a dominant majority, India has the third largest Muslim population in the world. Most of the child slaves that I interviewed in Bihar were Muslim, and they and their *dalit* Hindu cousins whom I spoke with in Nepal (Maoist insurgents controlled the town on the Nepalese side, so I did not need a visa to enter) faced the same basic trap: the only credit they could raise came from informal, often unscrupulous lenders. I interviewed three such lenders—together they had sold dozens of children into slavery.

The *madrassa's* imam, a short man with a long gray beard and a startlingly high voice, acknowledged that he had been a *dalal*, a word meaning "pimp" in Hindi, which now means "human trafficker." He had sold some *madrassa* students into loom work. He also expressed sympathy for the terrible ideology of Osama bin Laden. I was the first white American he had met, but he graciously fed me, and offered me his son's straw-and-mud *jhopari* for the evening. After I fell asleep on the hay, he poked his head in, burning with curiosity, and more than a bit of anger.

"We have heard," he said, "that America disturbs the peace of Islam."

It seemed that Americans might have a selfish interest in providing alternatives to slavery and *jihad* for his students. Communist terrorism and Islamist radicalism were not palatable to a Western visitor, but to thousands of families, they beat starvation or bondage.

Back in Shankargarh, Rampal defended the Naxalites, who had taken over nearby towns. He claimed that they had ensured that workers made the minimum wage, and promoted other grassroots development schemes. He had reached out to them, and told them that he sympathized with their cause, their methods, and, particularly, their desperation. Subsequently, state agents interrogated him about the contact. But he was unruffled: he felt he had nothing to hide.

"For the Naxalites," said Rampal, "there are no alternatives other than violence."

On March 4, 1998, Rampal formed an alliance with a man who shared his passion for freeing the slaves, but otherwise couldn't have been more different. On that day, Amar Saran, a refined, worldly Allahabad lawyer who would later become a High Court justice, visited Shankargarh for the first time. He was shocked by what he saw.

"An all-pervasive pall of depression" hung over the place, Saran recalled. Saran took dozens of pages of notes on village after village where every man, woman, and child was a slave. One Kol had shuttered his daughter in his *jhopari*. He was afraid to let her out for fear that the quarry contractor would rape her. Saran decided to serve as a pro bono adviser to Sankalp.

Rampal, then in his fourth year of working with the Kol, had learned some hard lessons about the difficulties in freeing them. In fact, he had learned early on that "freeing" them was impossible. They could only free themselves. But even if the Kol had a safe haven elsewhere, which they did not, most were too scared to run.

The problem was a confounding one for Saran, a soft-featured lawyer with a lilting British accent (his father, like my own, was Cambridge-educated). He had a direct, simple interpretation of the law. But he was also a pragmatist, and came to realize that in rural India, laws could only do so much. This particular situation called for a more forehanded approach.

Beginning in 1994, Sankalp encouraged the slaves in a nearby quarry to form a *mitra mandal*, a self-governing credit union. Each slave would scrape up a single rupee (about 3 cents) for the collective fund. Sankalp would then sponsor the slaves in a loan application from a bank. Soon, they would have enough money to pay off the debt of a single slave. The freed slave could then earn more, and contribute more to the credit union. It worked, but it was an agonizingly slow path to freedom. Also, it was illegal: the Bonded Labour Act forbade the payment of such debts because redemption inherently recognized the right of property in man.

Rampal and the slaves got confrontational. They tried simply placing red flags in the quarries and announcing to the contractors that they were free, that they would continue to work in the quarries, but would thenceforth keep the profits of their labor themselves. The flags did not stay long, and neither did the workers' hold on the quarries. The contractors, with the help of local authorities, swiftly regained their power. Slave resistance crumbled, as few workers had faith that the government would defend them in their newfound freedom. Many still thought of themselves as slaves.

Rampal and Saran converged on a new plan: Attain the leases so that the Kol could mine the quarries and retain the profits themselves. In a place where a law was often just a suggestion, they knew obtaining legal rights was just the first challenge, but Saran insisted it was an essential one.

After Saran's August 1998 visit, he began to study the quarries closely. Of course the contractors' claims on the lives of the slaves were illegal, but he soon found that most of their lease claims were also illegal. The area, officially, was forest land, but bribes and guns meant that Forest Department officials did not bother what Saran termed the "sand mafias."

The landlord of the forty-six quarrying villages that surrounded Shankargarh was a feudal raja whose family claim to the land was shaky at best, but predated the Raj. He leased the land to contractors like Ramesh Garg, but Saran thought he might convince him to lease it to the Kol instead. When that effort failed, Sankalp worked to win the leases through the courts.

Meanwhile, Sankalp also prepared the workers in several villages for a struggle with the contractors first by lessening their mortal fear, then by helping them organize for their post-liberation survival. The contractors, as predicted, reacted forcefully. One had his goons break up a meeting of the *mitra mandal* in his village, firing shots into the air, beating slaves, and setting their *jhoparis* ablaze.

On December 19, 1999, after back-and-forth lease decisions from the government, Sankalp organized a climactic meeting with hundreds of Kol to decide whether or not to seize quarries in one, massive collective action. Rampal termed the strategy *"halla bol,"* which means "attack." It would be a forceful move, and they discussed the probability that it would be met with a forceful response: they could be shot en masse. Amar Saran had earlier warned the Allahabad High Court of the "extreme likelihood of an explosive situation emerging and the law and order machinery completely breaking down in these areas." In spite of the danger, the group resolved "to give up being slaves from January 1, 2000, and to stop working under bondage to the contractors."

"They are not asking for the moon," Saran said after the meeting. "All that they want is a right to quarry stones and sands, educate their children and save their women from dishonor."

At eight o'clock in the morning on January 1, 2000, hundreds of slaves descended on the quarries with pickaxes, shovels, bows, and arrows. For a small group of the Kol, the first day of the new millennium would be their first day of liberty.

The rage the Kol had built up over generations could have led to a bloody explosion like Nat Turner's rebellion or John Brown's raid. A Naxalite-led insurgency would have led to a reversion to despotism, albeit of a different color. Still, few would have been surprised if the quarry slaves decided to "cut, plunder, murder and eat," as had their forebears, in order to redress the terror that they had lived with for generations.

But the Kol had little interest in revenge. What they wanted was the freedom to prosper. They seized fifteen out of the raja's forty-six quarries. The raja fought back using the local police, and the contractors fought back by beating up Kol resisters and Sankalp representatives. They burned several dozen *jhoparis*, destroying the slaves' meager food stores and immolating one Kol girl in the process. Despite the bloodshed, the Kol still clung to eight quarries.

Several dozen Kol returned to slavery. Most who went back to their masters did so to avoid starvation. Many who returned did so because the idea of ordering their own lives seemed overwhelming. All who returned did so because their fear conquered their desire for freedom. A few, however, clawed their way to liberty. Thanks largely to the quiet advocacy of Saran, the unflagging support of Rampal, but mostly to their own courage, over 4,000 slaves freed themselves and formed more than 200 microcredit *mitra mandals*. Sankalp backed Kol applications for bank loans, which the workers used to win leases for those eight quarries at auction from the Mines Commission. Their occupation was then recognized by law.

In a May 30, 2002, meeting with Saran, Allahabad's district magistrate called the Kol move "a silent revolution," and a profitable one for the government. In the first nine months after they received the lease, the Kol paid more in royalties to the district administration than the raja had paid in five decades of tenancy on the land. The liberation and rehabilitation of the Kol, which cost the government nothing, resulted in thousands of dollars flowing into state coffers.

I spoke with two dozen freed quarry slaves. Their lives were still constant struggles. Silicosis and tuberculosis still ravaged their elders. But they described a subtle shift. Previously, the struggle was for survival, and was fraught with daily humiliation. Now, with dignity, they struggled for the happiness of their families.

Despite Rampal's Communist sympathies, the linchpin of the sustained success of the Kol was the market in silica and gravel, the prices for which peaked at the very moment of the *halla bol*. The companies that bought the sand and the rocks did not care who produced it, as long as they did not have to pay any more. Sometimes, the liberated Kol were able to bring their prices below those of the contractors, who often colluded to cheat the buyers and support their own lifestyles.

"Competition is something which breaks the shackles of bondage," said Samar, a Sankalp ideologue. The antidote to slavery, in other words, is not communism. It is unfettered capitalism.

Within a year of the initial uprising, many Kol had income, and they had the freedom to do with it what they liked. Some branched out beyond quarry work. One man bought a local cow, sold the milk, earned income through animal husbandry, and bought another. Some started provisional stores, hawked bangles and perfume. With Sankalp's help, they planted 7,000 trees, and began growing their own food. They created microwatersheds, and started a beekeeping program. Young women began to use contraception and pressured their husbands to give up alcohol. Infant and child mortality dropped as sanitation improved. In six of the liberated villages, every child attended school. "The laborer is extremely flexible," Saran concluded. "He does not require the spoon feeding mentioned in the bonded labor rehabilitation manuals."

A bushy fellow named Bhola was a prime example of that self-sufficiency. At forty-five, he was the oldest man in Ghond, some three miles along a dirt road from Shankargarh. Ghond was the first village to win a lease.

Unlike Gonoo, when Bhola introduced himself, he led with his chest, not the top of his head. He was rail-thin and his face was dominated by a gray, walruslike mustache that pushed his cheeks into his eyes. He wore a dirty, stretched T-shirt and ragged canvas pants. His hands, like Gonoo's, were callused and worn smooth, but his face was oriented entirely differently. He grinned constantly. His eyes danced.

Over periodic quarry blasts, Bhola belted out his life story. He was eager to talk, and proud of his struggle—my translator could barely keep up as Bhola kept firing off unsolicited details. Like Gonoo, he had inherited slavery from his father and grandfather. As a child, he tended the water buffaloes of the quarry contractor, before joining his father as a quarry slave at age fifteen. He ran away once, but was recaptured. In 1985, his master sold his debt to another contractor. Bhola recalled admiring the new contractor's bicycle. Looking back, he realizes he was sold for about the same price as the bike. "I never thought of growing old," he said. "I only thought about the present, how to survive. I was in a trap."

In 1995, Sankalp began the long process of convincing Bhola and his fellow slaves to organize. Three years later, Bhola stared down his master and his village won a lease and its freedom.

At age thirty-eight, Bhola began to think about his future for the first time. He had lived on the same piece of land for over a decade, but never felt as if he owned it because he himself was owned by another man. Now he recognized that the land was, de facto if not de jure, his. And he realized that he could do something with it.

As he spoke, I thought of the American slave narratives, and of one unusually inspired fellow's thought on his emancipation. "Something begins to work up here," Robert Falls, a former American slave, recalled as he touched his forehead. "I begins to think and to know things. And I knowed then I could make a living for my own self, and I never had to be a slave no more."

Bhola showed me his original *jhopari*, a six-foot-high mud, stone, and grass structure. The hut now housed his one cow and the feed for his two water buffaloes, which stood by, chewing cud contentedly over a wide stone bowl. His new house was three times the height of the old one; it had ceramic shingles and a smooth, painted plaster over a bamboo frame. Nearby, his son had left the quarry and was farming a small family plot. The grain he grew fed the family, and sold at market in Shankargarh. Bhola's youngest daughter, the first literate member of his family, recently entered secondary school. "My children will not have to live the life that I lived," he said.

The situation was still unstable in Ghond and in all of the freed villages. The state had failed to cede full property rights to the Kol, an act that would have greatly reinforced their newfound freedom and unlocked what the Peruvian economist Hernando de Soto called "the mystery of capital."

But Bhola was building wealth nonetheless. In 2003, he bought a bicycle in Shankargarh for $30, although by 2006 he still didn't know how to ride it.

"I feel great in the sunlight," he said. "I can dream now."

On Christmas Day, 2005, Gonoo was cheerier than I had seen him in weeks. Over dinner in front of his *jhopari*, I found out why.

Knowing Gonoo had barely enough to feed his own family, let alone me, I had bought a chicken for $1.50 from a man who had six in a rusty wire coop on the main street in Shankargarh. Gonoo shoved the squawking thing in a tiny stone hutch next to his *jhopari* before the family began to cook. Dinner was a full-house production. His wife disassembled the bird on a flat rock, feathers blowing into the wind, entrails gathering in the dust and ash of the firepit. On a separate stone, Gonoo's eldest son Anuj ground an onion with a handmade pestle. Gonoo struggled to fashion chapattis with a tomato and two potatoes. It was a great, if not grand, Christmas dinner.

As the last light of the sun—made dark orange by the atmospheric silica—slipped below the horizon, Gonoo stoked the dung chips in the fire. It was below freezing, and we were swaddled in blankets. I felt as if Gonoo wanted to tell me something. I asked him what was on his mind, and he got giggly. He thanked me for the chicken, saying it was the first time he had eaten a bird in years. I thanked him for cooking it.

"I'm very glad you're here," he said. "I realize this [Christmas] is a big day for you."

Gonoo, a lax if not lapsed Hindu, had observed Diwali a month earlier. For him, the festival brought no joy, only memories of Vishnu, whom he sometimes dreamed was sleeping next to him. He asked if I was married. On my phone, I showed him a picture of my Italian ex-girlfriend, and explained that she had said no. He said she was lovely, and noted she covered her head like his wife. I said I took the picture when we were in Yemen, an explanation lost on Gonoo, who could name only one foreign country: America. The light of my cell phone drew Manuj, Gonoo's youngest.

"TV?" he asked.

He then stood up and belted out a Bollywood theme he had heard on a radio in the Lohagara market. The youngster had impressive recall, and unexpected volume. The pleasant smell of the burning chips dug deep into my sinuses as if I'd just had a good cry. I felt punchy, and soon all of us were laughing, but I wasn't quite sure what we were laughing at.

"So what's up?" I asked Gonoo, when we'd calmed down.

"Ramesh is gone," Gonoo said, looking off into the darkness.

The slavemaster had finally killed someone who mattered. Over the next three weeks, I filled in the details. The murder was the culmination of a fourteen-year feud between Garg and a distant cousin named Om Narayan Pandey. Pandey, another Brahmin quarry contractor, held dozens of slaves and had fourteen outstanding criminal charges against him.

The feud began, as did so many in the region, over money. Starting in

1992, the cousins competed in government auctions for tax collection contracts. Bidding was fierce because the payoff was big: the winner could tax a hundred small business owners, say that only forty paid, and pocket the difference.

Garg being a thug, and this being Shankargarh, competition over what would ordinarily be a bureaucratic position soon went the way of the gun. In the fall of 2003, Pandey shot Garg in the leg during a pitched battle that involved a half dozen men on either side. Everyone in Shankargarh knew what was coming next, they just didn't know when it would happen.

It happened at approximately 3:30 p.m. on September 5, 2005, on the highway near Kapari village. Garg, in a jeep, spotted Pandey riding with his son on a Yamaha motorcycle, and swerved to force them off the road. After Pandey struggled to his feet, Garg leaned out of the window and shot him with a country-made *katta* .315. Pandey's son, Pankash, hailed a *tempo* auto-rickshaw and carried his bleeding father to a hospital in Mirzapur. By the time they arrived, Pandey was dead.

Normally, if a Brahmin was killed in the area, the first response of the victim's family was not to report the crime but to kill the murderer. But because the hospital saw his dead father, Pankash Pandey filed charges against Ramesh Garg. Most assumed he still planned on exacting revenge on his own.

Garg was probably more afraid of retaliation than arrest. Whatever the reason, he fled, leaving the quarry to his foreman Babbulley, who most slaves considered heartless but less savage. It was the first time in Gonoo's adult life that his family was free of Garg's family.

"Why don't you escape?" I asked.

"Where would I go?" he said. "I have nowhere to go. They might not catch me, but I might be worse off than I am now. How would I eat?"

In slavery, there was comfort of a sort. And fear. Without the rations that Garg and now Babbulley allowed him, his family would soon starve. Moreover, Gonoo was convinced that Babbulley was in touch with Garg, and that Garg would soon return. "If Ramesh comes back, he will make us work for him," he said. "Or he will find us and beat us."

"But do you feel like legally you have to work for him?" I asked.

"I have to pay the debt," he said. "If I don't, there will be problems for me."

No one was laughing anymore. Gonoo was ashamed that he could not host me in his home, but there was simply no room. I told him there was no need to apologize, particularly as he had arranged for me and my translator to sleep in his neighbor's *jhopari*. It was the coldest night in seventy years in Shankargarh, but between the blankets and the hay, the simple little structure was transformed into a snuggery. As I fell asleep, I recalled the reaction of another American slave after Union soldiers freed him. "Say dey was gwine free de niggers en if it hadn' been for dem, we would been slaves till yet," Charlie Davis recalled. "Coase I rather be free den a slave, but we never have so much worryations den as people have dese days."

Now as then, mere emancipation did not mean freedom.

After a night of vomiting, I decided to see if I could find Ramesh Garg. My stomach wambled throughout the day. The chicken was one culprit, but my nerves were an accomplice. In the fall of 2000, shortly after the Sankalp-led uprising, a journalist came to Shankargarh to report on the quarry mafias for Rampal's old paper, *Aaj*. He was kidnapped, taken to a pig farm, shot in the back, and castrated. His murderers tossed his head in a pond in neighboring Rewa.

Rampal said that the family of Garg's murder victim would not help me, as they planned on killing Garg as soon as they found him. Villagers in Lohagara Dhal told me what they knew, but it wasn't much. They helped broaden my understanding of Garg's brutal and complete power, however. Many, like Gonoo, felt uncowed by daily violence for the first time in their lives. But their fear had not fled with Garg, and no one doubted that the brute would soon return.

The raja consistently rebuffed my requests for an interview, and the police were little help. At an outpost near Lohagara, I cornered one detective who still managed to dodge my questions by claiming he had sores in his mouth and thus could not speak. I drove a mile to Garg's headquarters in the Shankargarh market. Well over half of the Indian GDP comes from the informal sector, and that was well on display here. Provisional stores sold betel nut and strings of shiny plastic shampoo packets and soaps. Vendors piled short stacks of eggs and bowls of fried goods onto unpainted carts with bicycle wheels. A fat man grimaced with concentration as he fixed a shirt in the street with a hand-cranked sewing machine.

Police had boarded up the windows and doors of Garg's 16,000-square-foot house. Nearby they had also sealed the house of his brother Bhola, who was wanted in connection with the murder. I surreptitiously snapped a photograph from the back of the car, and realized when I looked at the image that I had captured a man, wrapped in a blanket, who glared at me as he passed by. Twenty minutes later, at Sankalp's office, Rampal said I had been spotted near Garg's home. Word traveled fast here, and I stood out.

At the hundred-year-old Shankargarh Police Station, several officers in khaki uniforms lounged in chairs in the courtyard. Next to them stood a 100-cubic-foot metal locker that held the possessions of Garg and his brother. The officers said they were not actively pursuing the brothers, but they hoped that by holding their property, the Gargs would be compelled to surrender. The victim's motorcycle lay at the other end of the station.

The Shankargarh precinct had no photographs of either Garg or his brother, but they kept a record of their rampant, unchecked violence in a giant ledger. I asked why Garg was not behind bars when, by all accounts, he had an established record as a serial killer.

"The Indian courts!" said one grinning officer, throwing up his hands.

They had arrested Garg after three of the prior murders, but the courts quickly released him on bail. Thanks to the famously glacial Indian justice system, he never stood in the dock.

I settled for hunting out Babbulley, the man who was Garg's overseer and, at the moment, his surrogate. At his house, I found only a surly dog and a surlier man, Babbulley's uncle, who growled at us to get off of his property.

Two weeks later, Gonoo told me Babbulley had gone on the *Magh Mela* pilgrimage at the confluence of the sacred rivers. There he would live ascetically, drinking only Ganges water and bathing thrice daily to wash away his sins. That was the theory, at least. In practice, the water was too fetid to drink, and his sins were too great to wash away in a month.

I went to "the king of all holy places" in Allahabad to try to find him. The floodplains were choked with sprawling rows of tents and make-shift temples with red and yellow prayer flags suspended high above. Here and there were quickly assembled *dhaba* restaurants and the odd emergency medical unit. A couple dozen polio vaccination volunteers in yellow trucker hats moved between the tents administering drops to children. Soot from bonfires fell thick. A line of tractors pulled pilgrims on enormous haystacks over a dirt road that cleaved the village. Others rode *tangas*, horse-drawn rickshaws with little platforms for passengers to sit cross-legged. High overhead black kites, with glass powder in their tethers, battled others with red and saffron sails.

In the mayhem of some 3 million pilgrims, I soon realized that finding the overseer was hopeless.

A week later, I got lucky. Gonoo said that Babbulley had returned.

It was a festival day in Lohagara Dhal. At one in the afternoon, five drunk men played cards in front of Gonoo's *jhopari*. Across the highway, several villagers filed into the simple brick temple built under Devnara-yan Garg. In the quarry, two women washed clothes in the brown pool. Near Babbulley's house, someone played a flute, and workers drank.

When we found Babbulley, he had anointed himself with white san-dal powder. Never at ease about using subterfuge, but knowing he would not speak to me otherwise, I told him I was writing an article about the Golden Quadrilateral, and wanted to ask about the basic ingredi-ents. Babbulley explained that he just managed the quarry and, after I pressed him, he acknowledged Ramesh Garg was the owner.

"Is that the same Ramesh that I heard about in connection with some murder case?" I asked.

"When Ramesh was here, due to a clash with another Brahmin, someone charged him with committing murder," he said. "So he fled. I don't believe he's committed the murder, though. At the time of the murder, he was at home."

"How do you find the workers for the quarry?" I asked.

"It's not complicated," he said. "They just have to be able to break the stones. No skills required."

"Do they all live here?"

"People come from Madhya Pradesh," he said, explaining that he will go to a *dalal*, or trafficker, to find more laborers. "But most live here and have for a couple of generations. It's an ancestral mode of livelihood." He claimed he paid the workers 1,600 rupees ($36) for breaking and loading stones into one truck, a claim previously denied by dozens of slaves and local officials.

"Do workers ever get advances, if they get sick, for example?" I asked.

"When we know that the laborer will stay to break the stones and return our payment," he said, "we give them an advance. And we take that out of his pay."

I asked him if the Kol were hard workers.

He raised his hands and grinned: "They can swing a twelve-kilogram [26-pound] hammer for eight hours with no break! It makes a great impact on their health. But blasting reduces the work."

"What happens if a worker that you give an advance to wants to leave before he pays it off?" I asked.

"I thought this was about road construction," he said, raising an eyebrow and refusing to answer my question.

After tea, I again asked him what happened if workers took a loan, and then wanted to leave.

"People don't try to skip out on the debt," he said. "They pay it back with their labor."

On my last day in India, to thank Gonoo for sharing his story, I took his family to an epic of a different sort. When I write, I often find that a good movie helps to loosen my thoughts. Given that the last time Gonoo saw a Bollywood film was also the last time he was free, I whimsically hoped that he might find a spark on the screen.

When I picked him up in a *tempo*, Gonoo had added several young cousins to the party. The littlest was a boy of about three, with black *kajal* around his eyes to protect him from evil. At Shankargarh's Kamlakar Cinema, named after the father of the raja, the movie tickets cost 12 rupees—about 25 cents. I bought ten, giving nine to Manuj, Gonoo's youngest son, whose eyes lit up. He had never seen a movie before. Barefoot, the boy pushed through the crowd of moviegoers and cows and presented the tickets to his father. Gonoo stood, bewildered, against the turquoise wall of the lobby, next to a dog that was curled asleep. In the corner stood a red ceramic spittoon. On the theater wall was an enormous dusty box, which locals assumed was a chicken coop. "In matter of fact, it is an air-conditioning unit," my translator explained. "It provides much pleasure in the time of summer."

We sat at the back of a large balcony. The seats were all worn through and uncomfortable, with stenciled numbers on the backs. As the curtain rose, the crowd hooted in the "2nd class" section below. The movie, *Zakhmi Sipahi* (Wounded Soldier), was a decade old. The projection was scratchy and poorly lit, and the soundtrack was almost inaudible thanks to an overwhelming bass. But what dated the film immediately were the costumes: the actors wore the tapered pants and upturned collars of a 1980s bubblegum teen flick.

The movie was vintage Mithun Chakravarti. Chakravarti, who played the hero, made his name starring in violent, simple pulp—called *masala* movies for their spicy flavor—aimed at lower-caste Indians. His character in this film was larger than life, the cinematic heir to Lord Rāma in the *Rāmāyana*. He was an epic demigod, a destroyer who smote seven villains with a single, flying roundhouse. His mullet feathered off his neck like the wings of a majestic falcon.

It was a terrible film, but accidentally hilarious. The villain was beyond evil. Like many *masala* baddies, he had a Bihari accent. At one point, for no apparent reason, he kicked an extra in a wheelchair down a flight of stairs. In the film's opening sequence, he shaved the head of a young boy, who would grow up to be Chakravarti's character, in order to shame the boy's father. I feared that was close to the bone for Gonoo, given Anuj's all too real encounter with Garg. Generally, I sensed that Gonoo absorbed even less than I did, though he stared straight ahead the whole time, transfixed by the flickering images.

A Gandhi motif recurred throughout the movie. One scene transitioned to the next via hamhanded zoom shots onto a portrait of the Mahatma. At one moment, for some unexplained reason, the villain held out a fifty-rupee note while he attempted to participate in the gang rape of a damsel. A tight shot on Gandhi's face on the bill was widened to reveal—who else?—Chakravarti, who then proceeded to unleash an orgy of ass-kicking.

Gonoo's wife shifted nervously during dance numbers, which included a belly dancer doing the Watusi on a giant chessboard with a backdrop of fountains that appeared lime green through the projector's aged filter. Her eyes, red and swollen, never left the screen. At one point, Manuj was about to explode with nervous energy and ran out during a gauzy love sequence, apparently to urinate. He then ran back so as not to miss another action scene.

The movie was three hours long, mercifully broken by an intermission. At half-time, I turned to Gonoo.

"You're going to have to explain that to me," I said. "I don't speak the language."

"I didn't understand it either," he said.

At the end, Chakravarti's character got his revenge when he shaved the head of the villain and tied him up in public to face the villagers' scorn. Chakravarti also tied up corrupt public officials. He showed them the rough hands of a shirtless, skinny, silent bonded laborer to shame them for failing to prevent his exploitation.

Afterward, I asked a keyed-up Manuj to tell me about the film. Manuj, who loved pop culture, had absorbed quite a bit of it and immediately identified the lead actor. Gonoo, by the end of the film, claimed to have taken at least one message from it. "I learned that political leaders take bribes," he said. "And they exploit everyone else."

That afternoon, Anuj, who had seen a movie twice before, cut his hair in a mullet like Chakravarti's, and told me, away from his father, that he was planning on marrying soon, and then going with his wife to Delhi. A trafficker had promised him he could earn $7 a month working in a sari loom. I expressed caution, as I had talked with several boys who had been enslaved after such an offer. But I was glad he was thinking beyond the quarry.

"I felt so free when Babulley told us Ramesh had fled," Anuj said. "And now that Ramesh is gone, my father is also *azad*—free. But when Ramesh returns, my father will be a slave, a *ghulam*, again."

I was not so foolish as to think that a film could break Gonoo's chains. But I introduced him to Rampal after the movie. When I called a Sankalp organizer a year later, he said that they had been working with Lohagara Dhal. Ramesh Garg never returned, but the village was a challenge to organize, as he had been the most brutal contractor in Shankargarh, and the terror of the slaves ran deep.

Perhaps, one day, if the local police will it, Garg will face justice. Perhaps, if the district magistrate wills it, the state will give the slaves title to the land that they have worked and lived on for generations. Perhaps, if the villagers will it, they will follow in the footsteps of their brothers and sisters in Ghond, and trade slavery for their fair share of India's tremendous growth.

Next to the picture of Frederick Douglass in my office, I now have a picture of Gonoo, one of only four ever taken of him. I hope, one day, I will find him again and show him the photograph. Perhaps, if he has willed it, he will be free.

9

Revelation:
Angels with Swords of Fire

Y ou will say it was quixotic. You
will say he was naive. But when John Miller went to war with India, he
did so because he interpreted American law literally, and because he saw
no other path to freeing millions of slaves.

On January 26, 2006, Miller flew to the Indian state of Tamil Nadu,
where he saw slavery so egregious that it prompted his lonely charge
against the elephant. A day earlier, in Riyadh, he had chastened the
Saudi crown prince over a slave whose masters had deformed her. Now
he visited one of the wealthiest states in India, which also had over a
million bonded laborers.

During his previous India trip, in October 2003, he met with survivors, some as young as fourteen, of the Delhi, Mumbai, and Calcutta
brothels. Miller's focus then, as it normally was that first year, was sex
slavery, which he correctly argued was the largest component of cross-
border trafficking. Miller successfully pressured the Mumbai govern-

ment to shut down traditional dance houses, some of which were fronts for prostitution.

On this, his second visit, Miller went through the looking glass and glimpsed, for the first time, the hidden majority of modern-day slaves. After landing, he drove several hours to a dusty, sun-soaked village in the Red Hills area where he met with tribal *dalits* from the Irula community. Like Gonoo's Kol, the Irula saw their ancestral forests closed off to them by government regulation. Many had now fallen into debt bondage in local rice mills. Also like Gonoo, their debts dated back generations. One man told Miller that he was paying off a debt that his grandfather incurred fifty years earlier when he took a loan for less than a dollar. Beginning at four every morning, men, women, and children worked barefoot in rice-drying units, pulling the world's most common staple from boiling water and spreading it onto scalding pavement. When the workers resisted or did not work fast enough, the masters beat them.

"I have been shocked a few times," Miller said. "But this was one of the bigger shocks. I realized that three generations were held—I mean, going back to grandfathers. And this makes it like historic slavery. They don't get out!"

Back in Washington, Miller confronted the visiting Indian labor secretary, K. M. Sahni. He asked Sahni why no master had been convicted, and he cited a study that found over 10,000 slaves in one small area. "Oh, we investigated that," said the secretary. "There was nobody in chains." Miller said that there were millions of slaves in India, and that the consensus among antislavery groups was that the government was doing nothing to free them.

"Give me the names of those organizations," Sahni responded, according to Miller, "and I'll make sure they're appropriately dealt with."

Miller's jaw dropped. He told the secretary that he was not relying on the reports alone, that he had talked with the slaves themselves. "I saw three generations in front of me," he said, his blood rising. "Sons, fathers, grandfathers! All of them enslaved! You can't call this something other than slavery."

Sahni ended the meeting, but Miller was not about to let the issue die. He was flummoxed that Indian officials, so responsive on the issue of sex trafficking, could so thoroughly deny the more widespread crime of debt bondage. He suspected it was because trafficking was a problem shared by many other nations, whereas large-scale debt bondage was only present on the Indian subcontinent, where the unreconstructed caste system allowed it to flourish. Their denials were due, in other words, to foolish national pride.

Miller decided to teach India a lesson that America was serious about abolition. If demoted to Tier Three, juggernaut or not, India would be staring down a loaded gun. If President Bush did not waive the decision, the United States would vote against India's requests to the World Bank, an organization that had provided India with $30 billion in aid since 1961. Moreover, direct foreign assistance from the United States totaled nearly $200 million annually. While billions of dollars in trade would be unaffected, sanctions would be molasses in India's development engine.

Miller was realistic. The odds were long that Condoleezza Rice would demote India to Tier Three. Even if she did, it was inconceivable that the president would allow sanctions. But an initial demotion would send a message to India: You may be our most populous ally, but we will hold you to account for also having the greatest population of slaves.

In March 2006, President Bush's first trip to India offered a chance for a shot across the bow. Miller leaned on the White House to address slavery in a private meeting between the president and Prime Minister Manmohan Singh.

But Bush was busy raising his glass in a black-tie celebration of a deal to share nuclear fuel and know-how with India. The deal was largely the work of Assistant Secretary of State for Arms Control Stephen G. Rademaker. A few months later, Rademaker left the State Department and signed a lucrative deal of his own to lobby for the government of India. The inconvenient fact of several million slaves was not something that either the president or the State Department's elite were going to bring up at such a happy moment.

Still, Miller held out hope. He believed in the law. More than that, he believed in a moral law that stands above men and nations.

He found that few of his original comrades in arms were by his side in the war against Indian slavery. With the exception of Congressman Christopher Smith, who called debt bondage "an abomination," the Horowitz coalition had no dog in the fight to free bonded labor slaves.

I asked Richard Land if he had heard about debt bondage. Land was the head of the political wing of the 16 million–strong Southern Baptist Convention, and a key Horowitz ally. "I have, but I haven't made it a part of a campaign," he said. "You know, you have to paint visual images that people can really grasp." Apparently, Gonoo was an inappropriate subject for such a painting. He was not a prostitute. He was not a martyr for Christ. Despite the fact that many of the bonded laborers in Pakistani brick kilns were Christians enslaved by Muslim masters, the Southern Baptist Convention was strangely silent on their plight.

If Miller was to succeed in relegating India to worst-offender status, where it deserved to be, he would not have the benefit of a letter-writing campaign, a publicity blitz via the Christian media. On his own, he would have to call forward his best "Johnson treatment," his best close-in lean, his best charm. It would be a struggle that he would take all the way to Secretary Condoleezza Rice. It would be an effort that he would never discuss publicly, even if he succeeded. But he wasn't in this for the accolades. He was in it for the slaves.

Four weeks after Miller shifted into high gear to try to convince her that Indian slaves mattered, Condoleezza Rice gave a command performance of her own to a group of people whose importance was self-evident. The June 2006 meeting of the Southern Baptist Convention (SBC) in Greensboro, North Carolina, came at a time when only a third of Americans approved of the job President Bush was doing. That approval rating had declined steadily since its peak after his 2005 State of the Union address, in which Michael Gerson had written a moving reference to the fight against human trafficking to remind Americans that "the freedom agenda" meant more than occupying Iraq. The SBC offered the administration another chance to change the subject before an adoring audience.

Viewed in historical context, Rice was an unlikely keynote speaker. She was pro-choice, a position that Richard Land likened to defending slavery. And she was the descendant of slaves, delivering the main address to an assembly which, in the words of its first president, would "promote slavery as a Bible institution."

The Southern Baptist Convention invited Rice, a Presbyterian, because their first choice, President Bush, was available to give only a disembodied five-minute televised address. In a meeting with Richard Land in the Eisenhower Executive Office Building, Karl Rove had suggested Vice President Dick Cheney as a replacement.

"Really?" said Land. "I don't think that will work."

"Why?" asked Rove.

"Well, there are a lot of reasons, but I'll cut to the chase," Land said. "Most Southern Baptists would have severe objections to the vocabulary that Cheney used in describing a rather impossible act to Senator [Patrick] Leahy." (Land was referring to the vice president's suggestion on the Senate floor that Leahy "fuck yourself.")

"Okay," Rove responded. "Well, who would you send?"

"I'd send Condoleezza Rice: Southern Baptists like her," said Land, who had orchestrated the 1995 apology for the convention's slaveholding roots, and unabashedly compared Bush to Lincoln.

After meeting her plane on the morning of June 14, the final day of the convention, Land escorted the secretary back to the Greensboro Coliseum. There she met with SBC president Bobby Welch, a former Green Beret who devoted himself to Christ after he was shot in the chest by a Vietcong sniper.

"Roll Tide," said Welch, referring to Alabama's cherished Crimson Tide football team.

"Roll Tide," responded the Alabaman Rice.

"They established communication early, on important elements of southern tradition," Land later explained.

They then knelt for an even more important southern tradition, and prayed together, before Rice walked out into the arena. Searing white sports lamps suspended from steel beams nine stories overhead lit up the floor, which normally hosts NCAA basketball tournaments, professional wrestling events, and monster truck rallies. As she approached the glass podium, a full orchestra and choir gave glory. The Coliseum was over-air-conditioned, but 12,000 congregants stood in ardent passion and cheered from the tiers around her.

The speech immediately took on the feeling of an old-time revival on the scale of a Billy Graham crusade. In uncharacteristically fiery prose, Rice channeled her grandfather and father, both Birmingham ministers. She searched her soul, and challenged the conscience of the nearly all-white congregation by remembering her ancestors who "in Mr. Jefferson's Constitution were three-fifths of a man."

She received twelve standing ovations. One came when Rice trumpeted the recent assassination of the terrorist Abu Musab al-Zarqawi. Two more came when she mentioned Danforth's peace deal in Sudan, and the administration's defense of international religious freedom. But the climax, resulting in the most thunderous applause, came halfway through the speech.

If not for America, then who would rally a great coalition and work to end the horrific international crime of human trafficking? Slavery did not end in the nineteenth century. It remains a tragic reality for thousands of people, mostly women and young girls, who are stolen and beaten and bought and sold like freight. Under President Bush's leadership, the United States has launched a new abolitionist movement to end the illicit trade in human beings. We are rooting out the perpetrators and helping to care for their victims. We are calling to account any nation that turns a blind eye to human trafficking. And we have made this promise to every person still held captive: So long as America has any— thing to say about it, slavery will have no place in the modern world.

The Coliseum erupted, flashbulbs popped, and Rice had to wait a full thirty seconds before the faithful calmed down enough for her to continue. At the end of the speech, the crowd once again bathed her in rapturous applause, and burst into a spontaneous rendition of "God Bless America." Reverend Welch approached her on the dais.

"They're going to be hard to contain," he shouted above the din.

He bowed his head, touched her back, and led a prayer as many in the rapt audience held their hands to the firmament.

"Dear Heavenly Father, we thank you now for this sweet lady whom you have protected and guided and blessed," Welch prayed. "And we pray to you now, that you'll send a band of angels with swords of fire, to camp out over her presence, and to protect her from the evil one—and harm that may be headed her way. Keep her safe, and bless her. You know how we have longed and yearned for such leadership as this, and we are grateful, Lord."

"That's nice," Rice said to Land, as she walked off the stage. "That is really nice."

That May, Miller tested Rice's words as he engaged in a high-level struggle to relegate India. It was a lonely, clandestine battle. Although the world would not know the details of the fight, India and other reprobate nations would take the measure of America's abolitionist intent based on its outcome.

The abolitionist had a powerful adversary. The U.S. Ambassador to India, David Mulford, was a trade guy, a candidate for Treasury Secretary, and a visceral opponent of putting Delhi on a shortlist for sanctions. Though he declined my request for an interview, State Department sources said that Mulford did not view debt bondage as slavery, despite American law, which defined it as such. Miller's staff tried to convince him with graphic pictures of bonded laborers. They had no effect.

Miller scored the first field goal when he convinced a skeptical Paula Dobriansky to drop India to Tier Three. But Mulford followed by making an end run to an old friend. Deputy Secretary of State Robert Zoellick had worked alongside Mulford in Reagan's Treasury Department, and the two shared a narrow focus on free trade. Now the number two person in the State Department, Zoellick overruled Dobriansky.

Flouting protocol, Miller made an end run of his own, outflanking Mulford by scheduling a meeting with Condoleezza Rice. If anyone, Rice, the descendant of slaves, might be moved to save Indian bonded laborers, whose slavery more resembled plantation bondage than anything Miller had encountered.

Miller's confrontation was a reckoning for the secretary, and a revelation for the antislavery czar. Rice gave him five minutes. The issue was too important for a sound bite, and Miller took more than an hour to plead the cause of the slaves of India and the other countries given a pass by Zoellick. He leaned hard on her to overrule her deputy and downgrade India to Tier Three.

In the end, Miller's well-learned politicking did not matter. Rice refused to demote India from the toothless "Watch List" of Tier Two, a status the Indian government swiftly and publicly dismissed. Ambassador Mulford softened even that light slap by gushing to Delhi that it was "recognizing trafficking is an important issue" and "taking action" to stop it. America would not call to account a nation that turned a blind eye to the bondage of millions of its own citizens.

Following the secretary's denial of the slaves, Miller was set adrift. Although he normally strides with determination, if wildly, Miller's head was down as he walked rudderless back from C Street. He then confided to his staff that he was contemplating resigning.

Meanwhile, the administration's second most passionate abolitionist was also in the final throes of his service. Hours after Rice gave her speech to the Southern Baptist Convention, Michael Gerson announced his departure. He had been Bush's conscience since the early days of the first campaign and, like Miller, he had done battle with Zoellick over human rights. Now Gerson's resignation meant that Miller lost his line-in at the White House. Without that connection, the Bush team's articulated abolitionism dissolved.

"My sense is that the president cares," Frank Wolf said in December

2006. "After you go below that, you're not really sure how much concern there is. I think the trafficking issue is fading."

Others who visited the Gerson-less Oval Office to discuss trafficking reported being met with blank stares. That spring, a graduate student asked a general question about the role of legalized prostitution in sex slavery.

"It sounds like I'm dodging here," said Bush, confused. "But again, you know more about this subject than I, and I will be glad to call Condi and talk to her about our policy."

Without Gerson, who had skillfully blended antislavery initiatives into the national security agenda, the Iraq War finally buried Wilberforce passions. Just as Vietnam undid Lyndon Johnson's War on Poverty, Iraq undid Bush's war on slavery. On average, the Bush administration spent as much money in two days to free Iraqis as it did in six years to free slaves.

Still, Miller kept fighting. He had at least one historical precedent going for him: two centuries earlier, war with Napoleon stalled William Wilberforce and Thomas Clarkson's struggle, but they pushed on to abolish the slave trade. While Wilberforce's faith sustained him, Clarkson's waned, and he moved away from the Anglican Church, to which he had planned to dedicate his life.

Like Clarkson, the administration's third most effective abolitionist stepped away from national religious oligarchs. After Jack Danforth brokered the peace deal in Sudan, he served as UN Ambassador until he abruptly resigned in the fall of 2004. At the time he said that he wanted to spend more time with his wife, but Reverend Danforth had additional reasons for departing.

"By a series of recent initiatives, Republicans have transformed our party into the political arm of conservative Christians," he wrote on March 30, 2006, in the *New York Times*. "Our current fixation on a religious agenda has turned us in the wrong direction."

Those conservative Christians soon reverted back to a domestic focus. Even before the Republican-led Congress shuddered and collapsed in the fall of 2006, the faith-driven core of the Horowitz coalition had shifted its attention back to gays and abortion. Without Evangelical pressure, the administration allowed the field of Sudanese peace that Danforth had tilled to lie fallow. Meanwhile Khartoum, refreshed from the pause and unenthused to relinquish key southern oil fields, began to rearm the slave-raiding militias.

Nearing the end of his fourth year in office, Miller looked around and found himself the lone helmsman of an abolitionist ship that was caught in the doldrums of Washington.

"My mind has been literally bent like a Bow to one gloomy subject," Thomas Clarkson wrote to a clergyman in 1793. "I am often suddenly seized with Giddiness & Cramps. I feel an unpleasant ringing in my Ears, my Hands frequently tremble. Cold sweats suddenly come upon Me. . . . I find myself weak, easily fatigued, & out of Breath. My recollection is also on the Decline."

While John Miller's breakdown was less pronounced, it was nonetheless unmistakable. It would be easy to blame it on the travel. Miller visited more than fifty countries, many of them several times. Normally absentminded, his memory faded rapidly on those trips, and he often lost his passport or his tickets. Despite occasionally getting exercise in a pool above his Virginia apartment, his health also fell apart. For Miller, all of these were symptoms.

He claimed it wasn't the battle over India alone that prompted him to resign. But the internal battles wore him down, and shook his faith in his government. He was frustrated with the State Department bureaucracy, and regularly livid at the stultifying delays it caused in his work. It would not have mattered so much if he headed some division in the Department of Agriculture. But his responsibility was a bit dearer: if he did not show up for work, slaves would die in bondage.

"You get consumed with this," he said one afternoon, looking skywards in a rare moment of self-reflection. "You get consumed. You start meeting these people. These victims. These survivors. And then you get consumed."

As we talked late one evening in September 2006, I told him I'd release him from my interrogation so that he could go back to his personal life.

"What personal life?" he asked, without irony.

He and his wife June divorced in December 2004, the same month he originally pledged to leave his post and return home to Seattle. His son Rip had asked him if they could travel together on one of his advocacy trips. But Miller didn't have time to take the seventeen-year-old to a Nationals game, let alone Thailand. After six weeks at Montana State, Rip dropped out, told his father he would join the army, but wound up working the night shift polishing floors at the local Wal-Mart. A year later he joined the Marines.

At sixty-eight, Miller lived alone in an unfurnished high-rise apartment in Arlington. "It's not that sad," he said, trying to smile through it. He couldn't cook, but there was a good noodle café around the corner from his apartment where stroganoff cost only $5, which suited his salary, since he took a pay cut after becoming an ambassador. His staff chipped in and gave him a serving set around Christmas and a plant for his birthday. He recently adorned one wall with a print by the African-American artist Jacob Lawrence. He even bought a sofa.

"In some ways this is an unreal existence," he said, his voice trailing for a moment. Then, in a flash, the same milewide grin that I saw when I first met him returned. He described his recent visit to an innovative project in Indonesia that provided trafficking survivors with retraining and income-generation packages.

"Ben, this was enough to make my day!"

10

A Little Hope

I first read her story in a fall 1999 wire report headlined "Girl's Case Sheds Light on Haitian Practice of Servitude." The details of her bondage were brutal but sketchy, and the Miami newspapers never published her name. Five years later, the indictment of her captor only referred to the victim by her initials, "W.N.," as is policy in federal cases involving the rape of a minor. After the police freed her, the Haitian-American community in suburban Miami began calling her *Ti Lespwa*, or "Little Hope."

Little Hope's biography belied her nickname. She was born in the Haitian capital on January 11, 1987, amidst the chaos following Baby Doc's ouster. Her birth certificate bears her father's name, Wilben. It is the only record she has that he existed.

Her mother, Immacula led a hard life but did her best to shield her daughter. Immacula made just enough to feed them both by cleaning the house of a wealthy Port-au-Prince family. At age four, the little girl began working alongside her mother, washing the family's clothes, and taking care of the family's handicapped child. Once, when Little Hope refused to run an errand to buy bread, Immacula raised a hand against her. It was the first and last time she did so. At night, Immacula always bathed her daughter. When the blackouts came, she held her child as they slept on the floor of their one-room shack.

On Sundays, Immacula would style her daughter's hair. One day, she brought home a blouse and skirt for Little Hope. Thenceforth, the girl insisted on wearing the outfit every Sunday until it was threadbare. In August 1992, Hurricane Andrew passed near Haiti. The winds and rain battered the capital, but Little Hope felt safe in her mother's arms.

Those arms soon went from thin to gaunt, however, as her mother suffered from a mysterious illness that sapped her energy, left her soaked with sweat at night, and ravaged her body. After Little Hope's sixth birthday in 1993, Immacula died of AIDS. Her employer paid for the funeral, and as Little Hope stood over her mother's open casket, she said good-bye.

The woman who had employed her mother took in the girl as a restavèk, a child slave. Without her mother, Little Hope's life was loveless. But her lot was better than that of many other restavèks, as her mistress fed her regularly and, in keeping with a promise to Immacula, sent her to school. Still, domestic duties impeded her schoolwork. The house, with two stories and a dozen rooms, was a lot for the young girl to clean, and without automated appliances, she had to wash the dishes, clothes, and diapers by hand.

One day in 1996, Marie Pompee, sister of the mistress, came to visit. An American citizen, Marie was the breadwinner for her relatives back on the island, visiting frequently and bringing clothes and money from her home in Miami. She was normally well dressed, favoring gold jewelry and pantsuits, well fed and well coiffed. To Little Hope, she—and America—meant comfort and luxury.

Marie now told the nine-year-old that she would send for her. For the first time since her mother died, the girl felt hope. Perhaps sensing her optimism, Marie quickly put the girl in her place.

"If I bring you to America," Marie told her, "you will be my slave."

While Marie's admonition served as a stark warning that she would not shed her chains upon arrival, Little Hope still yearned to see America. "The brightest beacon for freedom and opportunity in the world," as President Bush called the United States after 9/11, blinded the girl to the prison she was entering. She was not the only inmate. Annually, traffickers now take more slaves into the United States than seventeenth-century slave traders transported to pre-independence America.

Counting slaves today is a tricky business. As John Miller is fond of saying, slaves don't stand in line, raise their hands, and wait for the census to register them. Particularly in America, captors often build up slaves' fear of authority to keep them hidden. But even cautious officials in the U.S. government estimate that traffickers turn up to 17,500 humans into slaves on American soil every year. Put another way, assuming you read at an average speed—about 250 words per minute—by the time you finish this chapter, another person will have entered bondage in the United States.

With an average term of enslavement lasting at least three years, there are now some 50,000 slaves in the United States. Most victims come from Asia or Mexico, although several thousand are Eastern European, Central American, or African. U.S. officials have discovered slaves from over three dozen countries. Nearly all came to American shores willingly, desperate for prosperity and liberty, blending seamlessly with the 60 million others who enter the country every year. Some come legally, though most disappear amid an already invisible group: the roughly 12 million illegal immigrants in the United States. Too often, they find that the bondage they fled in their homelands still festers in the "land of liberty."

As in South Asia, usurious lenders and traffickers trap thousands in agricultural debt bondage. In a 2004 report entitled *Hidden Slaves*, Kevin Bales and the University of California-Berkeley estimated that one in ten slaves in America is a bonded farm laborer. Take Florida's $62 billion agriculture, in which outreach groups and police have found hundreds of slaves, predominantly Mexican. Those probably represent many more undiscovered bonded laborers. And yet the federal government has only prosecuted some half dozen cases of slavery in Florida's migrant farming camps.

As in Europe, human smuggling rings and mom-and-pop traffickers annually import thousands of women to be forced prostitutes. The Bales study, based largely on recent press reports of 131 cases of slavery, estimated that nearly half of the slaves languish in underground brothels, illicit massage parlors, or tightly controlled streetwalking operations. It is likely that the number of forced prostitutes is in the thousands. In 1999, the Immigration and Naturalization Service reported that over 250 American brothels held trafficked women. Today, despite hundreds of raids, many brothels remain open, and traffickers avoid detection by rotating their slaves.

As in Southeast Asia, the United States has its shameful hubs of child prostitution. The average age at which a prostitute first sells her body is fourteen and, as in Romania, traffickers here enslave both immigrant and native-born children. The problem has been a focus of the Bush administration. Through its "Innocence Lost" initiative, the Department of Justice has launched task forces in twenty-seven cities to arrest pimps and child traffickers.

As in the Middle East, domestic slaves in America, concealed in private homes, suffer in silent fear of beatings by their masters, and deportation by immigration authorities. According to the Bales study, a third of the known cases of bondage involved domestic servants—though the actual proportion is probably much higher.

And as in Haiti, restavèks, smuggled into America by their Haitian masters, have turned up in cities and suburbs as far north as Connecticut. Child protection hot lines in Miami's Little Haiti receive dozens of calls about restavèks every year, yet it normally takes a murder for the rest of the country to hear of the bondage. On January 3, 1978, a seventeen-year-old restavèk named Lyonel Dor, having endured years of abuse, killed his mistress with a pipe as she rested in her Brooklyn apartment. Twenty years later, a twelve-year-old girl named Marie

Joseph was enslaved in a Miami home. Kept out of school and out of sight, her bondage only came to light after she was killed in the crossfire of a drug battle as she worked for the family at a local flea market.

The new American slavery is as scattered and as diverse as the American population. Slaves have been found in over a hundred American cities over the last decade, though California, New York, Florida, and Texas—the main ports of entry for immigrants—have the highest concentrations of trafficking victims.

Immigrants, the lifeblood of America, usually come into the country only if they have the means to pay for the journey. Now, some human smugglers offer the chance to immigrate with little or no money down. The offer always comes with strings attached, however. And sometimes, it comes with chains.

One morning in 1996, Little Hope prepared to enter a new world. Marie had hired a human smuggler, who coached the girl on what to say and how to act with American customs officials. When the smuggler showed her the passport of another girl, who looked sufficiently similar, Little Hope sensed the risk involved but put her faith in the woman. And despite the slavery that she knew awaited her, she was excited to come to a land where she might be able to transcend her bondage.

At Miami International Airport, the customs officer did not give Little Hope a second look. Every year, some 10,000 children arrive unaccompanied in the United States. Although a third wind up sexually exploited by adults, prior to 9/11 and the Trafficking Victims Protection Act, the checks on their entry were few. To the customs officer, Little Hope was just another young black Haitian girl, and the older black Haitian lady that accompanied her was her guardian.

The smuggler drove Little Hope to Miami. On the way, the girl took in the new world with its clean lines and smooth roads. Masses of cars replaced masses of animals and people. Towering buildings replaced towering piles of garbage. It was all alien, and sterile. In Miami, Marie and her husband, Willy Pompee Sr., both forty, gave cash to the smuggler, and drove the girl to their large suburban home in Miami Lakes. The size of the place impressed the nine-year-old but also daunted her: it would be a lot to clean. And despite the two adult children living at home, the Pompees also would force her to care for the two youngest children, a baby and a four-year-old.

The Pompees ran Willy's Rags, Inc., a business in what Haitian Americans refer to as the *pepe* trade, repackaging clothing cast off by Americans, and reselling it to Haitians at a markup. *Pepe* is the primary element of most Haitians' wardrobes, and ragmen send millions of pounds of used clothing to the nation every year. By cutting corners, Willy Senior, who regularly traveled between Port-au-Prince and Miami, had become wealthy.

What had been a difficult situation of forced servitude for Little Hope in Haiti became violent slavery in Miami. From the beginning, she had the feeling that Marie resented her presence, and that the children hated her. Marie gave her a small bed in a guest room but told her she was to eat in the kitchen while the family ate together in front of the television. Once or twice, the family took her with them to fast-food restaurants, but normally they would leave her at home and feed her leftovers after they returned.

The Pompees berated their slave when she wasn't working hard enough. If neighborhood children came over to play, Little Hope would not talk to them except to ask, eyes downcast, if they would mind if she cleaned around them. At other times, Marie called her a whore, "like your mother," and beat her with a leather martinet she had imported from Haiti. If the baby cried too much, or the dog crapped in the garage, Little Hope knew to expect the whip. The beatings were often so ferocious that the girl thought Marie aimed to kill her. Willy Senior never physically abused Little Hope, and he occasionally intervened to lessen his wife's blows.

The eldest son, Willy Junior, was a muscled, dour fellow. A military school recently had expelled him, and now he was a video game addict. From that first day, there was something about him that scared Little Hope.

To comply with state law, Marie sent the girl to a big public elementary school in the neighborhood. Every Saturday, and most days after class, Willy Junior took her to sort incoming clothes at the family's *pepe* warehouse. None of the other children worked there. Always exhausted, Little Hope struggled in class, but one teacher took sympathy on the quiet girl and awarded her an "Outstanding Citizenship Award."

One night, a few weeks after Little Hope arrived in America, the hulking eighteen-year-old Willy Junior slipped into her bed. He told her to be quiet. She didn't know what was happening—no one had ever taught her about sex—but she knew it hurt, and she knew it was wrong. After he was finished, Willy Junior told her she would wind up on the street in Haiti if she said anything.

Despite his threat, the pain and bleeding she suffered the next day terrified her, and she told Marie what happened. Marie accused her of lying. When Willy Junior found out she had talked, he threatened to kill her if she did so again. The rape continued, and became more ferocious, occasionally leaving Little Hope with difficulty walking. When the young man entered her room, she would curl up and pretend she was elsewhere, in another house, with another family, perhaps with her own—even though she no longer had one.

Marie forbade Little Hope from leaving the house alone, but some days she escaped via a medium familiar to all American youngsters—television. She would watch when the others were not around, and what she saw looked like the America that used to appear in her dreams. On MTV, the R&B singer Mary J. Blige dazzled her. *The Oprah Winfrey Show* gave her courage, not because she understood all of the dialogue—her English was weak, as the family addressed her in Creole—but because in Winfrey, Little Hope saw a reflection of who she might become, were she free.

In 1997, the Pompees paid $351,000 for a house in a pristine, gated neighborhood in Pembroke Pines, a suburb some twenty miles north of Miami. Behind the new white walls and vertical blinds of the 4,100-square-foot home, Little Hope's slavery continued. Now a mattress on the floor replaced her bed, and another mattress in the garage awaited her if she misbehaved.

One Saturday afternoon in 1998, the Pompees left Little Hope at home alone. Impulsively, she ran away after they left. She didn't get far, and knocked on a neighbor's door down the street. Another ten-year-old girl answered, and invited her in. Little Hope did not tell the girl, whose name was Cherokie, about her bondage, as she could not trust a stranger that quickly. But Cherokie and her sister, Melissa, were kind to the visitor, and warmed up Hot Pocket sandwiches for her in the family microwave. Then they watched a movie on television. It was a small, short-lived respite—fearful of beatings, Little Hope returned home.

Between the flickering images on television that afternoon with the neighbors, and a few stolen moments at school, Little Hope began to realize that the trap she found herself in was not America. Though she knew she would never feel as safe as she did in her mother's arms, she began to imagine a world where she could be secure without being the property of another person.

One evening in July 1999, as Little Hope was cleaning the house, something on television made her drop her dust rag. An advertisement for the John Casablancas Modeling and Career Center beckoned young women with promises of self-esteem and a glamorous new life. The commercial ended, and a phone number flashed on the screen.

Catalina Restrepo, the twenty-two-year-old intern who fielded her call at the Fort Lauderdale branch, was polite, but quickly got off the phone with the strange little girl. Working the evening shift at the modeling agency, she had fielded prank calls before. But Little Hope called back—three times that evening. Then, the next evening, she called back again. After a week of such calls, Restrepo, bemused and a bit curious at the girl's persistence, began talking to her. Little Hope told her that she wanted to be a model so she could leave the place where she was living. Restrepo said that, at twelve, she was too young. When she persisted,

Restrepo said that if she was serious, because she was under eighteen, she would have to come in with her parents.

"I don't have no parents," she whispered. "I was adopted."

"Oh, well, they can bring you," said Restrepo.

"No, they can't," said Little Hope.

After two weeks of halting conversations, often ending suddenly with a click when one of the Pompees came close, Little Hope began to hint at her slavery. Once, Restrepo asked her what she was doing as she heard the girl fumbling. The girl said that she was cleaning. Restrepo quickly sensed, based on the frequency that she heard the same fumbling, that her tasks were more than ordinary chores. Finally, Little Hope confided that the Pompees forced her to work, and put her into a closet when she resisted. To Restrepo, the story at first seemed exaggerated, a Cinderella fantasy of a little girl angry at her wicked stepmother.

That August, as Little Hope got to know her new phone friend, Marie enrolled her in a new school, Florida International Academy, a free, predominantly African-American school in Opa-Locka. The academy had opened in August 1998; during its first year, students, nearly all of whom came from very poor families, had to use portable toilets, as there was no running water. There were significant staffing problems, as no one wanted to work in a school where several of the students already had criminal records on charges including assault and grand theft. The school board had threatened to shut the place down over building code violations, but the ad hoc principal, a tiny, brave, and controversial woman in her fifties named Sonia Cossie Mitchell, held it together. Marie did not send her own children to the school, which, measured by test scores, was one of the lowest-performing public schools in the country.

Her new teachers required Little Hope to bring basic school supplies, but Marie refused to provide them. So the girl borrowed pencils, and pulled paper out of the garbage when she saw it. Mitchell noticed her staring out of the window during class, and found that she never did her homework. She was stern with the girl, assuming that she was lazy and disorganized.

"Until today I blame myself," Mitchell later said. "How could I have been teaching this child and not know something was wrong?"

On September 9, 1999, Little Hope told Catalina Restrepo something chilling. "My brother comes into the room where I sleep at night and does something to me," she said. "And it really hurts."

One of Restrepo's supervisors, a former schoolteacher who was alert to signs of child sexual abuse, called the police, who transferred the modeling agent to an automated child welfare line. Eventually, a representative from the Department of Children and Families (DCF) called her back—and openly doubted Little Hope's claims.

Nonetheless, the following day, a DCF officer called to arrange an evening visit to the Pompees. Several hours later, a harried social worker came to the house. She spoke briefly to Little Hope in front of Marie, then left, satisfied that there was no abuse, and apparently unfazed that she had interviewed the child in the presence of the alleged abuser. After she left, Marie thrashed Little Hope, and told her she would be back on the streets of Port-au-Prince if she opened her mouth again.

Still, in secret, the girl kept calling the modeling agency, and the agency clerks kept calling child services. Independently, Little Hope's principal, Sonia Mitchell, had called DCF as well to express her own concerns about the girl. Child services made no meaningful follow-up.

On the morning of September 28, Little Hope, as usual, was late to school because of her cleaning responsibilities. This time, Mitchell who was pulling double duty and teaching Little Hope's class, noticed the girl walking gingerly and clutching her stomach in pain. She called in the custodian to watch the other students, and took the girl into the hallway. Little Hope, eyes downcast, said that her "brother" had kicked her.

Mitchell put her hand on Little Hope's distended stomach, and the girl grimaced.

"Wait a minute," said Mitchell in her silvery West Indian accent. "Let's go in my office."

Mitchell was not a doctor, but she could tell the symptoms did not fit the story. She pressed Little Hope. Finally, the girl sheepishly admitted the pain was farther down—a venereal issue—and lifted her skirt. She was bleeding. Mitchell asked if the blood was from her period. Breaking down, Little Hope blurted out the truth through sobs. The blood was from rough sex. Mitchell said she would call her parents, but the girl begged her not to tell them.

At the end of that school day, Restrepo and her mother showed up unannounced. Ostensibly, they had come because Little Hope had said that she had neither lunch money nor school supplies. Restrepo now brought her both. Mitchell called the two women into her office, where they compared notes.

Mitchell reported that Little Hope regularly had bruises, was often underfed, and always tardy. As they spoke, Mitchell summoned Little Hope. Restrepo, meeting the girl for the first time, gave her a chocolate. It melted immediately in her hand. Restrepo felt her forehead and realized the girl had a fever.

Just then, Restrepo saw Willy Junior approaching. All three women had serious concerns about allowing her to go home with the twenty-year-old. But Mitchell knew from experience that the only alternative was to call the police. After five fruitless calls to child services that month, she had become disillusioned. She feared the police would only return the girl to the home, where Marie or Willy Junior might punish her for speaking out.

Torn, Mitchell held the girl close. She decided that she would call the police anyway, but realized that, in that moment, she had to send Little Hope back with Willy Junior.

The next morning, Mitchell called the Opa-Locka police, who said it wasn't their problem because Little Hope lived in Broward County. The Broward police passed the buck back to Opa-Locka. Fed up, Mitchell called the Opa-Locka police again.

"Look," she said, "if you don't investigate, I'm calling the TV news."

That perseverance changed the girl's life. The police came, and after interviewing Little Hope, they drove the girl, crying hysterically, to a sexual assault treatment center in Fort Lauderdale. There they gave her a series of tests, and found out that she had been raped, sodomized, and was suffering from a range of infections, including hepatitis, and a painful sexually transmitted disease.

Recognizing that, in addition to rape, Little Hope may have endured slavery, the police called the Department of Justice office in Miami. Scott Ray, a sharp-featured federal prosecutor who had recently worked on an involuntary servitude case, taped the girl's deposition. Immediately, the FBI launched an investigation.

Meanwhile, Willy Junior went to pick up Little Hope from school as usual. One of Mitchell's colleagues told him that she was with the police, and he peeled out in a panic. The next day, police issued a warrant for his arrest.

In the span of a few harrowing hours, Little Hope had become free at last. That night, as the TV news played in her hospital room, she saw the flashing lights of police cruisers reflected off the Pompees' house, which still had the boards up after Hurricane Floyd. For three years as a slave in that house, television had been her escape, her window on the outside world. Now she had gone through that window, and she felt very alone on the other side.

Scott Ray, the U.S. Attorney who led the case against the Pompees, faced a daunting challenge. State-level prosecutors had conclusive evidence that Little Hope suffered violent rape. If convicted under Florida law, Willy Junior could face the death penalty, as the victim was a minor. But Florida had no antitrafficking laws, and at the federal level, it would be another year before President Clinton signed the Trafficking Victims Protection Act.

As Ray built a case, his tools were few, and his department's antislavery track record was long but inglorious. In 1870, shortly after Frederick Douglass spoke to the last meeting of the American Anti-Slavery Society, Congress created the Department of Justice to finish the work of abolition. The department faced a slippery target, as chattel slavery

soon gave way to debt bondage during Reconstruction. In the twentieth century, the department prosecuted only a handful of slavery cases:
traffickers became adept at concealing their victims deep within different waves of immigrants, whose cultures and languages were often
impenetrable for American officials.

At the time of Little Hope's rescue, Ray was one of a tiny group of
dedicated prosecutors who volunteered to take on modern-day slavery.
Despite Attorney General Janet Reno's personal interest in the issue,
the Department of Justice prosecuted only twenty-five slavery cases in
1999. But those attorneys who worked on the issue were an intense lot,
and, like John Miller, they tended to become more focused and more
determined as they came face-to-face with victims and survivors.

In order for a jury to convict the Pompees of involuntary servitude,
Ray would need to counter the defense that the family took the girl in
to save her from the Haitian street, and that they subsequently made
her a beloved member of the family. The Pompees' legal team immediately went about attacking Little Hope as a damaged child, who had
learned promiscuity from her mother, a prostitute. They claimed that
neighbors had complained after she snuck out of the house to have sex
with neighborhood boys. They claimed that Marie Pompee sent the girl
to the same private school and the same family doctor as her own children. They claimed that Marie had begun adoption proceedings, that
she treated the girl lavishly, that she showed her love with a roomful
of clothes and toys. Marie would not have forced the girl to work, they
claimed, because she paid a maid to clean the house twice a week.

Ray quickly disproved all of those claims, while physical evidence
bore out Little Hope's story. The Pembroke Pines police officer who
first searched the Pompees' home found a mattress in the garage with
feces and rotting food next to it, and a small pile of Little Hope's ragged
clothing in a bathroom cabinet. A week later, the FBI seized all family
pictures from the home—not one included the girl, who had lived with
the family in Haiti and America for the better part of six years. The
agents canvassed the neighborhood. Not one neighbor reported that
the child had been promiscuous, and few had seen the child unaccom-

panied outside of the home. Several said they had seen Marie publicly humiliate her.

As Ray built the case, police officials searched aggressively for Willy Junior and his father. The morning after police issued an arrest warrant for the son, the father turned up on the manifest of an American Airlines flight scheduled to leave for Port-au-Prince. Botched communication between detectives, customs officials, and an airline dispatcher in Texas meant the pilot, confused, defied an order to return Willy Senior to the gate. While the customs officials waited for the plane to turn around, they watched, slack-jawed, as it took flight. Two hours later, Willy Senior disappeared on the streets of Port-au-Prince. Though he held a round-trip ticket, he never used the return portion. Rather than face the death penalty, Willy Junior remained a fugitive as well, presumably hidden in Haiti with his father.

Meanwhile, during that first week after her rescue, the extent of Little Hope's injuries—both physical and emotional—became apparent. The Pompees had never taken her to the dentist, and only once, for school vaccinations, had they taken her to the doctor. Now nurses treated her for undernourishment, gave her antibiotics for her infections, and a dentist pulled two rotted teeth. Catalina Restrepo and Sonia Mitchell both visited her. Restrepo brought her dental floss, and showed her how to use it.

Her bruises soon healed, but the girl's ability to trust remained shattered. And despite the nickname given to her by the Haitian-American community, which was outraged at her abuse, Little Hope's future seemed dark. As the full details of her slavery emerged, those around her were shocked.

"I just thought this girl is going to be warped for the rest of her life," Mitchell said. "For a human being to go through that at that tender age—I tremble when I think about her case."

Little Hope's real name is Williathe Narcisse. Eight years after her rescue, she carries her five-foot-three frame at a dignified, deliberate pace—her own speed. She has smooth black skin and a winning smile that lights up her face. She loves to talk. Having read her file, and talked to her lawyers and caseworker before I met her, I was startled by her openness. I came to Miami expecting to find a victim. I found a survivor.

We sat down for lunch a few miles from the house where the Pompees had stolen three years of her life. She was renting a room in a gated neighborhood across from a shopping mall, and she was in her first year at nearby Broward Community College. In many ways she was a typical college kid. She had a stackful of discount cards for restaurants and retail stores—all of which she dutifully signed with her name and self-appointed nickname, "Hello Kitty." She loved hip-hop, and the ring tone on her cell phone was her favorite song, "This Is Why I'm Hot." She had a MySpace Web page that led with a quote from Diana Ross: "You can't just sit there and wait for people to give you that golden dream. You've got to get out there and make it happen for yourself."

Three months earlier, Williathe had turned twenty years old. She wanted to have a party: for most of her life she never even knew the date of her birthday, and she was making up for lost celebrations. But first-year college transitions meant she had no one to invite.

"I don't have any friends," she said. "My only friend is God, now."

For a while, she was close with the daughter of one of the foster mothers who took her in after the rescue. Now, the daughter was in her third year at the University of Florida.

"Are you still friends, then?" I asked.

"Yeah, but she's popular," Williathe said.

"What does that mean?"

"She's *popular*. Per-son-al-it-y," she explained, enunciating each syllable.

"You don't think you have personality?" I asked.

"I have personality," she said. "But I don't think people get mine as fast as they do hers."

Between classes, homework, and a job in the evenings at a retail clothing store, she had little time for self-pity. As she had since childhood, Williathe would fantasize about where she would like to be. But now she writes those fantasies down, believing that by rendering them thus, they will morph into achievable goals. In the short term, she wants to get a higher-paying summer job so that she can save up for a car—a necessity in Pembroke Pines, where public buses are not very convenient. Her postgraduation plans are more ambitious. Her teachers have told her that she should be a lawyer, "but I want to be a talk show host, like Oprah. I love her spirit."

She still has scars from Marie's whip, but the scars that affect her every day are ones that I couldn't see when I first met her. On our second meeting, she opened up about them. "Did you ever watch the show *Monk*?" she asked, referring to a sitcom about an obsessive-compulsive detective. "I'm like Monk."

The obsessions started as soon as the state placed her in a foster home. She would wash herself perpetually, taking three long baths every afternoon. She would stare at herself in the mirror and scrub her face, calling herself ugly. She would swab countertops and stack pots, even if the kitchen was neat. Nightmares were a constant. Sometimes she would break down during the day, collapsing in the shower and screaming that her hair was falling out; at other times, she heard voices in her head that told her to kill. The state paid for medication and five different therapists before she turned eighteen. But as soon as she began to feel secure, she had to move to a new setting.

"Foster care was a hell: I went through twenty-some homes," she said. "I don't know the exact number. Most of the people do it for money. I was looking for love so bad, and when love was there, I didn't know. I didn't know."

At times, while waiting for another foster spot to open up, she found herself in a nearby Department of Children and Families facility. Once, she ran away with a backpack and her two stuffed animals.

"I didn't know where I was running, I was just running," she said. "I just wanted to get away. I was just walking in the street. That's how they found me."

———

In the spring of 2004, Williathe's fragile mental health put Scott Ray, the lead prosecutor, in a bind. To prove the Pompees had forced her into involuntary servitude, he would need to put the teenager on the stand. There she would have to recount the worst things that ever happened to her, in front of a hostile audience of Marie's family members. Marie's lawyer would aim to undermine Williathe's credibility, and to blame what abuse did occur on the men in the household—who were now safely beyond the grasp of American justice.

Because slavery was so hard to prove—particularly in cases like Williathe's, where the bondage occurred before the Trafficking Victims Protection Act, which expanded the definition of coercion—Ray had learned the value of companion charges. In sex-trafficking cases, he would also charge a violation of the Mann Act, otherwise known as the White Slave Traffic Act of 1910. Under the Mann Act, prosecutors never had to prove that a woman was enslaved; all they had to prove was that the defendant had taken her across state lines "for the purpose of prostitution or debauchery, or for any other immoral purpose."

In Williathe's case, Ray charged Marie with a different companion crime: harboring an illegal alien. The charge was self-evident, and when Marie pled guilty in June 2004, Ray did not press for an involuntary servitude indictment. He knew Marie could face up to ten years in jail on the harboring charge alone, and he did not want to subject Williathe to the ferocity of open court.

In Fort Lauderdale on July 1, 2004, Marie's sentencing was a circus. Marie begged the forgiveness of the district court judge, but not of Williathe, who was not there. "I would like to apologize not only to the court, but to you personally for whatever happened to the child," Marie sniffled. "I was just helping a kid and I didn't realize that helping someone would bring me so many problems!"

The Pompees showed up en masse to speak on Marie's behalf, and to denigrate Williathe. Marie's cousin, twenty-three-year-old Veronica DuPont, testified that Williathe was a liar, and that privately the girl had admitted she concocted the entire story. She was "set up like a princess," DuPont said.

In the end, the judge sentenced Marie Pompee to just six months in prison, saying he believed her claim that she did not know about the sexual abuse. As Marie stood up to surrender, DuPont and other relatives wailed and cried that God was the ultimate judge.

"I'm kind of mad she didn't pay for what she did," Williathe later said of Marie. "But then again, her going to jail for more years can't take my pain away."

To foster families and therapists who only briefly intersected with Williathe during her teenage years, it seemed that the real slavery that she suffered under the Pompees had yielded to a form of emotional bondage, visible in the obsessive cleaning and ritualistic self-abuse. To her teachers and other students in overcrowded state schools, she was just a troubled kid. No one understood the struggle that she waged every day.

"I would have friends—well, associates—in high school to whom I sometimes would tell the story of my rescue, and they'd say, 'I remember that!'" Williathe said. "And then they'd start to feel sorry for me, and I told them not to feel sorry for me because I don't feel sorry for myself."

Around the time Marie lost her freedom, Williathe began to realize hers. Early in high school, she would beat herself up for bad grades. Math was a real stumbling block. But she also began to ask her teachers when she didn't understand what she was doing wrong. Williathe was a lot of things in those years of recovery, but she was not weak.

As her reading improved, she began to expose herself to more and more literature. She started out with music and celebrity magazines. She read the autobiography of the hardscrabble rapper DMX. Much more deeply, she saw her own life reflected in Celie, the main character of Alice Walker's novel *The Color Purple*, who overcame physical and sexual abuse and found her own strength in a society that considered her worthless.

She passed enough courses to graduate from her public high school, but extreme anxiety sank her every time she tried to pass the Florida Comprehensive Assessment Test, a requirement for graduation. Williathe seemed destined, like half of her classmates, never to get her diploma.

No one adopted the girl, but in high school, the state assigned a tough but caring social worker, Mike Stevens, to help guide her development. Despite having well over a hundred cases in his portfolio, Stevens took an active interest in Williathe. In August 2005, with Stevens's encouragement, she transferred to Life Skills charter school, a free school for children who have trouble in traditional school settings.

In the smaller classes of the new school, Williathe bloomed. Outside of class, she got her first paying job, at a local Target department store. Then she won an essay contest put on by a hip-hop radio station— where she soon secured an internship. The station employees treated her like family, and when the CEO of an R&B record company heard her life story, she offered Williathe a scholarship provided she wrote an essay explaining why she wanted to attend college.

On June 10, 2006, Williathe woke up at 8 a.m. vibrating with energy. This was graduation day, and as the salutatorian of her class, she was to give a speech. She recalled one of the happiest moments of her childhood, when her mother had given her a blouse and skirt combination. Now, with her own money, she bought a bejeweled brown skirt and a gilded white top.

Wearing her new outfit along with the school mortarboard, she glowed, but choked up when she gave the speech that she had rehearsed so thoroughly. There was an awkward silence, until someone in the audience shouted encouragement.

"I started to cry because I wished my mom was in the audience," Williathe said. "That's what really got to me."

She recovered and finished the speech.

"I'm not the best role model, but here's a little advice," she said. "Never give up on yourself."

Ever since police took custody of Williathe that fall day in 1999, the United States, on paper, has made strides toward ending bondage. And the Bush administration could claim to have moved the issue into the public eye. President Bush and his attorneys general frequently highlighted their antitrafficking successes in speeches when other elements of their domestic agenda foundered. But the administration's record did not match its self-congratulation. At the end of the Bush era, America is still a far cry from completing the "unfinished work" that Lincoln spoke of in his Gettysburg Address.

A few passionate and apolitical attorneys in the Civil Rights Division of the Department of Justice, who had worked tirelessly to free slaves beginning in the early Clinton years, quietly registered successes. In the six years after the 2000 Trafficking Victims Protection Act, created partly as a result of their pressure, the division increased prosecutions by 600 percent, and convictions by 300 percent. Meanwhile, twenty-seven states passed antitrafficking laws—the maximum sentence in Florida, for example, is now thirty years in prison.

But the magnitude of the problem dwarfed the surge in prosecutions and state-level laws. Assuming the government estimates are correct, America liberated less than 2 percent of its modern-day slaves in the six years after the TVPA. John Miller routinely conceded to foreign officials that the United States would probably rank itself a Tier Two country—not ending slavery, but making significant efforts to do so.

In part, politics bears the blame for the shortfall. Just as they lobbied John Miller and the State Department to eliminate the distinction between voluntary and involuntary commercial sex, the feminists and Evangelicals of Michael Horowitz's coalition contorted the TVPA into a mandate for the Justice Department to enforce nonexistent federal laws against consensual adult prostitution. The result is a domestic policy that reflects the same confusion as foreign policy regarding the essential question: What is a slave?

Despite the fact that less than half of all American slaves are forced prostitutes, more than three quarters of all prosecutions involve sex-for-hire. Certainly, traffickers annually coerce thousands of women and girls into forced prostitution. But privately, Justice Department officials who actually dealt with victims were galled that the Horowitz coalition expected them to find moral equivalency in the victimization of a $90,000-dollar-a-year call girl in Georgetown, who kept her own income and worked for herself, and a fourteen-year-old girl, raped fifteen times a day in a fetid trailer in a migrant labor camp.

The Civil Rights Division resisted Horowitz's pressure to use all of its limited resources on massive pimp "roll-ups," instead succeeding in prosecuting several large-scale operations of genuinely forced prostitution and labor. The same month that I visited Miami, Scott Ray's office announced three more indictments of Miami-area women for restavèk slavery.

Still, many U.S. attorneys, unfamiliar with human trafficking, focused only on organized commercial sex, to the exclusion of much more deeply hidden bondage in all fields.

Looked at more broadly, the U.S. antitrafficking strategy was essentially a game of whac-a-mole, or more precisely, whac-a-pimp. While the TVPA, thanks largely to the effort of the late Senator Paul Wellstone, provided for domestic and overseas prevention programs, the Bush administration knew it would get many more public relations miles out of a high-profile arrest in New Jersey than out of a microcredit program in Mexico.

And forced prostitutes, once police found them, were usually the easiest to identify as slaves, particularly if they were underage. In contrast, without extensive investigation, factory slaves might appear simply to be underpaid sweatshop workers; farm slaves, fearing deportation, would rarely identify themselves; and neighbors might overlook domestic child slaves as merely chore-burdened adopted children. Thus, while the average sex-trafficking operation lasted up to two and half years, the average slave labor operation lasted nearly seven years.

Williathe found freedom only because two women of conscience brushed up against her. Today, local police and child service workers are much more sensitive to trafficking than they were in 1999. But their reach in a free society is limited. And though the government can raise general consciousness, it cannot legislate the consciences of individual Americans.

On our final day together, Williathe and I drove to the Pompees' house. After her husband and son fled justice, Marie Pompee had lost her home, along with her business and her freedom. Now, for the first time since her rescue, Williathe was returning to the site of her bondage.

Pembroke Pines could be anywhere in America, save for the smattering of palm trees. Off the highway, we drove past dozens of national chain restaurants, gas stations, and department stores. At the edge of town lay a series of lovely, if prefabricated and outwardly identical, gated communities. Williathe, who had not seen the house for eight years, was as lost as I was in the placid labyrinth. As we drove, I asked if she wanted to speak to Marie ever again.

"No. I still have hatred in my heart," she said. "And I'm trying to get it out. She lied, she didn't admit what she did. She knew that I was being raped, and she said she didn't know."

Finally, Williathe recognized a man-made pond that was dug near the neighborhood. As the guard was off duty at the guardpost, and several houses we dialed at random would not buzz us in, I charged in behind a school bus before the gate came down.

The neighborhood was an affluent sanctuary. Curved, evenly numbered streets, silky smooth save for well-marked speed bumps, slid between white sidewalks and well-manicured emerald lawns. Uniform white mailboxes marked driveways, many with SUVs. Every house had a built-up, testaceous tile roof, a hallmark of construction in South Florida. Few strangers came here, and neighbors working on their lawns stopped and stared as we rolled slowly by.

Williathe was very quiet. We had been talking about hip-hop on the ride in, as I tried to lighten the mood. Now her throat tightened. At the end of a long drive was the Pompees' house, a tall white structure, more spartan than the others, but nonetheless impressive.

"What are you feeling?" I asked.

"Nothing," she said. "Nothing."

I turned the car around, and we headed out in silence. On the road out, we passed a house that seemed more alive than the others on the block—more open because it sat on a corner and had inviting French doors.

"That's it!" exclaimed Williathe. "That's Cherokie and Melissa's house!"

As we pulled into the roundabout, Williathe got out and rang the doorbell.

"What should I say?" she asked nervously, as we waited.

"Ask them if they remember you," I said.

A teenage girl answered the door, and Williathe asked if Cherokie and Melissa still lived there. She nodded, as Cherokie came around the corner.

"Do you remember me?" Williathe asked, smiling for the first time.

"Yes." Cherokie smiled back.

"How old are you now?" Williathe asked.

"Nineteen," Cherokie said.

"Are you in college?"

"Yeah: BCC," Cherokie said.

"Me too!"

Cherokie invited us in as she wrote down her contact information for Williathe.

"Now you know how to reach me," she said, as we turned to walk out. Williathe, who always had more friends than she knew, saw that Cherokie was still one of them.

Epilogue

A War Worth Fighting

You might wonder what became of the slaves I found in bondage. What happened to the young Romanian woman whose owner offered her in trade for a used car? Did she escape that fetid Bucharest brothel? Did police rescue her, after I told them of her predicament? Did she finally make the sad exit from this world, as she had attempted to do so many times before?

And what of Gonoo Lal Kol, his family, and the other villagers in Lohagara Dhal? Did they seize the moment of their master's flight and break their chains? What of those unseen slaves whom traffickers offered to sell to me? What of the three girls that I haggled for in Istanbul? Did they escape the grasp of the pimp's colleagues in Odessa? What of the girl the child broker offered for $50 in Port-au-Prince? Did he sell her to a caring home? Or did a sadist buy her instead?

I wish I could tell you that they are all okay. I wish I could tell you that they are all alive and whole, even if they aren't free. I can't tell you that. I don't know what has happened to them. Their fate haunts me.

Before I met those slaves and those traffickers, I told myself that I would observe, not engage. When I began the five-year process of investigation and writing, I intended to make a work of journalism, not of advocacy. My models, Samantha Power's and Philip Gourevitch's books on genocide, dealt brilliantly and unobtrusively with terrible human problems, and did so with sensitivity and diligence. The difference, I soon realized, was that my subjects weren't dead.

There was one instance where I interfered egregiously—principles be damned. Recall Camsease Exille, the girl whose mother wrested her from slavery with my help in Port-au-Prince. After her long walk to freedom, she faced long odds at home in Brésillienne. At thirteen, she was illiterate, as her mistress had forsaken her education during her years in bondage. Her mother had saved enough to pay for the first two or three months at the local school. After that, Camsease would have to drop out and work with her parents. Tuition for a full year, plus the entrance fee, was $87. I offered her a scholarship that year, and every year that she stayed in school.

Several months later, on December 23, 2005, I was in a ramshackle Internet café in a tiny town in Bihar, India's poorest state. To my surprise, I had an e-mail from Limyè Lavi, the only aid organization to have contact with Brésillienne. Through several intermediaries and a translator, Camsease had sent a choppy but heartfelt thank-you note, and an update on her progress in school. She had drafted the original, in Creole, by herself. She ended the note by writing: "It's me, your child, Came Suze you took out of the misery at Delmas 34."

That was the only Christmas gift I got that year. It was the only one I needed.

George W. Bush did more to free modern-day slaves than any other president. But on the subject of human bondage, history does not grade on a curve.

Critics will conclude that his administration's abolitionist efforts can be summed up in three words: sparkle and fade. And media malaise reflected that waning government attention: there were less than half as many English-language news stories mentioning modern-day slavery in 2006 as there were in 2004.

Following John Miller's resignation, his deputies carried on his struggle to demote India for countenancing more slaves than any other country. While they won the support of John Negroponte, a career diplomat who had replaced Robert Zoellick as the new number two in the State Department, ultimately Condoleezza Rice turned her back on Indian slaves once again in 2007.

Administration defenders will counter that, despite many missteps, Miller had led a bold attack on a disgracefully overlooked crime against humanity. He personified an optimistic approach that abolition, real abolition, was possible. It was an attitude that stood in marked contrast to the cynicism of many international organizations. But he oversaw a policy that was defective before his arrival, and after his departure.

The deepest flaws in American strategy began with ambiguity on some of the most fundamental questions. Foremost among these: What is a slave? In this book, a slave is someone who is forced to work, through fraud or threat of violence, for no pay beyond subsistence. I did not meet one Washington policymaker—out of two dozen that I interviewed—who could give me so concise a definition.

To the dominant coalition so brilliantly assembled and led by Michael Horowitz, the only slaves—anyway, the only slaves worthy of American attention—were prostitutes. And all prostitutes were slaves. Theirs was a circular logic that dumbfounded those who regularly aided real slaves, real prostitutes, and really enslaved prostitutes.

Horowitz argued vigorously for a separation of sex trafficking from other types of slavery, so as not to blur the lines between prostitution and labor. And that is fine. Ending prostitution is a noble goal, and if a society deems the best way to do so is to make it illegal, then government should enforce the prohibition. But such enforcement should not come at the cost of the humanity of the women involved. John Miller finally understood this. After meeting with hundreds of sex slaves, he supported vigorous penalties for pimps, traffickers, and clients; quietly, he believed that a just and compassionate society would not punish the prostitutes themselves.

And commercial sex slavery represents only a fraction of the overall phenomenon of modern-day bondage. Horowitz defended his exclusive, hard-line prohibitionist focus on prostitution by saying that ending that practice would lead to trickle-down abolition of the much larger phenomena of debt bondage and labor slavery of all types. Such reasoning is illogical—and immoral.

Gonoo's slavery was no more tolerable that that of Tatiana. Williathe's rape was no more acceptable than that inflicted on Natasha. American law, drafted by Democrats and Republicans alike, is clear: the 2000 Trafficking Victims Protection Act defines trafficking into labor as trafficking. As such, it is an American burden to combat this crime just as it is to combat sex slavery. But Horowitz's view, adopted by many in the Republican-controlled Congress and the Bush administration, was that one slave's emancipation would have to wait for that of another. That view threatened to put our nation on the wrong side of history.

The second major flaw of the Bush administration's antislavery strategy was that it lacked creative approaches to prevention. Half of the world's population lives on less than $2 per day, and the vast majority are not slaves. Certainly, lax law enforcement or outright corruption facilitates trafficking. But denying the central role of poverty in modern-day slavery is like denying the central role of gravity in rainfall.

Horowitz detests "root cause types" who bloat his streamlined agenda with "utopian overreach" and "the promulgation of unachievable goals." He argues that poverty alleviation is unimportant in the fight against trafficking, and that it is utopian to think that all forms of slavery can be eradicated.

I respectfully disagree. Slavery has been with us for more than 5,000 years, yet with concentrated and coordinated effort, we can eliminate it in a generation. As Kevin Bales has clarified, while there are more slaves today than ever before, they represent the smallest percent of the global population in bondage at any one time.

The end of slavery cannot wait for the end of poverty, but any realistic strategy of global abolition must involve some elements of targeted poverty alleviation. Yet handouts, like mere emancipation, will drain budgets and not bring long-term freedom to slaves. Thanks largely to the late Paul Wellstone, the TVPA included "economic alternatives to prevent and deter trafficking" through microcredit programs and grants to nongovernmental organizations. Even as Wellstone was drafting that legislation, microcredit groups like the Grameen Bank, started after its founder encountered a bonded laborer in his native Bangladesh, were proving that the poorest of the poor could build their own wealth.

Governments bear responsibility for some elements of abolition, but where they are unwilling or unable to do so, civil society and the private sector must join the fight. For example, if the Haitian government were to fulfill its constitutional obligation to provide free, universal elementary education, it would radically shrink the restavèk population. This will not happen any time soon, as Haiti struggles merely to remain viable as a nation. Therefore, international organizations would do well to intervene through local partners on behalf of the nation's children.

The most common trigger of debt bondage is a health crisis. Where nations cannot meet the most basic obligations to protect the well-being of their citizens, international organizations, private businesses, and local aid groups must bond together to ensure the safeguards. A "War on Diarrhea" may not have the same sexy ring as a "War on Slavery," but when diarrhea kills an infant every three minutes in India, is it not worth investing $2.00 per slavery-prone person for a LifeStraw that provides clean drinking water for one year?

Where slavery results from war, governments must make peace. Jack Danforth's negotiated armistice in Sudan brought the slave raids to a halt. The government in Khartoum, which sponsored those raids, now bears the responsibility to free the slaves who still languish in the north. In lieu of meaningful international pressure, the outlook is bleak: as of May 2007, Sudan's government was still sponsoring mass slave raids—this time to depopulate South Darfur.

Governments must enforce antislavery laws. The Bush administration cited thousands of trafficking prosecutions as evidence that foreign governments responded to American pressure. Although there is no measurable correlation between overall trafficking rates and prosecutions, robust police action is a vital fight in a larger war. Slavery is a crime of international concern, and UN member states must hold one another accountable for countenancing slavery—through multilateral coercion if necessary.

Often the best thing that government can do is step out of the way. In South Asia, where over half the world's slaves toil, millions of desperately poor people squat on land that the state owns. If they were to receive title to that land, many would own an asset for the first time in their lives. If those new landholders had access to legitimate microcredit, they would be less vulnerable to usurious lenders, traffickers, and slavemasters. Instead, slowly, they could build wealth.

The free market can be the world's most effective device for ending poverty. If governments and trade organization enforce the rules of the game, fair markets also can be the world's best devices for ending slavery. Abolitionists in the late eighteenth and early nineteenth centuries only succeeded because of the support of powerful industrialists. More recently, when the major chocolate companies agreed to an industry-wide eradication of forced labor, they did so as a result of American pressure, but also because abolition just makes good business sense.

A handful of social entrepreneurs are already taking a creative new approach to ending an age-old plague. Though it is not the largest such organization—and certainly not the best funded—Bales's Washington-based Free the Slaves is the most effective such alliance that I encountered. Under the group's umbrella, nine locally based partners currently tailor-make strategies to prevent trafficking, free slaves, and effectively rehabilitate the emancipated. Their approach is to equip survivors with knowledge of their rights and the ability to earn their own incomes—and not to make them wards of the state.

As I write now from northern Cambodia, my tour of modern-day slavery seems woefully incomplete. In Africa, I spoke in passing with forced child soldiers; but in this book I give them, and 120 thousand like them across that continent, nowhere near the ink they deserve. From Brazilian charcoal works to Chinese brick kilns, I have left unexplored dozens of fields that credible reporters have found to be infected with unpaid labor, extracted through violence. Many of those fields contribute to items that you have in your home right now.

Here in the malarial forest I'm also surrounded by the sad ghosts of large acts of misguided "salvation." The outside world now knows of the utopian nightmare—the forced labor plantations, the genocide—of the Khmer Rouge; fewer have heard about the misery wrought by the peacekeepers sent to clean up afterwards. When UN forces deployed in March 1992, there were barely a thousand prostitutes in Phnom Penh. After many of the troops began buying girls outright as "wives" for their tours, the sex slave trade blossomed. In 2003, the Cambodian government, responding to American pressure, closed brothels across the country. Today, from Siem Reap to Sihanoukville, the red glow of hundreds of small, unregulated massage parlors, karaoke bars, and guest houses beckon. Inside are over thirty thousand prostitutes, a third of whom are younger than eighteen. Thousands are raped daily—but even experienced local NGOs don't know exactly how many are slaves.

Here I'm also reminded that a mass movement against slavery will only work if every single supporter performs simple acts of preventative abolition. In the heart of Siem Reap's old French Quarter, 4 miles from the vast, ornate quincunx temple of Angkor Wat, there is a four-star boutique hotel called Shinta Mani. The eighteen guest rooms are well appointed, with dark teak furnishings; the spa is luxurious; the service is crisp and unfailingly friendly; and the fish amok, a Khmer specialty, is exquisite. But what gives this hotel a truly transcendent beauty is its business model: by design, some 20 percent of its employees are local young men and women who were at risk for human trafficking. The Cambodian owner, Sokoun Chanpreda, saw his community decimated by war and slavery, and decided to set up a free hospitality training institute to provide a real alternative to families who might otherwise have pawned their children. When business began to take off, Chan-preda added a page to the room service menu, offering visitors a chance to order such items as piglets and wells for neighboring village families. As of this writing, guests have contributed nearly $200,000, changing the destinies of more than five hundred desperately poor households. A simple act, a great impact.

It takes all of us. The original abolitionists were a varied lot, and their successes were due in part to their varied battle plans. From John Brown's carbines and pikes to Charles Sumner's verbs and nouns, the antislavery vanguard used widely differing tools, but united in a common cause. Now, as then, all personalities are welcome. There are those that find the energies of John Eibner and Michael Horowitz misdirected, and to a certain extent I agree. But Eibner and Horowitz were pioneers in a nascent struggle, and for that they walk among the righteous.

Writing to a friend on April 10, 1861, Henry David Thoreau—torn between pacifism and abolitionism—warned of the dangers of reading newspaper articles about slavery and the rumbling disunion that would erupt into civil war two days later.

> As long as you know of it, you are *particeps criminis*. What business have you, if you are "an angel of light," to be pondering over the deeds of darkness?

Now, at the end of this book, you have a choice. You can return to your status as "an angel of light," and purge your memory of the stories you read.

Or you can get your hands dirty. You can lobby elected officials to make comprehensive abolition of all forms of slavery a central goal of American foreign and domestic policies. More directly, you can contribute to the small but growing number of groups—several of which are highlighted in the Acknowledgments of this book—that take a rigorous and holistic approach to fighting bondage. I encourage you to learn more about one of the best such organizations, Free the Slaves, at www.freetheslaves.net.

Slavery is today much less visible than it was in Thoreau's day, so it isn't hard to pretend that it is long dead. In your mind, if you like, you can imagine it consigned to history books. I wish I could do the same.

Notes

Author's Note

xv   *That year, there were 3.8 million slaves*: Amy Lifson, "Voices of the Slave Trade," *Humanities*, vol. 23, no. 2 (March–April 2002).

xvi *In Russia at the time*: See Victor Serge, *From Serfdom to Proletarian Revolution* (1930).

1. The Riches of the Poor

4   *The annual budget for the health care*: Todd Howland, "In Haiti, Rhetoric Trumps Human Rights," *Boston Globe*, August 16, 2005, p. A15.

4   *Haiti has the highest prevalence*: Beverly Bell, *Walking on Fire* (Ithaca, NY: Cornell University Press, 2001), p. 20.

4   *"The younger ones are even more kinker"*: "Port au Prince Street Action: May 08, 2004," *World Sex Guide*; accessed October 15, 2005.

5   *The average fifteen-year-old child slave*: Based on a UN-sponsored 1984 study. One can extrapolate from other economic indicators that the gap would be even greater today. Cited in Debbie Sontag, "The Littlest Slaves in Haiti: If a Child Is Only Poor and Hungry, He Is One of the Lucky Ones," *Miami Herald* (Tropic Magazine), December 30, 1990.

6   *If you arrive in the afternoon*: Adapted in part from Jocelyn McCalla and Merrie Archer, *Restavèk No More: Eliminating Child Slavery in Haiti: A Report by the National Coalition for Haitian Rights*, April 18, 2002.

6   *At any time of day, you will*: The author has no knowledge that Le Réseau (The Network) barbershop is supportive of Benavil's work.

7   *Nationwide, the number of restavèks ballooned*: U.S. Department of State, *Haiti Human Rights Practices, 1992*, March 1993; 1998 UNICEF study cited in U.S. Department of State, *2005 Trafficking in Persons Report*; McCalla and Archer, *Restavèk No More*. Haitian government estimates for 2006 place the total figure between 90,000 and 120,000, though no comprehensive study was performed.

7   *Normally, this client is lower middle class*: Cited in Linda Goyette, "Haiti's Invisible Children Are Seen Everywhere," *Calgary Herald*, March 21, 1999, p. A7.

8   *Out of every 1,000*: Haïti Enquête: Mortalité, Morbidité, et Utilisation des Services, 2002 (Port-au-Prince: Institut Haïtien de l'Enfance); and State of the World's Children, UNICEF, 2005.

8   *More than 80 percent*: Carol J. Williams, "A Nation Loses Its Childhood," *Los Angeles Times*, November 21, 2003, p. A1.

8   *the average girl, 1.3*: State of the World's Children, UNICEF, 2005.

8   *But the dangled diamond necklace*: From a 1998 study, commissioned by UNICEF, and conducted by the Psychological Institute of the Family (Institut Psycho-Social de la Famille, or IPSOFA) cited in McCalla and Archer, *Restavèk No More*.

9   *Like many female restavèks*: "Campaign to End Child Servitude in Haiti: A Joint Initiative of Beyond Borders and the Limyè Lavi Foundation," January 2005. One expert at a 1984 conference on restavèks organized by the Duvalier regime recalled: "The Haitian poet living in Montreal, Jean Richard Laforest, in a nice text on domestic rape, admits that, as an adult, he cannot bring a sexual act to completion without thinking of the

little maid who served as his sexual initiator." Eddy Clesca cited in Sontag, "The Littlest Slaves in Haiti."

9   *When police, acting on a tip*: Tim Padgett, "Of Haitian Bondage; America's newest immigrants have brought with them a nefarious practice—child slavery," *Time*, March 5, 2001, p. 50; Carolyn Salazar, "One in 10 Children in Haiti Is Enslaved, Activists Contend," *Miami Herald*, April 13, 2002, p. B5; and Patrick Smikle, "Haiti: Slavery in Modern Times?" IPS-Inter Press Service, October 18, 1999.

12 *Now Haiti has more slaves*: 1791 figure from Roger Plant, *Sugar and Modern Slavery* (London: Zed Books, 1987), pp. 6–7.

12 *One hundred and seventy years after*: "Les enfants qui naîtront des mariages entre esclaves seront esclaves et appartiendront aux maîtres des femmes esclaves et non à ceux de leurs maris, si le mari et la femme ont des maîtres différents."—Louis XIV, *Le code noir*, Article XII (Versailles, 1685).

13 *At age twelve*: Mildred Aristide, *L'Enfant en Domesticité en Haïti: Produit d'un fosse historique* (Port-au-Prince: Imprimerie Henri Deschamps, 2003), p. 101.

13 *Rural parents, he noted with concern*: Cited in Edner Brutus, *Instruction Publique en Haïti* (Port-au-Prince: Imprimerie de l'Etat, 1948), p. 23.

13 *The first leaders of Haiti*: Ibid., p. 83.

13 *Despite these efforts*: A sum reduced to 60 million francs in 1838, and finally paid off in 1883.

14 *"O, come, Augustine!"*: Harriet Beecher Stowe, *Uncle Tom's Cabin; or, Life Among The Lowly, Vol. II* (Boston: John P. Jewett & Company, 1852), p. 76.

14 *Seeking, in President Thomas Jefferson's words*: Cited in Letta Tayler, "Haiti: A Legacy of Neglect," *Newsday*, January 1, 2006, p. 10.

14 *"If any good reason exists"*: Abraham Lincoln, Annual Message to Congress, Washington, DC, December 3, 1861.

14 *He remarked to his son Kermit*: Theodore Roosevelt, "Events Since Columbus's Discovery," (letter to Kermit), November 14, 1906 in Joseph Bucklin Bishop, *Theodore Roosevelt's Letters To His Children* (New York: Charles Scribner's Sons, 1919), p. 177.

15 *"Universal suffrage in Hayti"*: Theodore Roosevelt, *An Autobiography* (New York: Charles Scribner's Sons, 1920), p. 163.

15 *Four years later, at a meeting*: The League of Nations established the Temporary Slavery Commission in the spring of 1924 in an attempt to address criticism over continuing slavery. It was neutered by the colonial powers.

15 *Haiti's former minister of agriculture*: Suzanne Miers, *Slavery in the Twentieth Century: The Evolution of a Global Problem* (Walnut Creek, CA: AltaMira Press, 2003), pp. 106–109.

16 *While restavèk abuse occasionally*: Haiti Solidarity International study conducted by Jean Lhérisson in coordination with UNICEF, cited in Jacky Delorme, *Haiti: Tarnished Children*, International Confederation of Free Trade Unions (ICFTU), January 2004, pp. 1–18.

16 *"It is the destiny of the people"*: Jean-Claude ("Baby Doc") Duvalier quoted in V. S. Naipaul, *The Return of Eva Perón* (New York: Alfred A. Knopf, 1980), p. 199.

16 *"Children of Haiti,"*: Jean-Bertrand Aristide quoted in David Adams, "Haitian Child Slaves Look to New President to Save Them From a Life of Abuse," *The Independent* (London), February 26, 1991, p. 12.

16 *"The Haitian left"*: U.S. Embassy of Haiti, "Confidential Cablegram," Port-au-Prince, April 1, 1994, pp. 2–3, quoted in Bell, *Walking on Fire*, p. 21.

17 *Nancy Ely-Raphael, the Deputy Assistant Secretary of State*: Ely-Raphel cited in Tom Squitieri, "Defiant Military Regime 'Turning Haiti into Hell,'" *USA Today*, July 14, 1994, p. 10A.

17 *"Haiti is not worth"*: Rep. Phil Crane (R-IL), *Congressional Record*, October 6, 1994, p. H11095.

17 *Two months after the restoration*: Padgett, "Of Haitian Bondage," *Time*, May 4, 2001.

17 *The hot line was normally unmanned*: Mathilde Flambert, an aristocrat whom Aristide appointed as minister of social affairs to appease the Haitian elite, was fatalistic, but asked for more cash nonetheless. "We can't resolve this problem right away. It is deeply entrenched and has always existed in our country," she said in June 2000. "Little by little, we will build more [shelters] if we get more money."—Interview with Kathy Slobogin, CNN, June 25, 2000.

18 *"I believe it is the moral obligation"*: Jean-Robert Cadet, "Capitol Hill Hearing Testimony, Senate Foreign Relations Committee," Federal Document Clearing House Congressional Testimony, Dirksen Senate Office Building, Washington, DC, September 28, 2000.

19 *Widowed at forty:* Statistic cited in Bell, *Walking on Fire,* p. 19.

23 *On January 1, 2004, Aristide:* Lydia Polgreen, "200 Years After Napoleon, Haiti Finds Little to Celebrate," *New York Times,* January 2, 2004, p. A3.

23 *The rebel leader Louis-Jodel Chamblain:* Ibid.

24 *"The Interim Government of Haiti":* U.S. Department of State, *2005 Trafficking in Persons Report,* July 2005.

24 *From its air-conditioned and heavily fortified headquarters:* See, e.g., "Les fondements de la pratique de la domesticité des enfants en Haïti" (December 2002), co-issued by UNDP, UNICEF, ILO, Save the Children-Canada and Save the Children-UK, under the imprimatur of the Haitian Ministry of Social Affairs.

30 *As a comparison, in Burundi:* Poorest country as measured by 2005 per capita GDP—J. P. Slavin, "Restavèk: Four-year-old Servants in Haiti," *Thursday's Child* (2002).

30 *Nationwide, the average woman:* Don Bohning, "Haiti Struggles for Space: Burdened by Swelling Population, the Nation Searches for a Way Out," *Miami Herald,* June 22, 1999, p. 1A.

34 *Haiti has the highest rate of corporal punishment:* Hugo Merveille, "Haiti: Violence—A bad legacy bequeathed to kids," Panos Institute, Washington, DC, November 2002.

34 *After the February 2004 coup:* Ginger Thompson, "New Scourge in Haiti: A wave of kidnapping," *International Herald Tribune,* June 7, 2005, p. 4.

35 *When the* New York Times *columnist Nicholas Kristof returned:* Nicholas Kristof, "Back to the Brothel," *New York Times,* January 22, 2005, p. A15.

35 *"Do I have any regrets about being 'conned'":* Gregory Kane, "Slave Redemption a 'Racket'? Just take a look at the eyes," *Baltimore Sun,* June 2, 2002, p. 1B.

2. Genesis: A Drama in Three Acts

45 *The severely malnourished boys had been beaten:* Alicia Mundy, "The Real Deal," *Seattle Times,* August 21, 2005, p. 18.

45 *The previous year, Miller's office:* Colin L. Powell, "On the Rollout of the 2003 Trafficking in Persons Report," Released by the Office of the Spokesman, U.S. Department of State, Washington, DC, June 11, 2003.

46 *What they knew about Stalin:* John Miller, "Nixon and Hiss: The First Battle of the Cold War," *Seattle Times,* April 27, 1994, p. B7.

47 *On the night of his victory:* Jeffrey L. Pasley, "New House GOP Freshman Class Wary of Following Reagan's Budget Lead," *National Journal,* March 16, 1985, p. 584.

48 *"You have an obligation":* "Treasury Secretary, Virginia Congressman Tangle Over Slave Labor," Associated Press, March 6, 1986.

48 *Promising June that his D.C. days were over:* Though this was reported elsewhere, Miller said he could not remember whether he actually made a hard promise or not, but there was no question that "June did not enjoy Washington."

49 *The American Bar Association added its sense:* Mona Charen, "Leftist Nomination Whining Is Spectacular Chutzpah," *Cleveland Plain Dealer,* July 23, 1993, p. 5B.

51 *On January 11, 1998, Horowitz read a front-page* New York Times *article:* Michael Specter, "Contraband Women," *New York Times,* January 11, 1998, p. A1.

53 *Seizing its chance to savage Hillary Clinton:* Hillary Rodham Clinton interviewed on PBS *Wide Angle* with Jamie Rubin, September 25, 2003.

53 *Chuck Colson co-authored:* William J. Bennett and Charles W. Colson, "The Clintons Shrug at Sex Trafficking," *Wall Street Journal,* January 10, 2000, p. A26.

54 *In fact, only 5 percent of Sudanese were Christian:* Deborah Scroggins, *Emma's War: An Aid Worker, A Warlord, Radical Islam, and the Politics of Oil—A True Story of Love and Death in Sudan* (New York: Pantheon Books, 2002), p. 83.

55 *"The government of Sudan's military trains":* Frank Wolf, Jim Lehrer, and Sudanese ambassador Abdalla Ahmed Abdalla, "Another Somalia," *MacNeil/Lehrer NewsHour,* May 4, 1993.

55 *"The Government of Sudan's self-declared jihad"*: John Eibner, Capitol Hill Hearing Testimony, House Committee on International Relations, Subcommittee on Africa, March 22, 1995.

56 *"We must isolate this regime"*: Gus Constantine, "Wolf at Sudan's Door, Charging Slavery, Rights Violations," *Washington Times*, March 23, 1995, p. A13.

56 *On December 6, 2000*: William Jefferson Clinton, "Remarks by the President at Human Rights Day Observance," Presidential Hall, Dwight D. Eisenhower Executive Office Building, December 6, 2000.

57 *Danforth, who once described himself*: John C. Danforth, *Resurrection: The Confirmation of Clarence Thomas* (New York: Viking Penguin, 1994), p. 207.

59 *she had hard numbers*: Victor Malarek, *The Natashas: Inside the New Global Sex Trade* (New York: Arcade Publishing, 2003), p. 199.

59 *In a* Washington Post *op-ed*: Gary Haugen, "State's Blind Eye on Sexual Slavery," *Washington Post*, June 15, 2002, p. A23.

3. Those Whom Their Right Hands Possess

63 *Some Dinka parents used*: Francis Mading Deng, *The Dinka of the Sudan* (Prospect Heights, IL: Waveland Press, 1972), p. 137.

64 *On the second day of their journey*: Murahileen is derived from the word *murhal*, referring to the seasonal migration routes of the *baggara*.

67 *Yet before Eibner, Americans ignored slavery's recrudescence*: Not to be confused with the subsequent, equally grotesque genocide in Darfur.

68 *Stückelberger's "Christian duty"*: Quoted in Cameron Duodo, "Africa's New Slaves: Slave Trade Thrives in Sudan," *South Africa Mail and Guardian*, January 28, 2000.

69 *one of the "undiscovered holy men"*: Jacobs quoted in Allen D. Hertzke, *"Freeing God's Children": The Unlikely Alliance for Global Human Rights* (Lanham, MD: Rowman & Littlefield, 2004), p. 111.

69 *"I thought it was good to give up"*: Melanie Burney, "Students Protest Slavery in Sudan," *Philadelphia Inquirer*, May 19, 2001, p. B2.

69 *Garang condemned "the genocidal character"*: John Garang, "Address to the United Nations Human Rights Commission by Dr. John Garang, Chairman, SPLM and C-in-C, SPLA," Geneva, March 24, 1999.

70 *"Knowing that tens of thousands"*: Eibner quoted in Ian Fisher, "Selling Sudan's Slaves into Freedom," *New York Times*, April 25, 1999, p. A10.

70 *An impoverished elderly woman*: Richard Woodbury "The Children's Crusade; How fourth- and fifth-graders in Colorado are buying the freedom of slaves in a faraway land," *Time*, December 21, 1998, p. 44.

70 *"because they are no longer isolated"*: Quoted in Robert Hutchison, *Their Kingdom Come: Inside the Secret World of Opus Dei* (New York: Thomas Dunne Books, 1999), p. 424.

71 *After the British ousted the Mahdists*: In the 1970s, the American war correspondent Richard Critchfield visited Neetil, a village in the Nuba Mountains, and another area where the Arab north meets the African south. A Khartoum University law student had tipped him off that dozens of children had been sold to *baggara* to be used to tend cattle. "These children could be carried off by the camel Arabs without anybody knowing about it," the student told Critchfield. "They sever their tendons to keep them from running away. I'm convinced it still goes on." Each child, reportedly, was sold by impoverished families to the tribesmen in exchange for an annual payment of one cow to the child's father.

Shocked and fascinated, Critchfield set out to find the truth, and managed to spend a week living in a *zariba* with several slaves. One slave named the Wali told him that when his father had stopped coming to receive the annual payment, the Wali's master simply kept the cows for himself and obliged the boy to keep working. Critchfield writes: "Despite his bleak circumstances, the Wali seemed to be an exceptionally happy person; he took pleasure in small things and I frankly enjoyed the days accompanying him. He had never seen a white man before and thought I looked gruesome. 'Your hair,' he said one day, 'is like dead grass blowing in the wind.'"—Richard Critchfield, *Villages* (New York: Anchor Press/Doubleday, 1981), pp. 38–39.

72 *John Garang lent credibility*: Throughout the war, state-controlled television in Sudan displayed images of a glorious patriotic Holy War against the infidels. Most Khartoumers were not fooled, but had no choice but to fight. Recruits in other parts of the north came willingly, drawn to the Popular Defense Force by the call of defending the faith against the infidels. After six weeks of physical training and reinforcement of their radical Islamist instruction, they would be sent south to fight alongside the *murahileen*.

72 *During the dry season, between November and April*: Jok Madut Jok, *War and Slavery in Sudan* (Philadelphia: University of Pennsylvania Press, 2001), pp. 29–30.

72 *Elderly men, unable to run*: "The Tears of Orphans—No Future Without Human Rights," *Amnesty International* (February 1995).

73 *"Captives' hands were pierced"*: Sheila Rule, "Guns Tipping Cruel Balance in the Sudan," *New York Times*, May 4, 1986, p. A17.

73 *A herdsman nailed together*: *Slavery, Abduction and Forced Servitude in Sudan: Report of the International Eminent Persons Group*, Khartoum. May 22, 2002, p. 55.

73 *And as was true during the zenith of the Ottoman Empire*: Ehud R. Toledano, "Ottoman Concepts of Slavery in the Period of Reform, 1830s–1880s," in Martin A. Klein, ed., *Breaking the Chains: Slavery, Bondage, and Emancipation in Modern Africa and Asia* (Madison: University of Wisconsin Press, 1993), pp. 43, 59.

73 *During the rule of al-Mahdi's grandfather*: Zubeir Pasha, trans. and recorded by H. C. Jackson of the Sudan Civil Service, *Black Ivory or The Story of El Zubeir Pasha, Slaver and Sultan. As Told by Himself* (Khartoum: Sudan Press, 1913), p. 108.

74 *They were offered Dinka children*: Augustine Lado and Betty Hinds, "Where Slavery Isn't History," *Washington Post*, October 1, 1993, p. C3.

74 *The new leader, Lieutenant General Omar al-Bashir*: From the time he was a commander in southwest Sudan, al-Bashir himself kept a number of Dinka and Nuer slaves in his home—*New African* (July 1990), cited in Lado and Hinds, "Where Slavery Isn't History," p. C3.

75 *"based upon hearsay"*: Ahmed Suliman, "In Sudan, Slavery Is a Criminal Offense," *New York Times*, July 30, 1994, p. A18.

75 *The state-controlled media*: Ken Ringle, "The Next Rushdie?; Gáspár Bíró Spoke Out. Sudan's Government Condemned Him," *Washington Post*, March 26, 1994, p. D1.

75 *In it, the NIF said that Bíró's report*: Cited in David G. Littman, "Human Rights and Human Wrongs," *National Review*, January 19, 2003.

75 *Ahmed el-Mufti, a lawyer with the Sudanese Justice Ministry*: As proof, el-Mufti's group publicly returned twenty-seven abducted boys to John Garang's hometown in Bor. El-Mufti claimed they had been taken north for "education," but the boys' fathers told vastly different stories. Police had kidnapped their boys, they said, and forced them to convert to Islam and perform manual labor in a town north of Khartoum—Nhial Bol, "Sudan-Human Rights: Children Reunited with Families," *Inter-Press Service*, January 9, 1997. When Amnesty International issued a scathing 1995 report on slavery in Sudan, el-Mufti said that the organization had "become a patron" of the SPLM, and that British intelligence, MI5, provided their funding. Ahmed El-Mufti quoted in "Sudan Opposes Amnesty Visit," *Agence France-Presse*, May 22, 1995.

75 *"We don't want to speculate about his fate"*: Quoted in UN Commission on Human Rights, *Report of the United Nations High Commissioner for Human Rights and Follow-Up to the World Conference on Human Rights*, E/CN.4/2003/NGO/225, March 17, 2003.

76 *Under his guidance, the average raiding party*: Richard Miniter, "The False Promise of Slave Redemption," *Atlantic Monthly* (July 1999), p. 63.

76 *The horsemen were to "wipe out" the rebels*: "Government Militia Sent to Wipe Out Rebels in Bahr el-Ghazal," *Agence France-Presse*, June 9, 1992.

77 *But afterward, leaders on both sides*: John C. Danforth, confirmation hearing at the Senate Foreign Relations Committee, Washington, DC, June 17, 2004.

77 *The Bush administration responded*: John C. Danforth, "Assessment from the President's Special Envoy for Peace in Sudan," U.S. Department of State, April 21, 2003.

77 *"The Bush administration would do well"*: John Eibner, "Another Front," *National Review*, March 25, 2003.

77 *"There is probably no issue"*: John C. Danforth, "Report to the President of the United States on the Outlook for Peace in Sudan," April 26, 2002, p. 15.

81 *"The real Soudan"*: Winston S. Churchill, *The River War: An Account of the Reconquest of the Sudan* (1902; Holicong, PA: Wildside Press, 2002), p. 7.

81 *In 1840, at the behest of the Egyptian viceroy*: Muhammad Ali sent a dispatch to his commander in chief pillaging Sudan: "You are aware that the end of all our effort and this expense is to procure negroes. Please show zeal in carrying out our wishes in this capital matter."—cited in Paul E. Lovejoy, *Transformations in Slavery: A History of Slavery in Africa* (Cambridge: Cambridge University Press, 1983), p. 153.

81 *The Dinka called the period*: John Ryle, *Warriors of the White Nile: The Dinka* (Amsterdam: Time-Life Books, 1982), p. 28.

81 *Children were in loose-fitting fatigues*: "A revolution always needs people, women, children, all kinds of people," Commander Abdel Gadir Hamid Mahdi, 3rd Commander in the SPLA, told me; "some children insist on being with us."

82 *By 2001, a glut of guns*: "Kalashnikovs for Chickens: Small Arms Boom in East Africa," *checkpoint-online.ch*, July 8, 2001.

82 *In early 1987, after al-Mahdi began*: Alan Whitaker, "Slavery in Sudan," *Sudan Times*, October 8, 1988.

82 *By 1990, as supply swelled*: "Slavery: By Any Other Name," *The Economist*, January 6, 1990.

82 *Despite his title, he was a critic*: See Scroggins, *Emma's War*, passim.

83 *"rarely troubled with vermin"*. Georg Schweinfurth, trans. Ellen E. Frewer, *The Heart of Africa: Three Years' Travels and Adventures in the Unexplored Regions of Central Africa from 1868 to 1871*, Vol. I (New York: Harper & Bros., 1874), p. 158.

84 *He recalled restless nights*: Ibid.

84 *Now it was cloudy*: *Habub* is Arabic for "phenomenon," a reference to the sandstorms' ability to turn day to night in minutes. My father, visiting Khartoum while in His Majesty's Colonial Service in 1951, described one "which darkened the town as a London fog in November used to darken Holmes's Baker Street, but leaving dust everywhere, inside and out."—A. N. Skinner, "Pilgrimage in Reverse," *Nigerian Field*, XVI (1951), p. 6. I experienced several of similar magnitude, making even minimal movements impossible, in my time in both North and South Sudan.

85 *Mainline human rights groups*: In 1990, the Anti-Slavery Society changed its name to Anti-Slavery International.

85 *One official, the Civil Commissioner of the most raided country*: The same official has also been quoted as saying that the number was 50,000–60,000 and gave a radio interview in which he said 100,000. The total population of Aweil West is no more than 350,000.

87 *"the Sudanese version"*: Colin Nickerson, "The Price of Freedom," *Boston Globe Magazine*, December 19, 1999, p. 15.

88 *"It's a show"*: "The Slave Trade," *CBS News 60 Minutes II*, May 15, 2002.

88 *"You can tell the difference"*: Charles Jacobs on "Talk of the Nation," National Public Radio, April 18, 2001.

88 *Jacobs had previously spun criticism*: Charles Jacobs, "Redeeming Values: Media says slave redemption is fiction," *National Review*, June 4, 2002.

89 *The skeleton balance sheet that he referred me to*: "Schweizer Spenden Spiegel: 2003," p. 16. Also see Hutchison, *Their Kingdom Come: Inside the Secret World of Opus Dei*, p. 424n.

90 *Instead, Eibner exchanged redemption money*: In 1997, Linda Slobodian photographed Eibner exchanging money with Justin Yaac at the Nairobi airport. Originally a gynecologist, Yaac headed external relations for the SPLA. In the late 1980s, Band Aid, Oxfam, and Save the Children gave the SPLM's humanitarian wing, the SRRA, $60,000 for its office operations in Nairobi. According to Deborah Scroggins, "the money disappeared into an Addis Ababa bank account." Soon thereafter, Yaac returned from Addis Ababa to Nairobi, roughed up the head of SRRA, a lawyer named Richard Mulla, and took his post.—*Emma's War*, p. 133. Eibner's defenders in the Sudanese opposition living in London said he exchanged money with "civilian authorities," meaning unelected SPLM officials, like Yaac, who did not have a primary military role.

90 *Karl Vick cited a claim*: Karl Vick, "Ripping Off Slave 'Redeemers': Rebels Exploit West-

erners' Efforts to Buy Emancipation for Sudanese," *Washington Post*, February 26, 2002, p. A1.

91 *In 2000, a report commissioned by the Canadian government*: John Harker, *Human Security in Sudan: The Report of a Canadian Assessment Mission Prepared for the Ministry of Foreign Affairs*, Ottawa, January 2000, pp. 39–40.

91 *According to Vick, a Dinka-speaking Italian priest*: Vick, "Ripping Off Slave 'Redeemers,'" p. A1.

95 *"The bureaucrats"—he curled his lips*: As I prepared a story for *Newsweek International* on his work, I told Eibner what I had recorded, and what I have reproduced here, during our travels together. He vigorously objected to any characterization of his work as fraudulent or militaristic, although he did not deny any of the specific quotes or occurrences.

95 *"The people of Sudan can now hope"*: "Sudan Peace Deal Signed," CNN, May 26, 2004.

95 *Pressed by the impending release*: Embassy of the Republic of Sudan press release: "Al-Bashir: Sudan Determined to End Abductions!" May 15, 2002.

96 *One hundred and nine members of Congress*: Joel Brinkley, "Surge in Violence in Sudan Erodes Hope," *New York Times*, November 7, 2005, p. A5.

97 *That same morning, another government entity*: At the time, CEAWC's returns were generally considered legitimate, if agonizingly slow, thanks to collaboration with Save the Children.

98 *Fewer than 25 percent*: Marc Lacey, "Rebels, Many in Teens, Disarm in Sudan's South," *New York Times*, January 27, 2004, p. A10.

101 *In the rare instances*: Robert M. Press, "Sudanese Sell Children to Avert Starvation," *Christian Science Monitor*, July 27, 1988, p. 9.

102 *As many as 1.4 million refugees*: Abraham McLaughlin, "How a Sudanese Boy Came to be named '1 o'clock,'" *Christian Science Monitor*, February 8, 2005, p. 1.

102 *And each day for the first two months*: Opheera McDoom, "Sudan Abductees Start New Life in South," *Sudan Tribune*, March 7, 2005.

102 *acculturation was the only way to survive*: *Slavery, Abduction and Forced Servitude in Sudan: Report of the International Eminent Persons Group*, May 22, 2002, p. 18.

104 *Discredited in the eyes of all*: It appears that Eibner finally recognized that Malong's aspiration to topple Khartoum was fantasy. While he never acknowledged them to be fraudulent, Eibner abandoned grand redemptions, although reports persisted about school fund-raisers to buy back slaves. Eibner claimed to offer cow vaccinations, a currency less prone to misuse, to masters in Darfur in order to win the release of slaves. Finally, CSI began delivering relief in the form of sorghum and survival kits to Darfurian refugees and reportedly funded a medical clinic in Aweil.

104 *Internationally, there was never serious discussion*: In his *New York Times* column shortly after the peace deal, Nicholas Kristof called for the Bush administration to take those responsible for the genocide in Darfur to the ICC, and two weeks later, a UN commission recommended the same move. The administration resisted, but called for 10,000 UN peacekeepers for Darfur, which the Security Council approved in March 2004.— Nicholas D. Kristof, "Why Should We Shield the Killers?" *New York Times*, February 2, 2005, p. A21.

4. A Moral Law That Stands Above Men and Nations

106 *"Slavery has been fruitful in giving itself names"*: Frederick Douglass, Speech to the American Anti-Slavery Society, Boston, May 10, 1865, in Diane Ravitch, ed., *The American Reader: Words That Moved a Nation* (New York: HarperCollins, 1990), pp. 270–71.

108 *"Michael Gerson is so gifted"*: Robert Kuttner, "The Ideological Imposter," reprinted in *The Best American Political Writing 2003* (New York: Thunder's Mouth Press, 2003), p. 63.

108 *One morning, arguing for $15 billion*: Gerson quoted in Jeffrey Goldberg, "The Believer; George W. Bush's loyal speechwriter," *The New Yorker*, February 13, 2006, p. 56.

109 *"Mike is the one always wondering"*: Karl Rove quoted in Carl Cannon, "Soul of a Conservative," *National Journal*, May 14, 2005.

109 *Without Rove, who with Vice President Dick Cheney*: Prior to Miller's arrival, the president had spoken out against Sudanese slavery at the insistence of the Horowitz coalition in May 2001. Citing Theodore Roosevelt, he argued that "there were crimes so monstrous that the American consciousness had to assert itself."—"Remarks by the President to the American Jewish Committee," National Building Museum, Washington, DC, May 3, 2001.

109 *Chuck Colson and the Southern Baptist Convention policy chief*: Richard Land interviewed for "The Jesus Factor," *PBS Frontline*, April 29, 2004.

110 *"one of the greatest crimes"*: George W. Bush, "Remarks by the President on Gorée Island," White House Office of the Press Secretary, July 8, 2003.

110 *It was vintage Gerson*: "That speech was completely ignored by history," Gerson told me in his West Wing office, "but I think it is, you know, in the Providence of God, one of the most important speeches." What he failed to mention was that God and Gerson were not solely responsible for the speech: as with much of his work, Matthew Scully and John McConnell were silent but active partners.

110 *Immediately afterward, the Bush-Cheney '04 Listserv*: G. Robert Hillman, "Bush Campaign Touts Africa Trip to Potential Donors," *Dallas Morning News*, July 16, 2003, p. 8A.

110 *Would "hasten the day when"*: George W. Bush, "Remarks at the National Training Conference on Human Trafficking," Tampa, Florida, July 16, 2004.

113 *"We must show new energy" and the remarks that follow*: George W. Bush, "Address to the United Nations General Assembly," UN Headquarters, New York, September 23, 2003.

114 *"We ought to be raising holy hell"*: Rep. Dan Burton, "The Ongoing Tragedy of International Slavery and Human Trafficking: An Overview," Subcommittee on Human Rights and Wellness of the Committee on Government Reform, U.S. House of Representatives, October 29, 2003 (Washington, DC: Government Printing Office, 2004), p. 8.

5. A Nation Within a Nation

117 *a vision in pink*: " 'Tatiana,' " she said, "is a name that I use for security reasons."

120 *In practice, the dictator's secret police*: Christopher Walker, "Dark Side of Liberty on Show in Romania's New Dawn," *The Times* (London), February 10, 1990.

121 *Ceauşescu prohibited his people*: Ibid.

123 *Many investors and aid organizations pulled out*: Rodica Gregorian and Elena Hura-Tudor, *Street Children and Juvenile Justice in Romania* (London: The Consortium for Street Children, December 2003), p. 12.

124 *but their $3.5 billion in annual remittances*: Barbara Limanowska, *Trafficking in Human Beings in South Eastern Europe* (Bosnia and Herzegovina: UNDP, November 2003), p. 91.

124 *Even as the Foreign Ministry officially listed*: Sebastian Lăzăroiu and Monica Alexandru, *Who Is the Next Victim? Vulnerability of young Romanian women to trafficking in human beings* (Bucharest: IOM, 2003), p. 12.

124 *"I went up to the barbarian man"*: Von Gauting cited in Isabel Fonseca, *Bury Me Standing: The Gypsies and Their Journey* (New York: Vintage Departures, 1996), pp. 184–85.

125 *One third of all Romani mothers*: E. Zamfir and C. Zamfir, *Gipsies Between Ignorance and Concern*: (Alternative Publisher, 1993), cited in Gregorian and Hura-Tudor, *Street Children and Juvenile Justice in Romania*, p. 17.

125 *Most parents were unemployed*: Fonseca, *Bury Me Standing*, pp. 15–16.

125 *In the nineteenth century, a British visitor*: James Samuelson, *Roumania Past and Present* (London: Longmans, Green & Co., 1882), p. 50.

127 *During the 1990s, as the orphanages closed*: Gregory Rodriguez, "Romanians Still Culturally Caged," *Christian Science Monitor*, January 9, 1998, p. 19.

127 *The kids lived in the sewers*: Several Western missionaries were convicted for their actions here. In one high-profile 1998 case, an Anglican priest named Michael John Taylor was caught in his underpants with a naked child in a dingy apartment around the corner.

127 *In this area, Ceauşescu had forcibly resettled*: See Fonseca, *Bury Me Standing*, pp. 166–67.

127 *The government still owned 90 percent*: Ciprian Domnisoru, "Bucharest City Hall

Makes Largest Investment Since the Revolution," *Bucharest Daily News*, July 11, 2006.

129 *She had bleached, rust-colored hair*: In Romani culture, a mentally retarded girl, a *dili*, is unmarriageable. Even if the girl were not retarded, however, she might have been sold. A phenomenon condemned by the EU but largely ignored by Romanian officials, child-bride selling still occurs between Romani families.

132 *Meanwhile, fewer than half of all trafficking victims*: "A Global Alliance Against Forced Labour," International Labour Organization, Geneva, May 2005.

133 *In England, 200 years after abolition*: David Harrison, "Women Sold as 'Fresh Meat': Authorities losing the battle against gangs that are selling teens into sexual slavery," *Vancouver Sun*, November 19, 2005, p. C10.

133 *Traffickers shot dead four Romanian girls*: Will Stewart, "Once We Sold Wine to the World, Now We Harvest Our Women as Sex Slaves to the West," *The Mail on Sunday* (London), October 13, 2002, pp. 32–33.

133 *In Rome, a pimp forced*: Sue Lloyd-Roberts, "The New Warlords," *Evening Standard* (London), June 14, 2002, pp. 18–19.

133 *"when Marina, a 25-year-old"*: Andrew Purvis and Jan Stojaspal, "Human Slavery; Eastern Europe has become the fastest-growing point of origin for the trafficking of females for sex," *Time*, February 19, 2001, p. 18.

133 *Albanian networks that took women*: Victor Malarek, *The Natashas: Inside the New Global Sex Trade* (New York: Arcade Publishing, 2003), p. 37.

134 *a decade later, the number was 147 million*: *National Human Development Report, Republic of Moldova*, UN Development Program at 20 (1999), cited in *Trafficking in Women: Moldova and Ukraine* (Minneapolis: Minnesota Advocates for Human Rights, December 2000), p. 8.

135 *Twenty million passports went missing*: Moisés Naím, *Illicit: How Smugglers, Traffickers, and Copycats Are Hijacking the Global Economy* (New York: Doubleday, 2005), p. 101.

138 *The guards had a reputation for sadism*: "U.S. Report: Romanian police commit human rights abuses," Associated Press, April 1, 2003.

138 *It was built on a rotting swamp*: *U.S. Department of State Country Report on Human Rights Practices 2005—Romania* (March 2006).

140 *He stuffed as many as eighty inmates*: Mort Rosenblum, "Romanian Government Reported Stepping Up Repression," Associated Press, August 20, 1983.

143 *At the time, three in four Romanian sex slaves*: Malarek, *The Natashas*, pp. 32–35; David Binder, "A Trafficking Transit Point, Romania Also Has Its Victims," MSNBC, June 2001.

143 *From there, the Russians sold the women*: See Malarek, *The Natashas*, p. 47.

144 *A destination-point pimp could earn*: See Roland-Pierre Paringaux, "Prostitution Takes a Turn for the West," *Le Monde*, May 24, 1998, cited in Donna M. Hughes, "The 'Natasha' Trade: The transnational shadow market of trafficking in women," *Journal of International Affairs*, vol. 53, no. 2 (Spring 2000), pp. 625–51.

144 *A 2003 study in the Netherlands*: See Anna Korvinus, *Trafficking in Human Beings: Fourth Report of the Dutch National Rapporteur (Supplementary Figures)* (The Hague: Bureau NRM, 2005), p. 23.

145 *The Cămătarii rolled Costache's profits*: See Naím, *Illicit*, p. 148.

145 *One Albanian syndicate came up with*: Purvis and Stojaspal, "Human Slavery," *Time*, February 19, 2001, p. 18.

146 *In June 2003, John Miller's boss*: Paula Dobriansky, "Remarks to Trafficking in Persons Conference," Helsinki, Finland, June 1–3, 2003.

146 *Investigators interviewed 13,000 women and children*: Limanowska, *Trafficking in Human Beings in South Eastern Europe*, p. 29; and Submitted statement of Mohammed Y. Mattar, *The Ongoing Tragedy of International Slavery and Human Trafficking: An Overview*, Subcommittee on Human Rights and Wellness of the Committee on Government Reform, U.S. House of Representatives, October 29, 2003 (Washington, DC: Government Printing Office, 2004), p. 100.

147 *On January 7, 2002, the brothers hosted*: "Maverick Businessman 'Witnessed' Assassination Attempt on Mafia Head," *Gazeta Sporturilor* (Bucharest), February 25, 2005.

147 *Ion Pitulescu, the police chief who had resigned*: Christian Levant, "Former Police General Warns Powerful Organized Crime Rings Present in Romania," *Evenimentul Zilei* (Bucharest), October 11, 2004.

151 *He drew from the waves of Romanians*: "60,000 Romanians, Bulgarians Smuggled into Spain: Report," Agence France-Presse, May 24, 2006; Naím, *Illicit*, p. 89.

151 *Romani tradition absolutely forbade*: See Fonseca, *Bury Me Standing*, pp. 133–34.

6. The New Middle Passage

153 *Now the nation was Europe's largest source*: Peter Baker, "In Struggling Moldova, Desperation Drives Decisions," *Washington Post*, November 7, 2002, p. A14.

154 *The day after we arrived*: Alecs Iancu, "Moldovan President Denies Receiving Official Invitation to Join EU with Romania," *Bucharest Daily News*, July 13, 2006.

156 *Across the country, a million Moldovans*: Julianna Arnold and Cornelia Doni, *USAID/Moldova Antitrafficking Assessment—Critical Gaps in and Recommendations for Antitrafficking Activities* (Washington, DC: Office of Women in Development, Bureau for Global Programs, Field Support and Research, USAID, October 2002), p. 5.

156 *Up to 400,000 women had been sold*: Preston Mendenhall, "Infiltrating Europe's Shameful Trade in Human Beings," MSNBC, June 2001.

156 *Officially, in 2005, they constituted nearly a fifth*: Michael Jandl, "Moldova Seeks Stability Amid Mass Emigration," *Insight* (Migration Policy Institute; December 2003).

157 *A jut-jawed Russian*: Most here were ethnic Moldovans, but Chişnău's Russian population had grown—in contrast with the Moldovan population—since independence.

158 *Bush administration policy reflected*: "It is a vicious myth that women and children who work as prostitutes have voluntarily chosen such a life for themselves."—U.S. Department of State, International Information Programs, *Fact Sheet: Sex Trafficking, the United States, and Europe*, Washington, DC, January 6, 2005.

158 *Still, the debate raged in Washington*: The Horowitz coalition framed the issue early and often. During the fight over the formulation of the 2000 Trafficking Victims Protection Act, Michael Horowitz easily won the battle to require strict prohibition. Over a hundred Evangelical and conservative groups followed up by lobbying President Bush to issue a February 2002 National Security Directive declaring that prostitution was inherently harmful. In 2003, Christopher Smith included a provision in the TVPA reauthorization that would "prohibit the use of funds to promote, support, or advocate the legalization or practice of prostitution." Submitted statement of Chris Smith in *The Ongoing Tragedy of International Slavery and Human Trafficking: An Overview*, p. 13. "There is a line between prostitution and slavery," Smith told me in his office, "but it's very threadbare. I've had prostitutes sitting right where you are. And they are broken women." After Smith's reauthorization, all antitrafficking groups that wanted U.S. funds had to pledge their loyalty to the Justinian principle of ending prostitution by fiat. Several organizations argued that the restriction hampered their ability to reach the most desperate victims. Some drew a distinction between prostitution and slavery. While many agreed the former should be a crime, they separated it from the latter, a universally recognized crime against humanity.

158 *Like most women who wound up*: Melissa Farley, Isin Baral, Merab Kiremire, and Ufuk Sezgin, "Prostitution in Five Countries: Violence and Posttraumatic Stress Disorder," in *Feminism & Psychology*, (1998), pp. 405–26.

159 *Jotting a note in 1859*: Lincoln cited in Michael S. Green, *Freedom, Union, and Power: Lincoln and His Party in the Civil War* (New York: Fordham University Press, 2004), p. 32.

160 *A majority of the prostitutes*: Farley, et al., "Prostitution and Trafficking in Nine Countries: An Update on Violence and Posttraumatic Stress Disorder," in Melissa Farley, ed., *Prostitution, Trafficking and Traumatic Stress* (New York: Haworth Maltreatment & Trauma Press, 2003), pp. 37, 47, 51, 53, and 57.

160 *And among trafficking victims*: "Trafficking Women's Symptoms Akin to Torture Victims," Reuters, July 26, 2006.

164 *In the 1990s, at a time when national polls*: Jana Costachi, "Trafficking in Human Beings in the Republic of Moldova," in Simona Zavratnik Zimic, *Women and Trafficking* (Ljubljana: Peace Institute, 2004), p. 100.

164 *According to a Council of Europe study*: "Council of Europe to Help Moldova Combat Slave Trade," ITAR-TASS news agency, May 8, 2001.

166 *In 2004, there were twenty-three antitrafficking raids*: "Moldovan Police Report Successes in Fight Against Human Trafficking," *Flux*, May 1, 2004.

166 *Moisés Naím, the editor of* Foreign Policy, *labeled Transnistria*: See Naím, *Illicit*, p. 58.

166 *Between October 2005 and April 2006*: European Union Border Assistance Mission report cited in "Moldova's Uncertain Future," *International Crisis Group Europe Report No. 175*, August 17, 2006, p. 6.

166 *Naím cited Moldovan claims*: Naím, *Illicit*, p. 57.

167 *Transnistrians sold their own women*: *Trafficking As It Is: A Statistical Profile, 2004–2005 Update* (Chişinău: International Organization for Migration, March 2006), p. 4.

167 *In 2001, President Igor Smirnov*: "Moldova: Country Reports on Human Rights Practices—2003," Bureau of Democracy, Human Rights, and Labor, U.S. Department of State, February 25, 2004.

169 *Sometimes, pimps held the women, literally*: In the summer of 2005, Turkish police pulled five Ukrainian girls from a windowless twenty-by-twenty-foot underground cell in the resort town of Antalya. The two men who owned them had rented them as sex slaves to local clients over the course of ten months.—Amberin Zaman, "Turkey One of Largest Markets for Trafficking of Women," *Irish Times*, February 3, 2006, p. 15.

174 *While masters at the other end*: Kevin Bales cited in Susan Llewelyn Leach, "Slavery Is Not Dead, Just Less Recognizable," *Christian Science Monitor*, September 1, 2004, p. 16.

175 *The Dubai murder sparked debate*: The membership covered every country on earth. In Mauritania, "Teegee" reported, women wore small leather pouches under their skirts, which they did not remove during sex because they contained "some kind of magic." In Fiji, "ratufreddie" reported, one could purchase an Indian girl for "2 hours of gymnastics" for $30.

175 *"Dh 40 huh . . ."*: "Lomion," *International Sex Guide* entry, March 19, 2006. Exact time unclear because Lomion deleted his original post.

175 *"You know . . . it's not so funny"*: "Nice Guy 99," *International Sex Guide* entry, March 19, 2006, 11:52PM.

175 *"Spent the last 10 years"*: "Lomion," *International Sex Guide* entry, March 20, 2006, 5:53 AM.

175 *"Where there are troops"*: "Lomion," *International Sex Guide* entry, February 10, 2005, 1:52PM.

176 *There, if he wanted, he could buy a girl*: Christien van den Anker, "Introduction: Combating Contemporary Slavery," in van den Anker, ed., *The Political Economy of New Slavery* (New York: Palgrave Macmillan, 2004), p. 6.

176 *But Lomion's dystopic Eden*: Stewart, "Once We Sold Wine to the World," pp. 32–33.

176 *On March 14, 2004, Lomion posted a review*: "Lomion," *International Sex Guide* entry, March 14, 2004, 11:22AM.

177 *While Miller testified that there was*: John R. Miller, "Combating Human Trafficking," Testimony before Committee on House International Relations Subcommittee on Africa, Global Human Rights and International Operations, March 9, 2005.

177 *"Think Bosnia is starting to go the way"*: "Lomion," *International Sex Guide* entry, April 1, 2006, 6:43PM.

177 *"Now comes a really crazy idea"*: "Rock Dog," *International Sex Guide* entry, February 7, 2006, 8:55AM.

177 *With 2 million women in forced prostitution*: Similarly, a pornographer told the *New York Times*'s Frank Rich: "We realized that when there are 700 million porn rentals a year, it can't just be a million perverts renting 700 videos each"—Frank Rich, "Naked Capitalists," *New York Times Magazine*, May 20, 2001, p. 51.

178 *But the stamp was only the first*: "Big Bob II," *International Sex Guide* entry, October 11, 2004, 11:46AM.

181 *Drug-smuggling arrests increased 300 percent*: Hassan M. Fattah, "Dubai Journal: Bustling Gulf City Finds It Has Imported a Drug Problem," *New York Times*, May 5, 2005, p. A4.

181 *"Our first modern slave revolt"*: Rami G. Khouri, "Slave Revolts and Arab Summits," *Jordan Times*, March 31, 2006.

183 *"Life goes on as usual"*: "Discerning," *International Sex Guide* entry, May 8, 2006, 7:00AM.

183 *"What choice?"*: "11 Bravo," *International Sex Guide* entry, May 3, 2006, 8:27AM.

183 *"Now, that country, which shall remain nameless"*: Michael J. Horowitz, "Hearing on Germany's World Cup Brothels," House International Relations Committee, Washington, DC, May 4, 2006.

184 *Mainstream Dutch antitrafficking*: Marjan Wijers, *La Strada, European Network Against Trafficking in Women* (Amsterdam: La Strada, 2005), p. 14.

185 *The bullet-riddled corpse*: Sietske Altink, *Stolen Lives: Trading Women into Sex and Slavery* (London: Scarlet Press, 1995), p. 48.

185 *The slave traders leaped at the easy money*: Janice G. Raymond, "Ten Reasons for *Not* Legalizing Prostitution and a Legal Response to the Demand for Prostitution," in Farley, ed., *Prostitution, Trafficking and Traumatic Stress*, p. 318.

185 *Four years later, they numbered*: Jenifer Chao, "Dutch Waking Up to Organized Crime in Their Midst," Associated Press, December 14, 1994.

185 *"Five years after the lifting of the ban"*: Job Cohen quoted in "Police ignore human trafficking," *NRC-handelsblad*, October 10, 2005.

7. John Miller's War

193 *But she also confirmed*: John R. Miller, "On-the-Record Briefing on the Release of Conference Document, 'Pathbreaking Strategies in the Global Fight Against Sex Trafficking,'" U.S. Department of State, May 29, 2003.

195 *"I see sanctions in which countries"*: Rep. Brad Sherman, "Global Trends in Trafficking and the Trafficking in Persons Report," Hearing of the International Terrorism, Nonproliferation and Human Rights Subcommittee of the House International Relations Committee, June 25, 2003.

197 *Even as he took the oath of office*: John R. Miller, "Swearing-in as Ambassador-at-Large," Benjamin Franklin Room, U.S. Department of State, September 7, 2004.

8. Children of Vishnu

203 *The 1866 photograph captured*: As he held no birth records, Douglass may have been slightly younger than this: late in life he determined that his birth date fell in February 1816, though historians maintain he was born in February 1818.

204 *He was a member of the Kol*: F.B. Bradley-Birt, *Chota Nagpur: A Little Known Province of the Empire* (New Delhi, 1903), p. 23, cited in G. S. Ghurye, *The Scheduled Tribes of India* (New Brunswick, NJ: Transaction Books, 1963), p. 10.

205 *Kevin Bales has estimated*: Kevin Bales, "The Social Psychology of Modern Slavery," *Scientific American* (April 2002), p. 86.

205 *Only through slave labor*: Kevin Bales, *Understanding Global Slavery: A Reader* (Berkeley: University of California Press, 2005), p. 1.

206 *An observer once described*: James M. Gregory, *Frederick Douglass: The Orator* (Springfield, IL: Willey & Co., 1893), p. 100.

210 *Two decades later, a survey of Madhya Pradesh*: Brahma Chellaney, "Debt-Bondage Labor Becomes Issue in India," Associated Press, March 25, 1982.

211 *In their folklore, the Kol were not always*: Walter G. Griffiths, *The Kol Tribe of Central India* (Calcutta: Asiatic Society, 1946), p. 210.

215 *Like much of the developing world*: Somini Sengupta, "On India's Despairing Farms, a Plague of Suicide," *New York Times*, September 19, 2006, p. A1.

218 *"We were induced to drink"*: Frederick Douglass, *My Bondage and My Freedom* (New York: Miller, Orton & Mulligan, 1885), pp. 255–56.

220 *To fix that, he recently reinitiated*: Peter Foster, "Teachers Seek Sterilization 'Volunteers,'" *Calgary Herald*, February 25, 2006, p. A19.

220 *Indira Gandhi's disastrous reign*: P. Sainath, *Everybody Loves a Good Drought* (New Delhi: Penguin Books, 1996), pp. 195–96.

221 *In Kol lore, elephants in dreams*: Griffiths, *The Kol Tribe of Central India*, p. 196.

222 *"Any truism about India"*: Shashi Tharoor, *India: From Midnight to the Millennium* (New York: HarperCollins, 1997), p. 8.

223 *Neighboring contractors had chosen Kol girls*: "India: Police pledge to defend tribal women," *The Hindu* (New Delhi), November 5, 1997, p. 15.

224 *"The bond of the slave is snapped"*: Mohandas Karamchand Gandhi, "Speech at AICC Meeting: 8 August 1942," in Rudrangshu Mukherjee, ed., *The Penguin Gandhi Reader* (New York: Penguin Books, 1993), p. 171.

227 *The Kol believe that when a sleeper dreams*: Griffiths, *The Kol Tribe of Central India*, p. 197.

229 *"This is an act so unnatural"*: William Lloyd Garrison, "American Colorphobia," *The Liberator*, June 11, 1847, in Mason I. Lowance, ed., *Against Slavery: An Abolitionist Reader* (New York: Penguin Books, 2000), pp. 117–18. British abolitionists, of course, were far out front on the slavery issue, and Garrison likely lifted, and watered down, Thomas Day's 1776 comment to an American correspondent: "Slavery . . . is a crime so monstrous against the human species that all those who practice it deserve to be extirpated from the earth."—Thomas Day (written in 1776, published in 1784), letter to American correspondent, cited in Vincent Carretta, ed., *Unchained Voices: An Anthology of Black Authors in the English-speaking World of the 18th Century* (Lexington: University Press of Kentucky, 1996), p. 6.

230 *"If untouchability lives"*: Gandhi, "Caste Has to Go: 16 November 1935," in Mukherjee, ed., *The Penguin Gandhi Reader*, p. 223.

231 *"We are going to enter a life of contradictions"*: Cited in A. M. Rajasekhariah, *B. R. Ambedkar: The Politics of Emancipation* (Bombay: Sindhu Publications, 1971), p. 285.

232 *At a community meeting*: Biharilal Sarkar, 30, Cuthbert & Wilkinson to Thomason, February 12, 1832, cited in Ranajit Guha, *Elementary Aspects of Peasant Insurgency in Colonial India* (Durham, NC: Duke University Press, 1999), p. 22.

233 *Now that some knew*: Gandhi, "Speech at AICC Meeting: 8 August 1942," in Mukherjee, ed., *The Penguin Gandhi Reader*, p. 171.

234 *"The experience of all ages and nations"*: Adam Smith, *Wealth of Nations*, Vol. I (1776) (New York: Modern Library, 1937), p. 365.

234 *Administrators in tribal areas estimated*: Randeep Ramesh, "Inside India's Hidden War," *The Guardian*, (London), May 9, 2006, p. 23.

235 *"It would not be an exaggeration"*: Manmohan Singh cited in "Focus on Good Governance: Prime Minister Singh," *Hindustan Times* (New Delhi), April 13, 2006.

239 *"They are not asking for the moon"*: Cited in Arindam Roy, "Breaking the Shackles," *Economic and Political Weekly*, February 5, 2000, p. 425.

239 *What they wanted was the freedom*: For a more detailed look at Sankalp's work with the Kol, see the Free the Slaves documentary *Silent Revolution* (April 2006), produced by Peggy Callahan. See also Zoe Trodd and Kevin Bales, *To Plead Our Own Cause: Narratives of Modern Slavery* (forthcoming, 2007).

240 *"The laborer is extremely flexible"*: Amar Saran to Margaret O'Grady of Anti-Slavery International, 2000.

241 *"Something begins to work up here"*: Robert Falls interviewed by Della Yoe for Work Projects Administration, *Slave Narratives: A Folk History of Slavery in the United States from Interviews with Former Slaves*. Vol. XV: *Tennessee* (Washington, DC, 1941), p. 16.

245 *"Say dey was gwine free"*: Charlie Davis interviewed by Annie Ruth Davis for Work Projects Administration, *Slave Narratives: A Folk History of Slavery in the United States from Interviews with Former Slaves*. Vol. XIV: *South Carolina, Part I* (Washington, DC, 1941), p. 245.

9. Revelation: Angels with Swords of Fire

252 *Now he visited one of the wealthiest states*: Anti-Slavery International, "Debt Bondage in India, Nepal and Pakistan," submitted to the UN Commission on Human Rights, Sub-Commission on the Promotion and Protection of Human Rights, Working Group on Contemporary Forms of Slavery, 25th Session, Geneva, June 14–23, 2000.

255 *That approval rating had declined steadily*: George W. Bush, second inaugural address, Washington, DC, January 20, 2005.

256 *And she was the descendant of slaves*: Rev. William Bullein Johnson cited in John Patrick

Daley, *When Slavery Was Called Freedom: Evangelicalism, Proslavery, and the Causes of the Civil War* (Lexington: University Press of Kentucky, 2002), p. 77.

257 *"If not for America"*: Condoleezza Rice, "Remarks at the Southern Baptist Convention Annual Meeting," Greensboro Coliseum, Greensboro, North Carolina, June 14, 2006.

258 *"Dear Heavenly Father"*: Bobby Welch, "Remarks at the Southern Baptist Convention Annual Meeting," Greensboro Coliseum, Greensboro, North Carolina, June 14, 2006.

259 *Ambassador Mulford softened*: David C. Mulford, "We Can Make a Difference in the Fight Against Human Trafficking," *The Times of India*, June 6, 2006.

260 *"It sounds like I'm dodging here"*: George W. Bush, "Remarks by President Bush on the Global War on Terror," Paul H. Nitze School of Advanced International Studies, Johns Hopkins University, Washington, DC, April 10, 2006.

260 *While Wilberforce's faith*: Thomas Clarkson to Archdeacon Plymley, August 27, 1793, cited in Adam Hochschild, *Bury the Chains: Prophets and Rebels in the Fight to Free an Empire's Slaves* (New York: Houghton Mifflin, 2006), p. 237.

260 *"By a series of recent initiatives"*: John C. Danforth, "In the Name of Politics," *New York Times*, March 30, 2006, p. A17.

261 *"My mind has been literally bent"*: Clarkson to Archdeacon Plymley, in Hochschild, *Bury the Chains*, p. 237.

10. A Little Hope

264 *"If I bring you to America"*: Through her lawyer, Marie Pompee declined my interview request, but denied enslaving Williathe.

265 *Take Florida's $62 billion agriculture industry*: Editorial, "End America's Denial of Farm Labor Reality," *Palm Beach Post*, December 14, 2003, p. 2E.

266 *In 1999, the Immigration and Naturalization Service*: Amy O'Neill Richard, *An Intelligence Monograph: International Trafficking in Women to the United States: A Contemporary Manifestation of Slavery and Organized Crime*, DCI Exceptional Intelligence Analyst Program, November 1999, p. 3.

267 *Every year, some 10,000 children*: Richard J. Estes and Neil Alan Weiner, *The Commercial Sexual Exploitation of Children in the U.S., Canada and Mexico* (Philadelphia: University of Pennsylvania School of Social Work, September 19, 2001), p. 39.

272 *She spoke briefly to Little Hope*: Williathe recalls that a police officer interviewed her, not a social worker. The government record is that a DCF staffer conducted the interview—and was subsequently fired when her actions came to light.

275 *A week later, the FBI seized all family pictures*: Willy Junior's lawyer later produced one photograph of Marie and Williathe smiling together.

279 *Under the Mann Act*: In 1986, Congress replaced the words "debauchery" and "any other immoral purpose" with more precise terminology.

279 *"I would like to apologize not only to the court"*: Cited in Ann O'Neill, "Pines Woman Sentenced for Harboring Alien," *Sun-Sentinel* (Fort Lauderdale), July 2, 2004, p. 1B.

279 *The Pompees showed up en masse*: Ibid.

281 *"I'm not the best role model"*: I am indebted to Darran Simon for this description, and for his logistical help. See Darran Simon, "Tragedy to Triumph: A trek of inspiration," *Miami Herald*, June 11, 2006, p. B1.

283 *Thus, while the average sex-trafficking operation*: Richard, *An Intelligence Monograph: International Trafficking in Women to the United States*, p. 3.

Epilogue: A War Worth Fighting

288 *My models*: See Samantha Power, *A Problem From Hell: America and the Age of Genocide* (New York: Basic Books, 2002); and Philip Gourevitch, *We Wish to Inform You That Tomorrow We Will Be Killed with Our Families: Stories from Rwanda* (New York: Picador, 1999).

290 *Horowitz detests*: Michael Horowitz, "Memorandum to Interested Parties RE: Passage of the End Demand Act," Washington, DC, January 6, 2006.

290 *As Kevin Bales has clarified*: Submitted statement of Bales, *The Ongoing Tragedy of International Slavery and Human Trafficking: An Overview*, p. 111.

292 *Often the best thing that government can do*: I am indebted to the Peruvian economist Hernando de Soto for these ideas—See Hernando de Soto, *The Mystery of Capital: Why Capitalism Triumphs in the West and Fails Everywhere Else* (New York: Basic Books, 2000).

293 *"As long as you know of it"*: Henry David Thoreau, Letter to Parker Pillsbury: April 10, 1861, in *The Correspondence of Henry David Thoreau*, ed. Walter Harding (New York: New York University Press, 1958), p. 611.

Acknowledgments

One evening in the spring of 2001, as I was finishing up a stint as his assistant at the Council on Foreign Relations in New York City, Walter Russell Mead took me out for dinner at a posh Madison Avenue bistro. Living in the city on the salary of an entry-level researcher, I rarely supplemented my diet with meat, so I ordered steak on Walter's coin. It was good.

But Walter gave me something much more valuable during that meal—the idea for this book. It came up casually. He had seen several reports in the Evangelical media about modern-day slavery and thought it was an underexplored issue.

"Wouldn't it be something if there were more slaves today than ever before?" he said.

I immediately bought *Disposable People*, a book by the modern-day slavery pioneer Kevin Bales, who asserted just that. On two assignments for *Newsweek International*, I began to put flesh on the numbers, and got a truer sense of what slavery was.

Thanks to Mead and Bales—and to my *Newsweek* editors, Marcus Mabry and Richard Ernsberger—the idea was born. The midwives who brought the book itself into the world were my agent, Geri Thoma, and my editor, Martin Beiser. Thoma's patience, Beiser's steady hand, and their combined sense of story made this, my first book, happen.

I am proud and lucky to count a deeply moral statesman, Richard Holbrooke, as a mentor and friend. His generosity in supporting this project—culminating in the Foreword that leads this edition—testifies to his commitment to abolition.

Maya Angelou wrote: "History, despite its wrenching pain, cannot be unlived. And if faced with courage, need not be lived again." Her words capture why I am foremost grateful to the individual victims and survivors of slavery who trusted me enough to bear witness to me. None were paid for their stories. They spoke because they believed that by sharing their own experiences, they might relieve the suffering of others. Bill Nelson, Camsease Exille, Muong Nyong Muong, "Tatiana," Natasha, "Gonoo" Lal Kol, Bhola, Williathe Narcisse—and well over a hundred others whose narratives did not make this book—pled not only their own cause but that of thousands of others who suffer in silence.

Ambassador John Miller's cooperation was selfless, as was that of Mark Taylor and the rest of his staff at the State Department's Office to Monitor and Combat Trafficking in Persons. Similarly, attorneys at the Civil Rights Division of the Department of Justice were tremendous resources. In particular, Senior Prosecutor Lou DeBaca—who has been fighting modern-day slavery longer than anyone else I met in the United States—generously shared his knowledge.

Mary Van Evera provided critical support during my early investigations, and my friends at the World Economic Forum were good enough to fly me within shouting distance of some of my destinations.

During my five years on the road, a number of families and individuals gave me shelter. Some also helped me overcome strange tropical diseases. Without their kindness, I would not be whole—and certainly would not have finished the book. Among those individuals who shared their homes were Trajean LaGuerre in Brésillienne; Michael Geilenfeld, who gave me a room in his orphanage, a reservoir of hope called Maison St. Josef in Port-au-Prince; Richard Morris, who has kept Port-au-Prince's Hotel Oloffson as wonderfully creepy as it was in Graham Greene's day; Padre Pierre "Pedro" Ruquoy in Batey No. 5 on the Dominican border; Philip Chol, Chol Changath, and Betty Kiden, who lent me a *tukul* for weeks in Malual Kon; Save the Children's Toby Kay, who did the same for me in Lokichokio; Reverend Santino Bol, who allowed me to pitch a tent in his *baay* in Marial Bai; Martha and Johnson Mugambi, who treated my illness and shared their beautiful Nairobi home; George

P. Pagoulatos and his wife, who also nursed me back to health at the Acropole Hotel, an oasis for foreign reporters in Khartoum; Buthina Bashir, Nazer Abdel Rahim, Safwan Mohamed, and Al-Mutaz Ahmed, who treated me like family in Omdurman; Elena Moldovan, my dear landlady in Bucharest, who opened her own flat; Sasha and Veronika Imperial, who made me feel at home in Chișinău; Herrmann Jungraith-mayr, who did the same in Marburg, Germany; Francisca "Francie" Hoogeveen and Peter Besselink, who created a room for me for weeks in their canalside apartment in Amsterdam; Father Raymond D'Souza, who allowed me to use his residence in Naini, India, as a base for nearly two months; the family of Nita Colaço, who provided sweet relief in their beautiful beachfront house in Goa; and finally, in Miami, Scott Cunningham, who let me push the boundaries of friendship by giving up his South Beach apartment during spring break.

Translators were critical. With rare exceptions, those who translated the slaves' stories that I use here were not working for any advocacy organization, and had no declared agenda. They were all remarkably professional in difficult circumstances. In particular, Laurie Richard-son was a fixer and a friend who guided me through rough patches in Port-au-Prince, as did her colleagues Djaloki Dessables, Carla Blunt-schli, and Ari Nicolas; Serge, a.k.a. Sean R. J. Sacra, was mature well beyond his years, and indispensable in my travels throughout Haiti. In Sudan, Ayaga Garang not only provided flawless translation but kept me from wilting in 120-degree heat on long bike rides between Malual Kon, Mangar Angui, and points between. Alexandru Petrache, in Bucharest, performed with a cool head at several pressurized moments. Elena Popa was a splendid interpreter in Chișinău. Chandni Sharma, a lawyer, brought knowledge of the subject and sensitivity to her translation. Rajneesh Yadav, a graduate student in agriculture, was precise and dogged in his translations around Lohagara Dhal; and "Kerem," in Istanbul, held it all together during our impromptu undercover work.

Many hands molded the manuscript. Everyone at Free Press—espe-cially Martin Beiser and his assistants, Kit Frick, Andrew Paulson, and

Kirsa Rein—was very tolerant of my rookie status. The Bard College classes of Walter Mead and John Ryle read chapters and gave them a good thrashing. Council on Foreign Relations junior staff study groups— kindly arranged by Bryan Gunderson, Eitan Goldstein, Scott Erwin, and Eliana Johnson—did the same. Ania Wajnberg and Michael Red- lener's salon also tore into the material. The library staff at the Council on Foreign Relations—Leigh Gusts, Michelle Baute, Connie Stagnaro, Ming Er Qiu, Marcia Sprules—provided top-notch research as always. Ib Ohlsson, the keeper of a dying art, drew the maps by hand.

A few key people provided counsel and criticism on the manuscript and on the undertaking as a whole. Alberto Ibargüen, a friend with an almost mystical knowledge of the media world, gave me good ideas on structuring the story. The late David Halberstam, whose tragic passing coincided with the last stage of this book, kept my spirits up when I was considering throwing in the towel at an early stage. Ginny Baumann at Free the Slaves was a voice of reason at every stage, and patiently read most chapters. Parag Khanna was a friend who kept me on task. Joaly Alcalá, Ashley Bommer, and Megan Quitkin assisted with the final manuscript; and other friends in New York managed not to forget me during long absences.

Many local journalists and foreign correspondents assisted in help- ing me find the stories. These included Reed Lindsay in Port-au-Prince; Elizabeth Drachman and Peyman Pejman in Dubai; Paul Radu and par- ticularly Petrică Răchită, who were my saviors in Bucharest and beyond; Alina Radu, a guiding hand throughout Moldova and Transnistria; and Darran Simon, who got me started in Miami.

I am indebted to several writers for their work, although not all of them are aware that I was trampling out their vintage. These include Deborah Sontag for her writing in the *Miami Herald* on restavèks; Joel Brinkley for his early pieces in the *New York Times* on U.S. efforts to combat trafficking; Isabel Fonseca for her marvelous work on the Roma, *Bury Me Standing*; Deborah Scroggins for her engrossing biog- raphy *Emma's War*, which I lugged with me across East Africa; Allen D. Hertzke's chronicle of Evangelical influence on modern American foreign policy, *Freeing God's Children*; and Victor Malarek for his book on sex trafficking, *The Natashas*.

Several nongovernmental experts provided guidance on the research, and feedback on the text. In the United States, these included Florrie Burke, Jean-Robert Cadet, Katherine Chon, Gigi Cohen, Alex Dupuy, Joseph Elder, Frank T. Griswold, Samantha Healy, Ann Jordan, Natasha G. Kohne, Michael F. McAuliffe, Jocelyn McCalla, Monika Parikh, John Prendergast, Jemera Rone, Ken Roth, John Ryle, Rabbi David Saperstein, and Mike Stephens. In Amsterdam and Utrecht, I learned a great deal from Sietske Altink, Sandra Claassen, Maria de Cock, Marieke van Doornick, and Niene Oepkes. Three representatives from the International Organization for Migration in Chișinău—Iraida Margineanu, Martin Andreas Wyss, and, particularly, Lidia Gorceag—went out of their way to show me their underappreciated but courageous work running Moldova's only shelter for trafficked women. Other experts in Moldova who informed my work include Michael H. Getto, Veronica Lupu, Nicolae Misail, Ion Oboroceanu, and Angelina Zaporojan-Pirgari. In Khartoum, James Aguer, Kate Halff, and Adele Swinska, all gave great background, as did Wendy Fenton in Nairobi. In Abu Dhabi, Dr. Ushari Mahmud provided me the back story on his investigation into Sudanese slavery—the first of the modern era. In Port-au-Prince, Martial N. Bailey, Godfroy "Gody" Boursiquot, Abdonel Doudou, and Alphonse Deo Nkunzimana, helped further my understanding of the restavèk problem. In Delhi, Kailash Satyarthi, a pioneering activist against bonded labor, provided an overview of the struggle since the practice was formally abolished in India. Bruno Deceukelier, an aid worker in Port-au-Prince, not only gave me good information on slavery in the sugar plantations in the Dominican Republic but took me on his sport bike across the border to see it up close.

I would particularly like to acknowledge a few neo-abolitionists who have guided my journey but whom I have underrepresented badly in this book. These people run tiny organizations that do magnificent work with scant resources; all deserve support:

In Haiti, Reverend Miguel Jean Baptiste, Clermei de Rameau (a.k.a.

Mammy Georges Rameau), Patrick Bernard, Wenes Jeanty, Gernie Grandpierre, Marie Pasal Douyan, and Leslie Jean Jumeau run Foyer Maurice Sixto, the oldest and largest shelter for restavèks in Port-au-Prince. On the other side of Port-au-Prince, a child psychologist named Nadine Burdet runs L'Escale, a tranquil shelter for escaped restavèks. Jean Marcel, the secretary of Action Chrétienne for Development School in Cité Soleil, maintains a school in the most dangerous six square miles in the western hemisphere. In Jacmel, Guerda Lexima Constant and Samson Joseph run Fondasyon Limyè Lavi—with stateside coordination from Coleen Hedglin and David Diggs of Beyond Borders. Limyè Lavi does tremendous work educating families to prevent them from surrendering their children to traffickers.

In Europe, Iana Matei runs Reaching Out, a shelter for trafficked women in Pitești, Romania; in Tiraspol, Transnistria, Oxana Alistratova runs an organization called Interaction that works to prevent women from being trafficked in the first place. In the Bijlmer district of Amsterdam, Pastor Tom Marfo's Christian Aid and Resources Foundation (CARF) is the only local organization conducting outreach to women trafficked from West Africa.

In Asia, Sharla Musabih directs City of Hope, which is, as I write, Dubai's only shelter for trafficked women. In Shankargarh, India, Rampal, Suneel Kumar, and their colleagues at Sankalp run an edgy but effective organization that empowers quarry slaves to seize their freedom. Washington-based Free the Slaves coordinates several very effective programs through their South Asia director, Supriya Awasthi. These include Father Raymond D'Souza's Diocesan Development and Welfare Society, which operates Bal Vikas Ashram, a project to free, shelter, and rehabilitate children enslaved in carpet looms; Ranjana Gaur's Social Action and Research Centre (SARC) in Varanasi, which focuses on the traffic in women; and Bhanuja Lal's Society for Human Development and Women's Empowerment (MSEMVS), which combats bonded labor, particularly carpet slavery.

Finally, I have to thank my parents, Meg and Neil Skinner, to whom this book is dedicated, and without whom . . .

Index

About the Author

A graduate of Wesleyan University, **E. Benjamin Skinner** was born in Wisconsin. He has reported on a wide range of subjects from Latin America, Africa, and the Middle East for such publications as *Newsweek International* and *Travel + Leisure*. He currently lives in Brooklyn. This is his first book.